Education and Labour Party Ideologies 1900–2001 and Beyond

In 1997 Tony Blair broke with tradition by naming education as a major priority for the General Election Manifesto. Despite this, Blair has been greatly criticised for his educational programme 1997–2001. Was he taking education away from traditional Labour values of fairness and equality? Was Blair's 'Third Way' just 'Thatcherism in Trousers'?

Denis Lawton approaches such questions by analysing Labour education policies since 1900 and shows that from the very beginning the Labour Party lacked unity and ideological coherence concerning education. Specifically, there has always been a tension between those like the early Fabians who saw educational reform in terms of economic efficiency, and the ethical socialists whose vision of a more moral society stressed the importance of social justice in education. After an assessment of Labour ideologies in the past, this book concludes with an examination of New Labour and the 'Third Way' in education and suggests some changes that will be necessary in the near future.

Education and Labour Party Ideologies 1900–2001 and Beyond is a fascinating account of education policies and ideologies of the Labour Party. It will be of interest to anyone researching the history of education or politics and education.

Denis Lawton is Emeritus Professor of Education at the Institute of Education, University of London.

Education and Labour Party Ideologies 1900–2001 and Beyond

Denis Lawton

RoutledgeFalmer
Taylor & Francis Group

LONDON AND NEW YORK

Woburn Education Series

First published 2005 by RoutledgeFalmer
2 Park Square, Milton Park, Abingdon, Oxon OX14 4RN

Simultaneously published in the USA and Canada
by RoutledgeFalmer
270 Madison Ave, New York, NY 10006

RoutledgeFalmer is an imprint of the Taylor & Francis Group

© 2005 Denis Lawton

Typeset in Goudy by BC Typesetting Ltd, Bristol
Printed and bound in Great Britain by
Antony Rowe Ltd, Chippenham, Wiltshire

British Library Cataloguing in Publication Data
A catalogue record for this book is available from the British Library

Library of Congress Cataloging in Publication Data
Lawton, Denis.
  Education and Labour Party ideologies, 1900–2001 and beyond/Denis Lawton.
    p.   cm.
  Includes bibliographical references and index.
  ISBN 0–415–34776–9 (hard: alk. paper) –
  ISBN 0–415–34777–7 (pbk.: alk. paper)
  1. Politics and education–Great Britain–History–20th century.
  2. Education and state–Great Britain–History–20th century.
  3. Labour Party (Great Britain)–History–20th century. I. Title.
  LC93.G7L265 2004
  379.42–dc22
                                                              2004004145

ISBN 0–415–34776–9 (hbk)
ISBN 0–415–34777–7 (pbk)

Contents

Foreword and acknowledgements

In the 1990s I wrote a critical account of Conservative education in *The Tory Mind on Education* (1994). After 1997, some friends and colleagues suggested that I should write a similar book on the Labour Party and education. I was attracted to this idea but realised that my stance would have to be different because I have been a member of the Labour Party since 1956. The book that I have written will nevertheless be, I hope, if not impartial, at least objective. It will be just as critical of the Labour Party as *The Tory Mind* was of the Conservatives, but for different reasons. I criticised the Tory Party because I disliked the Tory philosophy of the market and education. Their education policy was, however, generally consistent with their educational practice. Since 1997 I have found myself critical of the Labour Party because their educational practices do not sufficiently fit in with their socialist philosophy of equality and social justice.

The intention of the book is to explore three strands in the history of ideas and to examine relationships between them. The first is the history of the Labour Party since 1900 with particular reference to educational policies. The second is education and socialism, and the link between various interpretations of socialism and the Labour Party. The third strand is the development of educational ideas over the same period. That might be enough for one book but it would not be complete. For some socialists, for example, William Morris, education was not just another aspect of social policy, it was a completely dominating central concern. For Morris, true education was indistinguishable from socialism. I would agree with Morris but would express the relationship rather differently: I suggest that socialism must have a vision of a better society; there are many factors which contribute to the achievement of that vision: political, social, economic and educational. One of the points which emerges from this book is that few Labour politicians have seen the essential, dynamic relation between education and the goal of a better society. There have been some exceptions, but most politicians and political theorists have tended to regard education as one of the social services competing for time and limited finances. They see it as a drain on government resources rather than as part of the means of achieving a better society.

This book aims to analyse the educational policies and practices of the Labour Party since its foundation. That analysis includes a suggestion that it is necessary for politicians to understand the need for some kind of educational theory, in the same way as they need to have a theory of economics.

A theory of education would include ideas about human development (how children learn, and intelligence, for example); and ideas about curriculum (what content should be learned) and pedagogy (the teaching–learning experiences). Great educational theorists of the past from Plato to Rousseau and Dewey produced coherent theories of education and society – some better than others. But twentieth-century politicians have tended to replace educational theory by reducing complex ideas and practices to what they think of as 'common sense' but what is really over simplified and out-dated theory.

It is one of the purposes of this book to examine the relationship between socialist visions of a good society and educational ideas that would help to achieve that society. The Labour Party has not yet made enough progress in that direction.

In writing this book I have not tried to produce an historical study in the sense of generating new data from original sources. It seemed to me that there is a good deal of material already published on those subjects, and that what was needed was an attempt to bring the various strands together as a coherent but complex story. The end result may be, for some tastes, too speculative to count as history. I have also made a number of assumptions, or reached certain conclusions, that some may wish to challenge. For example, it seems to me that there is a powerful connection between different sets of educational ideas and ethical socialism, that contrast with the educational principles of Sidney Webb and some Fabians whose main interest in education was economic efficiency rather than superior quality of life in the ethical sense. I suggest that these two traditions have continued to exist within the Labour Party.

Acknowledgements

I would like to thank Professor Peter Gordon for encouraging me to write this book and to include it in his series on education. I am also grateful to Professor Clyde Chitty for discussions and helpful suggestions. Dr Clive Griggs also made a number of useful comments.

Anyone writing on this topic would have to be greatly indebted to the late Professor Brian Simon for his many volumes on the history of education.

I found Geoffrey Foote's *The Labour Party's Political Thought* (1997) very helpful in clarifying my ideas about ideologies within the Labour Party. I was, however, surprised, and perhaps relieved, to find that he had almost nothing to say about educational ideas and theories. I would also like to thank many other colleagues, too numerous to list, with whom I have discussed these ideas over many years.

1 Nineteenth-century background

By the turn of the century several of the major assumptions which had guided Victorian economic and social policy were being questioned. At the centre lay the body of ideas known as *laissez-faire*.

(John Stevenson in Pimlott, 1984, p. 15)

The history of the Labour Party begins in 1906, or 1900 if you prefer to date the founding of the Party from the establishment of the Labour Representation Committee (LRC). In any case, it is necessary to stress the importance to the Labour Party of various events, movements and ideas, including socialism, in the nineteenth century that have left some kind of permanent legacy. This chapter is intended to paint in that background but trying not to over-simplify an extremely complex story.

England in the nineteenth century

The nineteenth century opened with England at war with France. In the eighteenth century there had been two great changes – the Industrial Revolution and the French Revolution, both of which strongly influenced the development of education. France had been a commercial and colonial rival for centuries, and in 1800 Nelson was establishing British naval supremacy throughout the world; in 1815 Wellington (with a little help from the Prussians) would finally defeat Napoleon who had been seen not only as a military threat but, curiously, as a symbol of the subversive thinking of the Enlightenment and of the French Revolution and the wars that followed. A major result of the Industrial Revolution was urbanisation with all its advantages and disadvantages.

After 1815 there was much discontent in England: food prices were high but wages were low, with many workers unemployed. Working-class living conditions were often appalling. The government responded to the problem of disaffection with harsh, repressive legislation and incidents such as the notorious Peterloo 'massacre'. Elsewhere in Europe the scene generally became one of conservative political regimes, designed to put the clock back to pre-1789 ways of life. The intellectual ethos was also conservative, even reactionary. Such writers as Chateaubriand in France and many others in England were openly anti-democratic. Queen Victoria, much later in the century, declared that she would not wish to be a monarch in a democracy.

In 1848, there were uprisings in Germany, Italy and France which caused some alarm in Britain, but there was no serious threat of revolution in England apart from the Chartists who were by then in decline.

By the end of the century, Britain was less confident and becoming less powerful; for example, confidence had been shaken by the 'Great Depression' from about 1876. Although the seriousness of this setback has sometimes been exaggerated, there were fears at the time, by politicians and many others, that Germany and the USA were overtaking Britain industrially, in some respects, as well as in military power. At a more abstract level the Victorians were disturbed by Darwin's ideas about evolution (published in 1857).

After a series of conflicts, in Zululand, Afghanistan, China and the Crimea, the century ended with Britain again at war, the Boer War. It was significant that Britain was fighting an imperialist war far away from Europe, and not doing very well. A major difference between 1800 and 1900 was a changing attitude to the concept of imperialism which affected many aspects of life in Britain, including education. Queen Victoria had become Empress of India in 1876.

An age of reform

Despite a background of poverty and injustice in a rapidly urbanising society, the nineteenth century in England has often been referred to as an 'Age of Reform'. Partly as a result of the Chartist movement, Britain gradually approached the principle of one person one vote, as the franchise was extended. Before the end of the century, some precursors of the suffragettes were indicating that women's rights could not be ignored for ever (Married Women's Property Acts were passed in 1870 and 1882). Legislation to humanise working conditions in factories and mines was gradually introduced, but started from a low base: exploitation and oppression of men, women and children had been taken for granted, but public opinion was changing. Trade unions were developing; they were eventually accepted and legalised, and the TUC was established in 1868. Victorian morality changed in several respects that indicated an increase in humanitarianism: for example, the abolition of slavery and flogging in the army; better care for the sick and the wounded (personified by Florence Nightingale); more humane treatment of children – including in schools – the National Society for the Prevention of Cruelty to Children was founded in 1884 (preceded in 1824 by the Royal Society for the Prevention of Cruelty to Animals).

Parliamentary reforms

At the beginning of the nineteenth century discussions were taking place about the reform of Parliament, but many regarded the *status quo* as all but perfect, despite the existence of 'rotten boroughs', 'pocket boroughs', the possibility of MPs buying their seats, and other practices which came to be regarded as 'corrupt'. At the beginning of the century there were loose groupings of Whig and Tory members, but nothing like the tight discipline and control over parties that developed in the twentieth century; the system was only slowly moving towards the idea of a two-party system of government with a 'loyal opposition'. The King or Queen was regarded as a 'constitutional' monarch with limited powers, but certain royal prerogatives remained in England that from time to time caused constitutional problems, even minor crises.

The three Parliamentary Reform Acts during the century (1832, 1867 and 1884) gradually extended the franchise to members of the middle classes, and even to more affluent working-class men. This tended to sharpen the distinction between Tories and Liberals (who replaced the Whigs as the second major party). No one represented working-class and trade union interests as such, although the Liberal Party tended to be more sympathetic to some of the causes of the under-privileged, and even sponsored a few working men as parliamentary candidates, the Lib–Labs. The Liberal Party was certainly not a working-class party, and it was this vacuum that the Labour Party was to fill in the twentieth century, eventually replacing the Liberal Party as the main party of the left. Not many working men stood for Parliament in the 1868 general election, following the 1867 Reform Act. The Labour Representation League was set up in 1869 partly to make sure that working-class men eligible to vote were registered. But the League lacked money to support candidates or MPs. Trade unions were not yet in a position to provide financial help. The practical solution had seemed to be to work with the Liberal Party. So it might have remained had the Liberals been more co-operative, but in many constituencies they were hostile to working-class candidates: in the 1874 election only two working-class men were elected with Liberal support.

The idea of a separate party gradually gained ground although many trade unionists remained loyal to the Liberals. A major reason for the emergence of the Labour Party was that it was, above all, a party committed to working-class representation. As such, it brought together a number of quite different ideologies and traditions: Liberal, Radical, Fabian and various shades of socialist thinking including ethical socialism, Christian socialism and Marxism. It was not surprising that such a mixture would give rise to internal disputes about policies. Those looking forward to a revolution were a small minority, but there were varying degrees of attachment to 'class conflict' and opposition to capitalism. From the beginning the majority view was that parliamentary methods should be followed, and violence should be avoided.

Industrialisation and the roots of socialism

By the 1880s, socialist politics, as distinct from working-class politics, was developing: criticisms of *laissez-faire* capitalism were increasing, not only from theorists such as Robert Owen and Karl Marx, who was still little known, but in private and public discussions of various kinds, such as socialist clubs and debating societies. The word 'socialist', according to the *Oxford Dictionary*, was first used in the 1830s, but Tony Crosland found an earlier example in *The Co-operative Magazine* in 1827. It referred to the London 'Co-operators' whose socialism was based on an ethical view of society (Crosland, 1956, pp. 101–2). Much of the early use of the word in Britain was connected with Robert Owen (1771– 1859) whose vision of a better society was based on moral principles such as social justice. Some would say 'liberty, equality and fraternity', adding 'for all' to distinguish socialist doctrine from the less inclusive values of the revolting French bourgeoisie in 1789 who still linked rights with property. It would not be appropriate to attempt a comprehensive definition of socialism here; better to accept it as a general word that embraces a wide range of attitudes. Some socialists would agree with Clem Attlee: 'I joined the socialist movement because I did not like the kind of society we had and wanted something better' (*As it Happened*, 1954). I would, therefore, like to stress that socialism is a relatively modern idea resting on two post-Enlightenment concepts: first, the notion of progress; second, the principle that all adults should be treated equally – hence another possible connection between socialism and women's rights.

In addition, a number of non-socialist writers, for example Thomas Carlyle (1795–1881), were influential. Carlyle's view of society was essentially that of a romantic, right-wing radical who disliked the decadent, modern industrial society with its utilitarian emphasis on the cash-nexus and *laissez-faire* individualism which he regarded as morally inferior to the old paternalistic links that had involved duties and obligations. Carlyle was also critical of the landowning aristocracy who produced nothing (except piles of birds they shot from time to time). His thinking, although backward-looking in some respects, was seeking some kind of non-materialistic social philosophy. He had briefly flirted with the ideas of Saint-Simon, but was not attracted by Chartism, British socialism or even democracy. From the point of view of Labour ideas his importance was that he was highly critical of the existing society and was advocating something morally superior to the dominant values of Victorian Britain. Many early Labour leaders had read Carlyle and been influenced by him.

John Ruskin (1819–1900), was equally dissatisfied with industrialism. He recognised the impossibility of reverting to the old order, and saw the need for a new kind of society. Ruskin went further than criticising the ugliness of industrial society, setting up a model farm to be worked as a co-operative by a group of Sheffield socialists. The experiment failed but perhaps added credibility to his progressive sentiments. Ruskin was best known for his books on art and architecture but his mature writings contain interesting examples of powerful social criticism, for example, *Unto This Last* (1860–62). He also wrote letters to 'the working men of England' which were published as *Fors Clavigera* (1871–84). He said that the modern factory with its division of labour prevented a genuine relationship between a worker and his work; labour had become meaningless and was a burden rather than the joy it ought to be.

Ruskin frequently criticised nineteenth-century education for being based on wrong values such as competition rather than 'brotherhood'. He also believed that art should be a central concern of education for all – girls as well as boys. His writings influenced individuals as different as William Morris and Gandhi who claimed that reading Ruskin had changed the course of his life. C.P. Trevelyan who, as we shall see, moved from the Liberal Party to Labour, also expressed enthusiasm for Ruskin. Writers, on the right as well as on the left, had the effect of casting doubt on the values and practices of *laissez-faire* capitalism. Some readers of all classes were impressed by the kind of social criticism they found in Carlyle and Ruskin, and, a little later, in William Morris. All these writers helped to change public opinion. (Henry George's lecture tour of 1882 was also influential.)

To achieve radical reform it was necessary to have direct access to the power of Parliament. The Liberal Party had not gone far enough to satisfy working-class demands. There were considerable numbers of working men's clubs and local socialist societies but they were not suitable for organising elections or raising funds sufficient to pay MPs once they were elected. The Lib–Lab idea became increasingly discredited as a means of supporting working-class interests. This was the main reason for trade unions deciding to line up with such organisations as the Fabian Society and the Social Democratic Federation to get more working-class representatives elected to Parliament and to have a party organisation to support them once they were there. To say that the Labour Representation Committee (LRC) and, a few years later, the Labour Party was 'a broad church' is to underestimate the range of beliefs within 'Labourism' at the beginning of the twentieth century and the hostility between some of the groups. Not all of the groups or individuals within Labour gave education a high priority.

Education in the nineteenth century

Throughout the century two sharply different attitudes towards the education of the poor were developing. At the beginning of the nineteenth century, the prevailing upper-class view was that education was essentially a private matter and that if any interference by government were undertaken it should be to assist, but not to provide, a deliberately inferior kind of education for the children of the poor. Even the philosophical radicals, often regarded as educational reformers, did not advocate education of high quality for working-class children. They believed that in a modern society all children should be educated, but capitalism demanded different kinds of education and training for different classes: capitalism could not work if all children received exactly the same kind of education.

At the opposite extreme, the developing socialist view was that in the long run education should be free, with equal opportunity for all – girls as well as boys; in the short run action should be taken to give the children of the poor as much access to education as possible.

Some who have been referred to as reformers, such as Hannah More (1745–1833), were firmly in the first category – she believed in reading, but no writing, for children of the poor. Other 'reformers' wanted a limited amount of education for the poor, for religious and humanitarian reasons, but would have drawn the line a long way from equality. For example, in 1802 the elder Sir Robert Peel had introduced the 'Health and Morals of Apprentices Act' which limited the hours of work of pauper children employed as apprentices in factories to 12 hours a day. His intention was to prevent unscrupulous mill owners from having an unfair advantage over 'enlightened' employers. This was the first of a series of 'Factory Acts'; in some of the Acts education is referred to as part of the argument for limiting working hours, but the intention was to provide basic instruction, not to challenge 'middle-class education'.

In 1807 Samuel Whitbread introduced a Parochial Schools Bill proposing 2 years free schooling for children between 7 and 14. It was strongly opposed, among others, by Davies Giddy, MP, who claimed that education for the labouring classes 'would be prejudicial to their morals and happiness; it would teach them to despise their lot in life, instead of making them good servants in agriculture and other laborious employments. Instead of teaching them sub-ordination, it would render them fractious and refractory . . . it would enable them to read seditious pamphlets, vicious books . . . it would render them inso-lent to their superiors' (*Hansard* Vol. IX, 1178) quoted by Barnard (1961, p. 55).

Soon after this Robert Owen (1771–1858) published *A New View of Society* (1813) in which he described the school at his mill in New Lanark. Few industrialists followed his example, but in 1818 a committee which included James Mill and Henry Brougham started a school, following Owen's model, in Westminster, and in 1820, another in Spitalfields. They appointed Samuel Wilderspin (1792–1866) to take charge. He published an interesting book *On the Importance of Educating the Infant Children of the Poor* (1823). We will return to both Owen and Wilderspin in a later section on educational ideas.

In May 1816 Henry Brougham (1778–1868) had moved for a select com-mittee to enquire into the state of education among the poor. This was granted, Brougham became chairman and introduced a number of education Bills advocating some kind of state involvement, but none of them was passed. In 1833, the Radical MP, John Roebuck, asked the House to consider 'the means of establishing a system of National Education'. The scheme proposed was complex and was too ambitious to be acceptable to the Commons. But there was support for the more modest idea of giving some financial help towards the education of the poor, and a few days later Lord Althorp, Chancellor of the Exchequer, included in his budget a sum of £20,000 to be made available to the two religious societies (the Church of England National Society and the Non-Conformist British and Foreign Schools Society) to be spent on school buildings. In 1839 in order to make sure that the government money was being properly spent, a Committee of the Privy Council on Education was set up with authority to appoint two inspectors of schools, Her Majesty's Inspectors (HMI). This was not yet state education but there was an element of state control being introduced. Some advocates of working-class schools, for example, Hodgskin, objected very strongly to this development (see Simon, 1960, p. 215).

Both of the two religious societies ran their schools according to the monitorial system, a cheap but effective means of inculcating basic skills, especially the 'three Rs'. These schools had little in common with the schools envisaged by Robert Owen and Thomas Hodgskin where children learned by activity and discovery rather than mechanical rote learning.

The monitorial system clearly owed much to factory organisation. Even so, some critics thought that elementary schools were costing far too much. In 1858 a royal commission was appointed under the chairmanship of the Duke of Newcastle 'to enquire into the present state of Popular Education in England, and to consider and report what Measures, if any, are required for the extension of sound and cheap elementary instruction to all classes of the people'. The report (1861) drew attention to a number of unsatisfactory features of the existing system, and there was concern over the amount of money that was being spent on education. One of the recommendations, known as the revised code, set up a system of payment-by-results which was intended to ensure that education of the poor should be cheap and if possible efficient as well. The revised code, with payment-by-results, had the temporary effect of reducing costs: the annual grant fell from the peak of £813,000 in 1861 to £637,000 in 1865. But the counter-pressure on the government to do more resulted in 1870 in a dramatic change of direction.

In 1870 W.E. Forster, the Liberal vice-president of the council, introduced the Elementary Education Act which, for the first time, accepted the idea of education being provided out of public funds, on a national basis. Some saw the Act as a step forward, but H.G. Wells described it as 'Not an Act for a common universal education, it was an Act to educate the lower classes for employment on lower class lines, and with specially trained, inferior teachers' (1934, p. 93). The 1870 Act did not make education compulsory (although the new School Boards could apply compulsion locally by means of by-laws if they wished). This half-hearted approach was amended by another Act in 1876 which made schooling compulsory up to age 12 (with some exemptions). Elementary schooling was, however, still not free, and fees remained until 1891. Progress towards a national, but minimalist, system was slow and often grudging.

The attitude to extending education towards what we would now call 'secondary' was even more grudging. Some School Boards had encouraged schools to develop a curriculum beyond the three Rs as authorised by the codes. A few boards developed 'higher-grade' schools which were doing what came to be regarded as secondary work. The London School Board was one example, and in 1900 a local government auditor, Mr Cockerton, brought an action against the board in order to test the legality of the London Board's generosity. The High Court ruled that School Boards were not permitted to teach beyond the range of elementary subjects. The decision, (the *Cockerton* judgment) was upheld in 1901 by the Court of Appeal. This action was to demonstrate the need for education beyond what was offered as elementary, and served to stimulate the government to prepare the 1902 Education Act which will be discussed in Chapter 2.

Meanwhile, in 1886, Sir Richard Cross had been appointed chairman of a royal commission to enquire into elementary education since the 1870 Act. The committee failed to agree on some recommendations and in 1888 it issued a majority and a minority report. They were agreed that more schools with better provision were needed; that payment-by-results should be modified and relaxed; that the curriculum should be improved, emphasising science and technical instruction; and that a clear definition of 'elementary' should be set out. The main reason for having two reports was that there was a difference between two groups on the committee about voluntary schools (that is, denominational schools). The majority report supported voluntary schools and recommended that they, like board schools, should be supported from the rates, whereas the minority report disagreed, recommending that a non-denominational place should be available for all pupils whose parents wanted one.

In 1894 a Royal Commission on Secondary Education was set up, chaired by James Bryce. It was recognised that there was a vast gap between elementary schools and universities. This issue will be considered in Chapter 2 in the context of the 1902 Education Act. Finally, in 1899 the Board of Education Act was passed, replacing the Education Department by a new Board of Education, headed by a president.

Changing ideas in education

Schools in the sixteenth century and early seventeenth century had been guided by Renaissance theories of education. During the Commonwealth period some democratic notions of education were discussed, and one of the greatest education theorists of all time, Comenius, was invited to England to add to the debate. He left a permanent mark, but after the Restoration in 1660, education theory went into a decline which continued into the eighteenth century. One influential voice in England, however, was that of John Locke (1632–1704) who combined some advanced philosophical and psychological ideas with reactionary social attitudes. On the one hand, Locke revived the idea that the child should be at the centre of the educational process, and emphasised the importance of experience rather than rote learning. On the other hand, Locke's (1697) practical suggestion for educating the poor was that they should be set to work from the age of 3 in a 'school of industry' so that they could be compelled to earn their keep and not be a charge on the parish. This attractive idea was highly regarded by many, and William Pitt tried to revive the notion in 1796, but failed to get it started.

However, Locke's ideas influenced the Enlightenment writers in France, who developed a variety of theories on education. Jean Jacques Rousseau was the best known; he reinforced and perhaps exaggerated the child-centred views of Locke. Some of the educational ideas of the Enlightenment, not least those published in Diderot's great *Encyclopaedia* were regarded as socially disruptive. One suggestion was that education should be a state responsibility, not something controlled by the church; others feared giving too much power to any state. That was the view shared by William Godwin (1756–1836) in England. From about 1740 John Wesley (1703–91) covered the whole country, with an educational as well as a religious message. Many nineteenth-century Labour leaders had received some of their education in Wesleyian chapels.

Mention has already been made of Robert Owen and his socialist ideas on education. In 1818 Owen had visited Pestalozzi at Yverdon. Pestalozzi's theories, based to some extent on the romantic views of Rousseau, confirmed Owen's educational practices at New Lanark, stressing praise and enjoyment rather than punishment and mechanical obedience. Wilderspin also stressed kindness, patience, sympathy and seeing the learning task from the point of view of the child. This was very different from the mechanical rote learning practised in most nineteenth-century schools.

There is, of course, a connection between the romantic educational views of the followers of Rousseau and the writings of John Ruskin. Both stressed the importance of nature and the natural. Rousseau believed that the child was 'naturally' good but corrupted by an unjust society. Ruskin hated the unnatural industrial, urbanised developments of much of England in the nineteenth century. Both wanted a natural environment for the young. Rousseau's views also influenced R.L. Edgeworth (1744–1817) and his daughter Maria who wrote about education and developed ideas from their experiences in schools. All of this was in step with the developing nineteenth-century humanitarianism which, as we saw earlier in this chapter, changed the laws on slavery, employment of children, prisons and other harsh social practices. At the end of the nineteenth century some school inspectors were attempting to improve educational practice in elementary schools. In general it would be true to say that early socialists tended to support this kind of progressive attitude in education.

Education and socialism

Long before the establishment of the Labour Party, those of a radical, anti-establishment frame of mind displayed a considerable interest in education, mainly for reasons of social justice, but partly because they were concerned by the waste of talent. Brian Simon (1960) begins the first of his four *Studies in the History of Education* in the period beginning 1760, and showed that many eighteenth-century enthusiasts for educational reform were Dissenters, accustomed to challenging conventional views on many social as well as religious issues. Many of the early socialists saw the advance of education and political progress essentially as part of a single programme. For example, William Morris (1834–96) had a vision of a better society where 'labour would be pleasurable and education the right of all'. For Morris, as for Robert Owen, work was a primary human activity which should be an expression of an individual's personality and dignity; but *laissez-faire* industrialisation had not only destroyed craftsmanship but had turned work into a burden. Education should be part of the transformation of society, and for Morris it was an essential part, enriching work with uniquely human activities like art, literature and science. He was, however, not enthusiastic about schools as he knew them: they had ceased to exist in the utopian society in *News from Nowhere* (1897).

Socialist attitudes which grew in the last quarter of the nineteenth century involved a break with traditional liberal ideas: 'Socialist education programmes aimed directly to change the workers' outlook, to develop a new conception of the dignity of man. In this sense the importance of the early socialist movement, as Morris insisted, was primarily educational' (Simon, 1965, p. 18). But this kind of programme would necessarily involve much more leisure for working-class adults; to some extent this was anticipated by the development of working men's clubs with well-stocked libraries and education classes of various kinds, especially in economics and politics. Organisations with similar aspirations included Republican Societies, and others such as secular Sunday schools.

More recently, Kevin Manton (2001) has written an excellent study of socialism and education in the last two decades of the nineteenth century (specifically, the years 1882–1902). I will not try to summarise this rich source of evidence, but will make some reference to a few sections. Manton shows that some socialist writers such as F.J. Gould, Harry Lowerison, H.W. Hobart and the steadfast reformer Margaret McMillan were not only extremely critical of the nineteenth-century elementary school system, but were also dissatisfied with teachers and their trade union, the National Union of Elementary School Teachers (NUEST). Education for the lower orders was still minimalist and deliberately inferior. Manton suggests that there was not complete consensus on education among socialist writers, but a few generalisations are possible. For example, they preferred local control (School Boards) to centralised direction (or to the later large Local Education Authorities). They were rightly suspicious that the government might want to use schools to make future workers more compliant and obedient. They, unlike many teachers, were opposed to the use of corporal punishment in schools, for educational as well as humanitarian reasons. Socialists disliked the testing regime associated with payment-by-results because it distorted the true purpose of education as well as teaching methods. Their socialism was of the ethical rather than the economic kind, but they saw that educational process could not be separated from general social and economic reform. They objected to the competitive capitalist model of society that they saw strengthened by the curriculum and pedagogy of elementary schools; they tended to dislike artificial subjects and the emphasis on the three Rs, but to favour an integrated curriculum, emphasising social and moral issues.

It may have been no accident that at the very time when socialists and radicals were beginning to influence a number of the local School Boards, that they were swept away as part of the 'reforms' of the 1902 Act. The boards were replaced by the more conservative local education authorities, mostly in the counties, as we shall see in Chapter 2.

Meanwhile, Manton's book gives us interesting examples of 'socialist education' in the 1890s, especially as practised in socialist Sunday schools. It was suggested, for example, that the ideal was 'to draw out rather than to cram in' (p. 92). They believed that education should be enjoyable but also that children should acquire habits of hard work and a respect for work. One of the socialist writers, Harold Lowerison, had the opportunity to put theory into practice: having been dismissed from his school in Hackney for his socialist views, he set up his own 'Ruskin School-Home' in Norfolk. It was based on three beliefs: first, that education should take place within a natural setting rather than always in a classroom; second, that the correct way to instil a moral code was by example; and finally, that children at the school should be presented with the motto 'justice and gentleness' together with scientific rationalism. Manton points out that these views were shared by William Morris and Margaret McMillan, for example.

As we shall see in Chapter 2, however, there was another view of education within the Labour movement, associated with Sidney Webb and some Fabians, that was much more utilitarian, centralist (following the Fabian concern for economics and national efficiency).

Another interesting example of socialist education was provided by the efforts of Annie Besant (1847–1933), a Fabian and a member of the Social Democratic Federation. Having assisted the match-girls' struggle against their employers in 1888, Mrs Besant proceeded to help them to establish a trade union with a club as an educational centre for the girls. Trade unionists were particularly anxious to develop economic understanding among their members, but some saw their role in much wider educational terms. Simon (1965) points out that in Bradford:

> A remarkable number of societies and local clubs had become established by 1892, including not only a Fabian society, a Labour Church, a Trades Council and Trade Union branches but also twenty-three local Labour clubs all concentrating on the instruction rather than the entertainment of their members, numbering some three thousand.
>
> (p. 37)

Co-operative Societies were also important, at about this time, for the development of educational activities for their members.

Between 1870 and 1900 many workers broke away from the limited thinking of Liberal 'reforms' and were seeking an alternative to the Liberal Party. By the time the LRC was established in 1900 many were considering education in very ambitious ways – but this was by no means the unanimous view of the Labour movement, as we shall see when discussing the early Fabian Society.

Three different views of socialism and education at the end of the nineteenth century

The Fabian Society

The Fabian Society was founded in 1884 in London as a non-revolutionary socialist society organised for research, discussion and publications about the gradual reform of society, not as a political party. Bernard Shaw joined soon after its foundation and became an active member, writing influential policy papers. Beatrice and Sidney Webb joined in 1885 and were frequently at odds with other socialists, especially about imperialism. In the long run, some of their views on education hindered the development of socialist theory and practices in education. The Fabian Society still exists, but has shed many of the principles associated with Sidney Webb. Support for imperialism was based on the idea that with the development of the welfare state in Britain, a superior kind of society could be exported to all corners of the British empire. Thus they expressed support for the British position in the Boer War, when others in the Labour movement were strongly against the war. Their view of social progress and efficiency was essentially a top–down approach. They hoped to convert the leaders of society by rational argument so that their views could be improved from above – in Britain and the empire and maybe the world. Sidney Webb was involved in the foundation of the London School of Economics and Political Science (LSE) in 1895. His concern was partly to provide the civil service with graduates educated in the social sciences rather than classics.

Sidney Webb's elitist attitude towards an efficient society also coloured early Fabian policies on education. Sidney Webb's vision of secondary education might be summed up by his phrase 'capacity-catching': he wanted a more efficient but still inferior system of elementary education for the majority, from which a small minority would be selected for a superior grammar school education. This 'ladder of opportunity' became a crude alternative policy to the socialist 'broad highway' – that is, real secondary education for all. Kenneth Morgan (1987) sums it up nicely:

> One is struck with equal force by their selflessness and their soul-lessness, by their dedication and their lack of humanity. Gradgrind was never far beneath the surface . . . Publicly, the Webbs were a kind of machine. They appeared to show little interest in a wider culture beyond the dictates

of the 'housekeeping state'. They did not particularly admire the workers they were anxious to organise, educate and improve.

(pp. 55–6)

Some would say that Webb's view of education was anti-socialist. On several occasions in the twentieth century his ideas continued to distort the development of Labour education.

It was no coincidence that many of Webb's policies for secondary education were taken up by the Tory Party and incorporated into Balfour's Education Act (1902). The Webbs were intellectual rationalists who had failed to learn the lessons of the Enlightenment, especially the need to temper reason and efficiency with humanity and fraternity. Later they were very impressed by the 'efficiency' they witnessed in Stalin's Russia. It is significant that William Morris left the Fabian Society because he could not share their vision of modern efficiency.

The Social Democratic Federation

Henry Hyndman (1842–1921) was an old-Etonian barrister who had stood, unsuccessfully, as an independent Conservative in 1880. In 1881 he founded the Democratic Federation which was the first socialist political organisation or party in England. It was Marxist in its doctrines, but it was Marx as interpreted by H.M. Hyndman, who had first tried, unsuccessfully, to inject his socialist theories into the Conservative Party. Having failed to convince Disraeli, Hyndman reorganised the Democratic Federation as a separate political party in 1884. Both Marx and Engels, however, disapproved of Hyndman and refused to have anything to do with his party, the Social Democratic Federation (SDF). Hyndman had produced a book *England for All* (1881) that was almost entirely based on the ideas of Marx, although Hyndman failed to give Marx personal credit, referring only to 'a great thinker and original writer'. Marx treated this acknowledgement as an insult. Hyndman spoke to working-class audiences wearing a silk hat and frockcoat, severely criticising them for accepting the capitalist yoke. He had a low opinion of working-class ability to organise themselves, including trade unions. He over-simplified Marx's ideas and presented a superficial view of industrialised society, but his writings were influential, and for most people were the only introduction available to Marx. (No English translation of *Kapital* was yet available.)

William Morris was attracted to some of Hyndman's writing and, for a short while, was a member of the SDF. He supported the idea of revolution but disliked Hyndman himself. Hyndman, in 1884, also began a journal, *Justice*. Marx's daughter, Eleanor, and Edward Aveling joined the SDF: 'In fact, there was hardly a socialist in the decade that followed who did not join the SDF – and leave it soon after. As Engels calculated in 1894, one million people had passed through it, but only 4,500 had stayed' (Benn, 1992, p. 30). Morris and a few others formed a rival Socialist League which had itself faded away by about 1889. John Burns also joined the SDF and stayed a little longer (until 1891) – long enough to be prosecuted with Hyndman in 1886 for leading a revolutionary procession in London. By 1889 trade and employment had improved and support for the SDF revolution diminished. Hyndman, unlike Morris, did not see education as a central concern of his socialist agenda: Hyndman was focused on the evils of capitalism and the domination of the working class by the unfair economic system itself. The conditions of the working class, according to Hyndman, could only be improved by revolution, not by education and welfare.

The Independent Labour Party (ILP)

An alternative organisation, however, was already developing: Keir Hardie's ILP was originally non-Marxist although some members were influenced by Hyndman's ideas whilst rejecting his organisation. Hardie had tried co-operating with the Liberal Party, and had been a candidate for mid-Lanark in 1886 with some Liberal support – but not enough to get elected. He became convinced that the interests of the Liberal Party were not close enough to working-class needs, and turned, first, to the Scottish Labour Party, and later to the more broadly based Independent Labour Party.

In the next year, 1893, 120 delegates chaired by Hardie met in Bradford to discuss working-class representation in Parliament. As well as five delegates from the SDF, the Fabians, the Scottish Labour Party, local Labour organisations and trade unions were all represented. They came with a very wide range of political beliefs. Significantly, the title 'Socialist Labour Party' was rejected in favour of the 'Independent Labour Party'. The SDF soon left because the new organisation was committed to constitutionalism rather than revolution.

In 1895 the ILP fielded 28 candidates at the general election, but none, not even Keir Hardie himself, was elected. The working-class population had not yet adjusted to the idea of an independent party, tending to remain loyal to the Liberal Party or even to be attracted by Disraeli's 'One Nation' Tory Party. The ILP might have been destroyed by this setback in 1895, but it was not; Hardie was determined to succeed. He and the ILP became even less popular by their opposition to the Boer War; but the ILP did not collapse.

In the same year, 1899, the TUC authorised its Parliamentary Committee to call a special conference of working-class organisations who would co-operate to improve Labour representation in Parliament. The conference met in January 1900 and set up the Labour Representation Committee (LRC) supported by the ILP, trade unions and the Fabian Society. Ramsay MacDonald was elected secretary. The ILP continued its independent existence until after World War II, having disaffiliated from the Labour Party in 1932; it remained a powerful tradition within Labour.

Kenneth Morgan (1987) listed what Keir Hardie himself stood for as follows: the fight against unemployment, women's rights, democracy and equality, Republicanism (including the abolition of the House of Lords), civil liberties, local decision-making (including Home Rule for Ireland), world peace and anti-imperialism. He and the early Labour Party were also against class war, direct action (and especially revolution) and Marxism. Hardie and the Party were constitutionalist from the beginning. His views and attitudes influenced many of his colleagues and left a mark on the Labour Party. Caroline Benn saw Keir Hardie as a complex, but great, political figure despite attempts by some writers to play down his significance within the Labour movement.

Keir Hardie could not be expected to be an education theorist: he regretted his own missed opportunities, and although he was proud of his self-education, wanted more and better schooling for working-class boys as well as equality for girls. He was in no position to specify in detail an educational programme, although he did suggest that the curriculum ought to include lessons in 'thrift'. Hardie saw clearly that education had to be part of the socialist vision of a better society. Education was a means to freedom. He believed in education in a broad sense, wider than simply schooling or training for work. Without education, people might add to their material possessions but remain enslaved. In 1882 he said that it was culture, knowledge and learning that would liberate the working class from the selfish greed engendered by capitalism. The purpose of education was not to increase earnings but to improve quality of life (Benn, 1992, p. 431).

Another Labour leader who began as a member of the ILP was Ramsay MacDonald who joined in 1894. He was also attracted by the ethical, non-Marxist, socialism of the ILP, and like Keir Hardie he opposed World War I in 1914, regarding it as the outcome of the undemocratic, aristocratic type of diplomacy that had resulted in the triple entente (England, France and Russia). MacDonald resigned from the Chairmanship of the Labour Party on the issue of support for the war, blaming the influence of trade union members for moving the Labour Party in the direction of chauvinism, when they should have been supporting international socialism. We shall take up the story of MacDonald's influence on the ILP and the Labour Party in the next chapter.

The roots of ideology

It is always dangerous to attempt to relate whole organisations to sets of beliefs or ideologies: organisations are made up of individuals who usually vary considerably in their beliefs. Nevertheless, it is useful to try to put individuals into groups, provided that we do not over-generalise. With that proviso, I would accept Foote's (1997) view that in 1900 the three main (overlapping) groups within the LRC were the ILP, the Fabians and trade union representatives, with three different sets of beliefs and ideas. I have already suggested that the ILP was influenced by ethical socialist ideas, especially social justice and the dignity of human beings. The Fabians, especially Sidney Webb, had, since 1883, been working with a different set of principles, more concerned with economic efficiency, involving nationalised industries, rather than with social justice. Webb and some other Fabians had a vision of society very different from that of Keir Hardie, for example.

Finally, trade union representatives within the LRC, the group probably still closest to the radical wing of the Liberal Party, were more pragmatic and more specific, with a list of desirable changes to the laws affecting their members (including their voting rights). They wanted better working conditions and wages *for their members* rather than measures that would benefit society as a whole. However, the TUC often made more general policy statements, including many on education.

These three main groups had different sets of ideas – not yet clearly formulated nor even attempting to be coherent. In addition, we should not ignore Marxism: it was by no means a major influence, but there were individuals in all three organisations who were impressed by the writings of Hyndman, but probably not directly by Marx. Marxism was the only 'ideology' which had the advantage (and the disadvantage) of a sacred text *Das Kapital*, even if it was not often read and was frequently misunderstood.

Conclusion

Throughout the nineteenth century there was a tension between certain Victorian social values (such as Christian charity, compassion and justice), and the economic and utilitarian doctrines of Adam Smith, Bentham and others (such as *laissez-faire*, individualism, informed self-interest, and the small state). Marxism was, strangely, a combination of both moral concerns and economic analysis. The attraction of his position, even if it was wrong, was that it presented a holistic analysis of the ills of industrialised capitalist society, together with a vision of the future.

Towards the end of the nineteenth century, as Geoffrey Foote has shown, this resulted in three different (but overlapping) socialist belief systems: first, ethical (humanitarian) socialism; second, the economic and social efficiency model advocated by the Webbs (the Fabians); third, Marxism. Some ethical Victorian values helped to provide the ILP with a set of beliefs, often of a semi-religious kind. At roughly the same time, the Webbs took control of the Fabian Society and developed a programme for the good state, including public control of industry. At the same time, a variety of Marxism became the gospel according to Henry Hyndman and the SDF.

The three groups were, of course, overlapping and frequently changing. William Morris, for example, joined and left the Fabians and the SDF, partly because he did not like the individuals, but more importantly, because he found the beliefs unacceptable. (He did not live long enough to make a decision about the Labour Party.)

In the 1890s there was a growth of working-class movements of many different kinds – trade unions, temperance movements, debating clubs, 'socialist' churches. This was accompanied by the gradual perception that there was a real need for parliamentary representation better than the Liberal Party was willing to provide. This encouraged the emergence of a political organisation, the LRC, despite the fact that the Fabians at first doubted the value of having a separate Party but favoured the policy of permeating the Liberals and Conservatives with Fabian enlightened ideas. Similarly, some ethical socialists had first been attracted by the idea of forming a group within the Liberal Party; there was a respectable radical tradition within Liberalism but in the end it became clear that the Liberal Party could not represent both workers and their bosses. Marxists generally rejected the 'parliamentary' solution advocated by Labour, and waited for revolution. Nevertheless, some of their ideas were incorporated into socialist and Labour Party thinking.

This left two socialist visions: one of a better society based on a more moral, principled way of life, avoiding exploitation and inequalities; the other aiming for a more efficient society based on economic principles and a state with power to control economic life (in future chapters I will avoid the temptation to refer to this group as 'the Fabians', which is increasingly misleading as the twentieth and twenty-first centuries progress). Each vision had a different view of the good society and a different conception of education: the first based on co-operation and quality of life (including leisure) with an emphasis on the need for social change; the second based on economic criteria, better training for effective workers and good citizens, and with an emphasis on social order. The extent to which these two visions of society and education could be reconciled within a single party will be the concern of later chapters.

2   The early years 1900–39

Ideas and contradictions

Deriving from an elitist conception of society and a conservative estimate of the extent of ability, Webb's educational policy was associated less with the universalist, social-service ambitions of some champions of the School Boards than with a desire to promote merit wherever it could be discovered. Education had to be scaled to the abilities of the child, and the cultivation of excellence was the first priority.

(Barker, 1972, p. 15)

Britain and the empire 1900–39

The period covered by this chapter is dominated by war and the threat of war. War often has an effect on changes within political parties as well as stimulating the desire for some kinds of educational progress. But the aftermath of war may prevent the implementation of reforms – including education.

At the beginning of the twentieth century, Britain was at war with the Boers in South Africa, and a little later was coping with the Boxer Rising in China. Both events, as well as many other less dramatic occurrences were reactions against British imperialism, which was based on a philosophy and set of practices that would split British society in general and the Labour Party in particular. The struggle of the Boers may even have suggested to Gandhi that the British were not invincible and should be opposed in India. In 1905 there was a bitter territorial war between Russia and Japan, and it was the non-European country that was successful. The West was showing signs of decay: in 1917 the Russian Revolution shook the whole of Europe. Nearer home, the Triple Alliance between Germany, Austria and Italy had been signed and there were rumblings within the Habsburg Empire that would eventually lead to the Sarajevo assassination and World War I (1914–18).

After the defeat of Germany in 1918, some predicted that the Versailles Treaty would inevitably lead to another war, at least between France and Germany. Italy turned to Mussolini and fascism in 1922. And Germany soon moved in a similar ideological direction with Hitler and the Nazi regime. World War II was soon to follow. Several historians, notably Roy Lowe (1988), have stressed the importance of the rapid development of industrialisation during this period and its impact on education. Lowe links industrial change to the position of women, imperialism and the development of collectivist ideas. All of these factors were to play a part in the development of education. There is also an unanswered question: was education a catalyst for change? Or, did education still 'prop up' an outmoded social structure?

British politics 1900–39

The early years of the century witnessed demands in many countries for greater working-class representation in government. In England, as was reported in Chapter 1, in February 1900 a conference of British working-class and socialist organisations (the ILP, the SDF, Fabians and trade unionists) set up the Labour Representation Committee with Ramsay MacDonald as its secretary.

In 1901 Queen Victoria died and was replaced by Edward VII. This made little difference, except that some thought a new century reinforced by a new age – the Edwardian – was significant. Some, but not all, Labour politicians had opposed the Boer War from the beginning. Nevertheless, the Tories won the 'Khaki election' in 1902 with 402 MPs, and only 2 Labour MPs were elected.

In 1901 the Taff Vale Railway Company won an action against a trade union for damages caused by a strike of railwaymen. The trade union was declared responsible according to the law: had this legislation remained it would have been disastrous for the growing trade union movement. The apparent injustice encouraged agitation to change the law, and Labour was supported by some Liberals in this. But the Tory government refused to act and Labour had to wait for the next Parliament before any legislation more favourable to the working class was possible.

In 1906 there was a change of government. The Liberals under Campbell-Bannerman won a landslide victory, and Labour increased its number of seats to 30. The LRC was now officially transformed into the Labour Party. The new Liberal government made strike action legal (reversing the *Taff Vale* judgment), and Lloyd George as Chancellor of the Exchequer was assured of Labour support on the Old Age Pensions Act (1908). In 1910 there were two general elections (February and December). Labour increased its MPs to 40 and then to 42. The Labour Party, together with the Irish Nationalists held the balance of power between the Liberals and the Tories. Labour was able to bargain with the Liberals, agreeing to support some Liberal measures in return for legislation that would grant salaries for MPs (in 1912) and the Trade Union Act (1913).

There had been an important constitutional development in 1909 which gave rise to the two elections in 1910. The Lords, dominated by the Tory Party, refused to pass Lloyd George's 'People's budget', ignoring the convention that the House of Lords should not interfere with financial legislation. The budget was eventually passed when there was a threat of creating sufficient new peers to outvote the Tory majority in the Lords. A further advantage was that the Conservative peers also had to allow the Parliament Act of 1911 which restricted the ability of the Lords to delay any Act. In 1913 the Liberals also passed the Trade Union Act which reversed the *Osborne* judgment of 1910 that had prevented trade unions from funding political activities.

During the war years, 1914–18, there was a tendency for political parties to try to co-operate: a coalition government existed from 1915, at first under Asquith and later, 1916, under Lloyd George. A number of Labour MPs, including Keir Hardie and Ramsay MacDonald opposed the war. Hardie continued to attack the government on domestic issues, including education. In 1915, when a new by-law was introduced allowing children under 12 to leave school to work on farms, he protested that farmers were being given cheap labour taking priority over children's education. He would not accept that for children not intellectually bright 'schooling was a waste of money'. One of his favourite precepts was that it was time for education to be seen from a working-class point of view (Benn, 1992, p. 339).

Arthur Henderson, who took over as leader of the Labour Party when Ramsay MacDonald temporarily withdrew from the leadership, became a member of the War Cabinet. This did not prevent industrial unrest, however, especially in the latter part of the war. In the first post-war election in 1918, the Labour Party hoped to benefit from the extension of the vote to all men over 21 and most women over 30. Expecting to win at least 100 seats they only managed to get 63, and many leaders lost their own seats (including MacDonald, Lansbury, Snowden and Henderson).

The Labour Party, in 1918, adopted a constitution largely written by Sidney Webb which included a commitment to the nationalisation of the means of production (later clause 4). For the first time the Labour Party was openly committed to a socialist programme. From then onwards, individuals could join the Labour Party directly, rather than through affiliated bodies such as trade unions, the ILP or the Fabian Society. The TUC continued to be an important source of funding. But some were still dissatisfied with the Labour Party and considered other possibilities. For example, Sylvia Pankhurst started her own communist party. Others, including Emrys Hughes, preferred the ILP as an organisation, and voiced their disapproval of some Labour views on education (see discussion later in this chapter).

The Lloyd George coalition continued until 1922 when the Conservatives withdrew their support. The Conservative Party gained a big majority at the general election (when Labour MPs reached a total of 142). In 1923 Labour won a total of 191 seats, more than the Liberals' 159. Ramsay MacDonald, leader of the Labour Party since 1922, agreed to form a minority government in 1923 after the Tory government had been defeated over tariff reform. Labour remained in power for only ten months when the weakness of having to rely on the Liberals became apparent, and the first Labour government was defeated. The Conservative Party returned to power with a very comfortable majority over all other Parties, having won 419 seats. Whatever his faults, Lloyd George had been an advocate of better public education: this was not the case with the Conservatives who replaced him.

In 1929 the Labour Party had another chance to form a government, although with 288 seats against the Conservative's 260, once again MacDonald had to rely on support from the 59 Liberal MPs. It was not the best of times to form another government without a clear majority. The economic situation was reaching crisis point. Labour, with Philip Snowden as Chancellor of the Exchequer, attempted to pursue an 'orthodox' financial policy, in other words a capitalist rather than a socialist programme. In 1931, when international pressure and the banks forced the government to cut spending, including unemployment benefits, Snowden and MacDonald lost support, including that of most of the Labour MPs. Instead of resigning and handing over the poisoned chalice to the Tories or settling for a general election, Ramsay MacDonald accepted a suggestion from the King and the Tory leader, Stanley Baldwin, that he should remain as the Prime Minister of a 'National' government. For this MacDonald was expelled from the Labour Party and branded as a traitor. The Labour Party was badly divided and lost many seats at the 1931 general election. They retained only 52 MPs compared with the National Government's 554 (including 13 'National Labour'). The Labour Party did not fully recover from this catastrophic split until World War II: at the 1935 general election there were 154 Labour MPs against 432 Conservatives.

Educational developments, 1900–39

It will be convenient to discuss this period under the six headings:

1   the 1902 Education Act (the Balfour Act);
2   the 1918 Education Act (the Fisher Act);
3   education policies and events during the first Labour government;
4   the Conservative years, 1924–29 (including the Hadow Report, 1926);
5   education policies and events during the second Labour government;
6   other educational developments during the 1930s (including the 1936 Education Act).

The 1902 Education Act

Some of the background to this Act was briefly outlined in Chapter 1. During the last years of the nineteenth century some progress had been made towards an improved elementary school system: payment-by-results had virtually disappeared; some School Boards were improving their local schools as far as the rules permitted (and sometimes straying beyond the rules); 'higher grade' schools were popular in several boards. Brian Simon (1965, p. 179) estimated that by 1895 there were 67 higher grade schools with 25,000 students receiving good quality education). Some of those who were less than enthusiastic about 'education on the rates' had been convinced by the Boer War that our minimalist elementary system needed considerable improvement. On the other hand, there were many others who thought that education provided by the boards was too good, and the *Cockerton* judgment meant that School Boards would not be permitted to allow schools to develop work considered to be 'secondary', however great the local and national needs. Some politicians, including the Duke of Devonshire (President of the Board of Education) and his representative in the Commons, Sir John Gorst, were also disturbed by the way that democratically elected School Boards were interpreting their role. Moreover, the TUC and some new trade unionists were developing an attitude to education that was seen as dangerous: the TUC Circular and Resolution of 1900 said that 'the distinction of primary and secondary schools should be . . . strictly and solely educational, marking the successive stages of an educational curriculum; and not social, marking merely different grades of social rank' (quoted by Simon, 1965, p. 201). The TUC also demanded the provision of maintenance grants for workers' children, but specifically attacked the idea of the scholarship ladder: 'the system of providing secondary education only for the very small proportion of the workers' children who can come to the top after severe competition with their school fellows is to be strongly condemned' (quoted by Simon, 1965, p. 202). This was dangerous stuff as far as Devonshire, Gorst and also Morant were concerned.

The 1902 Act, usually referred to as the Balfour Act after the Conservative Prime Minister who took personal responsibility for the Bill, was mainly the work of Robert Morant, an able civil servant whose views on education were essentially based on upper-class assumptions about social stability. Morant wanted to restrict elementary schools to their traditional role, encourage the development of a limited number of secondary schools, and replace School Boards by a centrally directed system of education administered locally by 'safe' Local Education Authorities that would probably be dominated by squires and parsons.

In pursuit of these policies, Morant and Sir John Gorst, were assisted by the detailed planning of Sidney Webb who had recently published a Fabian pamphlet *The Educational Muddle and the Way Out* (1901). The explanation of this strange collusion is reasonably straightforward. The Bryce Committee had been set up as far back as 1894 to 'consider the best methods of establishing a well organised system of secondary education in England'. The report (1895) made a number of recommendations including the establishment of a single central authority for education, with local authorities responsible for secondary as well as elementary schools, and a scholarship system joining some elementary pupils to secondary places. None of these recommendations had been adopted by 1902. There was a muddle about secondary education that urgently needed attention. Secondary schools operated entirely outside the School Boards, some of which had accordingly set up alternative arrangements to secondary schools by stretching the elementary school structure. Leeds School Board had a high grade school in 1872 and other boards, including London, followed the example. There were also many schools funded by a separate government agency, the Science and Arts Department in South Kensington. To bureaucratically minded men like Morant and Webb, the untidiness was both inefficient and perhaps in danger of getting out of central control.

School Boards were, however, popular with liberals as well as socialists, and their abolition was seen as undemocratic and as a way of benefiting Anglican schools which could now receive state and local funding. Much of the Labour movement lined up with the Liberals to oppose the Bill, but the Labour Party (still officially the LRC) did not have an agreed position on education. Sidney and Beatrice Webb represented an extreme view, not even shared by all Fabians: 'Neither was by temper, instinct or training democratic. Sidney was a born bureaucrat; Beatrice a born aristocrat. In each case, the impulse was benevolent and entirely disinterested; in neither, equalitarian' (M.A. Hamilton, 1944, *Remembering My Good Friends*, quoted by Barker, 1972, p. 16).

In other parts of the Labour movement, the TUC and the Co-operative Societies were completely opposed to the Bill, strongly supporting School Boards. The ILP was, however, divided. The second Annual Conference of the LRC was in favour of School Boards and rejected a Fabian amendment supporting the Bill.

Sidney Webb had to some extent anticipated the 1902 Education Act in his work for the Technical Education Board of the London County Council where he had put into operation a workable 'ladder of opportunity'. Webb was firmly committed to selection rather than 'common schools' and wanted to develop what he described as 'the greatest capacity-catching machine the world has ever yet seen' (quoted by Barker, p. 16). Webb's views were, however, opposed by such socialists as Keir Hardie, Will Crooks, a Fabian MP, and Will Thorne of the SDF.

The Labour movement was already divided on education principles, especially on the issue of selection. The Labour movement was, however, also divided on the question of financial support for Church Schools which was part of the Bill. In general Labour supported free, compulsory, *secular* education, but there was considerable Roman Catholic pressure that prevented unanimity on the religious question, and this issue, which provoked noisy opposition to the Bill, tended to obscure what was later considered to be the more important educational questions about School Boards and selection. Meanwhile, Webb's pamphlet was made available to several thousand readers, and even before publication was offered at proof stage to Gorst who circulated it to others in the Tory Party as well as to those like Morant responsible for detailed drafting of the Bill.

The 1902 Act was passed despite furious protests. It is important in this chapter to stress two points: first, to dispel the myth of steady progress from the lack of any education system at the beginning of the nineteenth century, to the 1870 Education Act, and then with further advances from 1902 to 1944 – the reality was much more complex, and progress was contested and distorted at almost every point. Second, the 1902 events show that from the beginning, Labour lacked a clear, unified view about education priorities and policies.

This was not a purely educational debate: underlying the two views about the 1902 Act there were fundamentally different beliefs and attitudes about society, ranging from the Webbs' Fabian approach based on efficiency, to the ethical socialist tradition that emphasised social justice and quality of life. These two views remained throughout the twentieth century and into the twenty-first. The importance of this ideological division cannot be exaggerated.

The 1918 Education Act

The main effects of the 1902 Act had been, first, to abolish democratic School Boards and replace them by Local Education Authorities (counties and county boroughs that were mainly under Tory control); and, second, to drive a wedge between elementary schools for all working-class children and qualitatively different secondary schools. Only working-class children of exceptional ability would be permitted to join those children whose parents could pay the secondary school fees. Even some supporters of the 1902 Act were disappointed when it was interpreted in a restricted way by the new Board of Education: for example, Nottingham had planned four new grammar schools but received permission for only two, enhancing the exclusive element in the legislation. The NUT also objected to the decision by the Board of Education only to recognise secondary schools that charged fees. Morant intended the two school systems to be as distinct as possible, rigidly defined and joined only by a ladder for the exceptional.

This may have stimulated socialists to increase their activities:

> During the twelve years between the passing of the 1902 Act and the outbreak of war the Labour movement evolved a clear educational policy, one which sought not only to gain immediate improvements but also to secure fundamental changes in the structure of the educational system as a whole. This growing clarity reflected an increasing strength and maturity; it reflected also the growing influence of socialist thinking.
>
> (Simon, 1965, p. 249)

Partly because the 1902 Act was unpopular, there was a change of government in 1906. The Liberals had a good majority in the Commons but were easily outvoted in the Lords. The Liberal attempts to modify some of the 1902 Act were simply turned back by the Lords. Meanwhile, the TUC was increasingly active on education policy and from 1905 began to insist on the principle of equal opportunities in education. The LRC in the same year did not go quite as far, but demanded that technical and secondary education should be free.

During the Liberal government after 1906 there were a few minor victories concerned with welfare and health rather than education itself, but they helped to establish a general concern for children and the need to move away from child labour. It is also worth a mention, but not much more, that from May 1915 to October 1916, during the war-time coalition government, a Labour MP, Arthur Henderson, was President of the Board of Education. It was of limited importance because Henderson was not able to take any useful action on education during the war. But when Lloyd George replaced Asquith as Prime Minister in 1916, some interesting changes took place, including the appointment of the Liberal H.A.L. Fisher as President of the Board of Education, who insisted on having some real power. By this time there were considerable pressures on the government for social changes, including education. Part of the government motivation was the suspicion that German education was superior and that this was having some effect on the war effort. Fisher, former Vice-Chancellor of Sheffield University, was eager to make progress, although most of the discussion was still about education after the war. His Education Bill (1917) contained some progressive measures. There were two main proposals: first, full-time education for all up to the age of 14, with no exemptions; those who did not receive full-time education from 14–16 were to have part-time education up to 18 in continuation schools. Second, LEAs were requested to prepare plans for the development of education as a continuing process, including nursery schools for children under 5. Fisher carefully avoided any attempt to revive the arguments about Church Schools. The TUC expressed disappointment that the school leaving age was not to be 16 for all. But the reform was made even more modest when a group of employers conspired to have an amendment proposed (supported by some Labour MPs in Lancashire) that would postpone the provision of part-time education for 7 years. Only then was the Bill passed, shortly before the war came to an end.

Labour complaints about the Act may have been muted by the fact that they were still part of the war-time coalition government. Barker (1972) suggests that there were four kinds of Labour response to the Act: those who welcomed the Bill, passively; those who were generally sympathetic but wanted further reforms; those who opposed parts of the Bill; and finally, some who seemed to have taken no interest in the Bill at all. (The ILP's Parliamentary Report for 1918 made no mention of the Act) (Barker, 1972, p. 29).

Fisher was disappointed by the apparent lack of enthusiasm for his Bill on the part of the Labour Party inside the Commons. The explanation for some of this indifference was that many Labour MPs still wanted improvements in elementary school education itself, and others like the Lancashire MPs were reluctant to restrict the earning power of young members of families working in factories. In the 1918 election, however, the Labour Party increased its number of seats and adopted a new constitution, including the well-known clause 4 about public ownership of the means of production. In June 1918 a new document appeared, *Labour and the New Social Order,* setting out such objectives as a rationalised education system from nursery school to university, social equality, and reorganisation of society on the basis of co-operation, equality and participation. But universal secondary education was not specifically mentioned. R.H. Tawney was later to comment: 'In 1918, the Labour Party finally declared itself to be a Socialist Party. It supposed, and supposes, that it thereby became one. It is mistaken. It recorded a wish, that is all; the wish has not been fulfilled' (Tawney, 1934, p. 5).

Some socialists, including Emrys Hughes were disillusioned at this time with education practice as well as Labour policies:

> Emrys stopped teaching altogether in 1920. Even if he had not wanted to take up political work, he had come to hate the strict disciplinarian attitudes teachers were forced to display at that time and which the ILP soon turned against, calling the 'education of the masses and drudgery to both pupil and teacher', designed for a man to be kept subordinate. The working class 'do not want ladders . . . and patronage' but 'culture, independence and power'; not to know things but to know how to think of things, because 'it is much easier to mislead people who read but cannot think than people who think but cannot read'.
>
> > (Benn, p. 394, quoting from Hughes *Journal of a Coward*, and ILP leaflet, no. 4, *c.* 1917)

This is an interesting example of a Labour point of view, rejecting 'more of the same' as a policy for working-class education. Emrys Hughes, Keir Hardie's son-in-law, was firmly committed to the ethical socialist view of education and found the Webb efficiency model completely unacceptable.

The first Labour government, 1924

If the Fisher Act was modest it was at least a step in the right direction. But the reality of post-war conditions proved too strong even for Fisher's minor reforms. In 1921 a Committee on National Expenditure, chaired by Sir Eric Geddes, recommended that education grants be reduced by one-third. This 'Geddes Axe' put an end to any immediate education improvements, cut education expenditure and also reduced teachers' salaries. Little of any educational significance occurred until the first Labour government in 1924. By that date R.H. Tawney had produced for the Labour Party an ambitious document *Secondary Education for All: A Policy for Labour* (1922), followed by his popular version, *Education: The Labour Policy* (1924). Both proposed a reversal of the fundamental 1902 decision:

> The Labour Party is convinced that the only policy which is at once educationally sound and suited to a democratic community is one under which primary education and secondary education are organised as two stages in a single continuous process; secondary education being the education of the adolescent and primary education being education preparatory thereto.
>
> > (Tawney, 1922, p. 7)

Alarmed by this kind of rhetoric, the Conservative government was persuaded to ask the consultative committee of the Board of Education to review the whole question of post-11 provision, with the intention of 'dispelling the socialist and Labour war cry of secondary education for all' (Simon, 1974, p. 76). The Tories hoped that this diversion could be achieved before the Labour Party might come to power, but the consultative committee did not report until 1926 (the Hadow Report, *The Education of the Adolescent*) when the Conservatives were again in office (see below). Meanwhile, the Labour Party had a document which was at least an expression of socialist intentions, but Barker's judgment on it is highly critical:

> *Secondary Education for All* had two qualities which rendered it an almost perfect illustration of the character of the Labour Party which produced it. It drew on the concepts of citizenship, commonwealth, equality, and social justice, and set the educational system in the midst of the struggle to replace a divided materialistic society with one properly attuned to intellectual and spiritual values. But its proposals were taken directly from the educational system of its time and were no more and no less than an extension into general practice, and at a more generous level of expenditure, of particular experiments and ideas less well publicised than Tawney's.
>
> (p. 43)

Barker's intention was to show that Labour Party education policy was, despite their ideals, in practice insufficiently different from that of the Liberals or even the Conservatives. Nigel Haslewood (1981) has, however, pointed out that it is always important historically to distinguish between rhetoric and real policy intentions. Haslewood criticises Barker for comparing the Liberal and Conservative promises in their election manifestos of 1924 and 1929 with what Labour actually achieved, under extremely difficult circumstances in their first and second governments. There were also real differences between Labour and the Conservatives on the issue of equality of opportunity. Clive Griggs (2002) has also produced evidence showing that Labour and Tory thinking on education was very different in 1925. The delegation from the Trade Union Congress included Labour MPs and it was clear that they had little in common with the President of the Board, Lord Eustace Percy (see below).

Brian Simon in a somewhat different context (1974, p. 72) drew attention to the fact that in 1922–23 the Tories had been worried by teachers becoming attracted to the Labour Party because they perceived it as more sympathetic to the education service. It would seem that teachers in the 1920s were not under the impression that there was little difference between the Parties on education. Some of this difference was due to Tawney's consistent advocacy of 'secondary education for all' even if that slogan was open to a variety of interpretations.

Brian Simon (1974), however, criticised Tawney for failing to advocate comprehensive schools throughout the 1920s. Tawney certainly failed to rethink secondary education in terms other than the grammar school with its existing traditional curriculum. In accepting some of these criticisms of Tawney, Haslewood wanted to insist on the considerable achievements of Tawney, especially when he was defending his views on two fronts: from the Tories and some Liberals for advancing too quickly and advocating far too much spending; and from some of his own Labour Party who were not yet convinced that secondary education for all should be top of Labour's list of education priorities.

Labour's ten months in office were not wasted. The Labour President of the Board of Education was Charles Trevelyan, a convert from the Liberal Party who had served as a Junior Education Minister, 1908–14. He joined the Labour Party in 1919 and soon became a spokesman on education. His initial admiration of MacDonald turned to hostility when he experienced his lack of socialist values. Trevelyan's first act as president in 1924 was to withdraw circular 1190 which in 1922 had restricted expenditure on education. He also encouraged LEAs to use by-laws to raise the school leaving age, but they generally failed to take action.

Barker claims (p. 50) that Trevelyan probably did not have any contact with Tawney or with the Party's education advisory committee before taking office in 1924, but Tawney was not slow to make his views known to the president, and sent a memo from the advisory committee offering detailed advice on priorities: to improve conditions in elementary schools; to increase secondary places; to increase the number of free secondary places; to improve maintenance allowances; to abolish fees within five years; and that full-time education should take priority over continuation schools. Trevelyan acted on some of the committee's advice, but fudged the distinction between secondary education and senior elementary schools in a way that might have threatened the clear-cut policy of 'secondary education for all'. A quarrel between the president and the advisory committee was avoided, and without legislation Trevelyan encouraged LEAs to increase free places. But LEAs were reluctant to act individually on this issue – a national policy was essential.

Trevelyan was popular in the Party, but his action on free places, by giving approval to the process of selection, might also have been seen as moving against the principle of 'secondary education for all'. This was a familiar problem for Labour: the ultimate objective was secondary education for all, but meanwhile it was useful to improve the existing system. As I pointed out earlier, some in the Labour Party wanted to retain a selective system. When the Labour government fell, education was seen as one of two successes, second only to Wheatley's much praised Housing Act which had lasting benefits. Simon (1974) sums up the year (1924) perfectly:

> Short though the period had been, the Labour Government had tackled matters with considerable effect. Trevelyan had set foot on a concerted effort, across the board, to extend the school life of the majority beyond 14, furthering the appropriate arrangements while at the same time making direct moves to extend secondary education and make it free. It was, therefore, in a positive context that the conception of a general reorganisation of schools for those over 11 took root.
>
> (Simon, 1974, p. 84)

The Conservative years, 1924–9 (including the Hadow Report, 1926)

The performance of the first Labour government had disappointed some, but progress had been made despite the lack of a generally accepted set of education priorities (and the lack of any socialist theory on education). There were now three positions within the Party on secondary education: some wanted to develop elementary schools with good quality education for the whole 11–16 group; others following Sidney Webb's 1902 ideas, pursued the policy of secondary education for all on a selective basis, hoping to increase the number of free places and ensure that working-class children would get a fair share of those places (an improved ladder of opportunity); finally, there existed a more egalitarian view of secondary education for all (a broad highway approach based on common schools). The third option was as yet unclear and there was no theoretical description of what that kind of secondary education would mean in practice. No one had yet made any plans about the kind of curriculum that would be appropriate in the context of 'secondary education for all'.

The Conservative successor as President of the Board of Education was Lord Eustace Percy. One of his first acts was to abolish the grants to LEAs that encouraged free places in secondary schools: a clear difference between Labour and Tory was that Percy, reflecting the views of his Party, wanted secondary education to remain highly exclusive.

The confusion that existed on both sides of the House of Commons in 1925 can be seen by a private motion, introduced by a Labour member, Richardson, but backed by all parties, calling on LEAs to prepare schemes for full-time post-primary education for all up to 16, together with an increase in the percentage of free places in secondary schools. All three parties appeared to want more education for all, but they did not necessarily agree on priorities. Eustace Percy dismissed the idea of secondary education for all as merely 'pious' (Simon, 1974, p. 117). Barker suggests that they were all waiting for the Hadow Report, but this no longer seems completely plausible: reference has already been made to work by Griggs (2002) describing the delegation from the TUC and Labour Party to the President of the Board, Eustace Percy, when the Labour point of view met with no kind of positive response from the president. The parties were still divided on some issues, especially fees: most Labour MPs wanted abolition, whereas Tories approved of fees and did not want too many free places. Any impression that there was little difference between the parties was dispelled by the General Strike 1926 which divided the nation on most issues. Lord Eustace Percy was, however, soon embarked on a programme of education cuts in 1926–27.

At the Labour Party conference in 1926, reflecting a post-strike aggressive mood, there was a resolution from Manchester calling for education to play a part in 'abolishing the present and creating a new Order in Society'. This resolution was passed without difficulty, as was another from the Teachers' Labour League that protested against 'imperialist propaganda in schools, biased textbooks and the ritual celebration of Empire day' (Simon, 1974, p. 113). Both resolutions were then referred to the Education Advisory Committee and were suitably reworded as policy in *From Nursery School to University* (Labour Party, 1928). It would seem that the relation between education and a new order in society was not converted into either theory or practice, but the sentiment still worried Eustace Percy and many of his Tory colleagues.

The Hadow Report, 1926

The Consultative Committee for Education (chaired by H.H. Hadow) was asked by the Conservative administration in 1924 for a report on courses and curricula for children up to the age of 15 in schools other than secondary schools (i.e. other than grammar schools) covering both a good general education and a reasonable variety of curricula for children of varying tastes and abilities; in addition, advice was sought on the examination of end-of-course achievements.

We have seen that the original intention of the Conservatives was to provide an alternative to Labour's 'secondary education for all'. But soon after the committee had started work, the Labour government began its nine months of power (in 1924). This had an effect on the deliberations of the committee which included Tawney who had, ironically, been the person most responsible for the secondary education for all doctrine in 1922. (Tawney had been due to retire from the committee in 1924, but the Permanent Secretary of the Board, Selby-Bigge, ensured that he was reappointed.) The committee also included Albert Mansbridge (founder of the Workers Education Association) and several others with enlightened views on education. On the other hand, the committee also included Percy Jackson, who was the originator of the idea of developing an alternative to Labour's 'secondary education for all'. Since grammar schools were specifically excluded from the terms of reference, this could have limited the discussion of 11–16 schooling, but the committee overcame this difficulty by regretting the current educational terminology 'secondary education' referred to a type of education rather than to a 'stage' or 'age-group'; they then proceeded to discuss the general need for a primary stage followed at 11+ by a secondary stage for all adolescents. They even went further: acknowledging that to recommend that all forms of secondary education should be treated equally in terms of building, finance and organisation, was outside their terms of reference, but they suggested that should 'such a development occur we would be disposed to view it favourably' (Simon, 1974, p. 128).

The Hadow Report, *The Education of the Adolescent*, was published in December 1926. It recommended that primary education should end at 11, and that all should proceed to secondary schools until at least age 15; the principle of secondary education for all was accepted, but secondary schools might be either grammar or central (now to be called modern) schools, or senior divisions of elementary schools. 'All go forward, though along different paths. Selection by differentiation takes the place of selection by elimination.' How was not explained, but the different types of school would have distinctive curricula: secondary modern schools would have 'at least a four-year course from the age of 11+ with a realistic or practical trend in the last two years' (p. 95). The grammar schools would continue to 'pursue in the main a predominately literary or scientific curriculum' (p. 99). There would also be technical and trade schools, starting at age 13 for suitable pupils, in institutions 'developed so far as is possible in accordance with the needs and requirements of certain local industries' (p. 66). Primary education would end at 11+, and the term 'elementary' school would eventually disappear. Simon points out that only one person giving evidence to the Committee, J.H. Hallam, Chief Officer for Secondary Education in the West Riding, 'indicated how the problem of incorporating new divisions in the school system could be evaded, and a realistic approach made to children's needs, by adopting a single secondary school' (Simon, 1974, p. 131).

The Report was capable of a variety of interpretations, and in 1928 the Conservative government's Board of Education issued an explanatory pamphlet, *The New Prospect in Education*, that discussed the problems of reorganisation in LEAs. The Hadow Report was clearly incomplete, and the consultative committee would have to take up the question of secondary education again under the chairmanship of Will Spens. Its interim report, *The Spens Report on Secondary Education* (1938), will be discussed below. Meanwhile, in the years 1926–29 there were many different kinds of response to the report.

This is not the place to discuss all the responses to Hadow (1926) (see Simon, 1974, pp. 132ff.). It will be sufficient here to contrast the Conservative and Labour Parties. Labour MPs tabled a motion welcoming the Report and calling on the government to implement the kind of post-primary education advocated in it, together with raising the school leaving age. At its annual conference the Labour Party accepted a memorandum from its Education Advisory Committee which wanted to interpret the Hadow Report in a vaguely multilateral way (Simon, 1974, p. 136) and confirming support for its own policy in *Secondary Education for All* (Tawney 1922). Trevelyan readily accepted the motion as suitable 'marching orders' for a Labour Minister of Education.

The Conservative government claimed to accept the principles of the Report, but rejected the central Hadow recommendation about raising the school leaving age: Percy explained that he had no intention of disturbing the plans of LEAs which were based on the assumption that most children would complete their schooling at 14. He preferred to spend the limited resources available on an able minority. For Percy (and most Tories) the grammar school was a superior education for superior children. This at least provided the Labour Party with a ready-made policy: a negative attitude of hostility to the principle of a good education only for a minority; plus a positive principle of raising the school leaving age for all. The Hadow Report, all but rejected by the Tories, almost automatically became Labour Party policy. It will be necessary to return to the Hadow Report later in this Chapter and in Chapter 3 when the kind of thinking that persisted from Hadow 1926 to the Education Act 1944 (and beyond) will be examined.

The second Labour government, 1929–31

Trevelyan was again appointed President of the Board of Education. He had a shopping list but little cash to spend. Education was not top of the Prime Minister's list of priorities – unemployment and the economic situation were more urgent. Improved education on its own would not solve the ills of what was now seen as a sick society. Education and social reforms needed to progress side by side, and were hardly possible without a working majority.

The major issue for Trevelyan and those who wanted to carry on the battle for education was raising the school leaving age. Trevelyan was, however, unable to persuade the Prime Minister and some other Cabinet members that a leaving age of 15 was worth fighting for at that time. Apart from the problem of finding the money, MacDonald and Snowden were still worried about alienating members in Lancashire and Yorkshire. On the other hand, the Education Advisory Committee sent a deputation, including Tawney, to Trevelyan seeking an assurance that an Education Bill would be drafted without delay. Some Labour members also wanted to separate the school leaving age issue from unemployment. The Cabinet agreed that the school leaving age should be raised to 15 in 1931. However, Thomas, Snowden and MacDonald still resisted giving education priority on the legislation timetable. Trevelyan also faced Labour criticism for not improving maintenance allowances as promised at the 1927 conference, and for not abolishing means testing. This was unfair because the blame should have fallen on MacDonald and Snowden. Snowden's lack of interest in education is shown by the fact that in his autobiography he does not even mention the Labour education policies. He was not alone in regarding education as insignificant compared to Labour's financial problems.

A school leaving age of 15 was still opposed by Eustace Percy and most Tories. There was also an immediate financial problem: it would be essential to have enough public funds available to be able to reassure the Anglicans, Roman Catholics and Non-conformists that raising the school leaving age would not leave them with the task of finding the necessary cash; and it was difficult to satisfy the Anglicans without antagonising the Non-conformists who would object to Church of England schools being treated too favourably.

A Bill was introduced in October 1930, and Trevelyan was able to reach an agreement about more government money for voluntary schools in exchange for greater LEA control. Some Roman Catholics MPs were, however, still not prepared to trust the government, and introduced an amendment to the Bill delaying its implementation until financial provision was actually made for voluntary schools. In the end all of this was completely wasted effort: the House of Lords simply rejected the Bill. Trevelyan resigned in despair. Barker, whose research included a detailed analysis of Trevelyan's private papers concluded that:

> Trevelyan's had been the only voice of importance, apart from Mosley's, raised against MacDonald before the final break. The Lords' rejection of

his Bill in February 1931 had been for Trevelyan the confirmation of a growing feeling of political impotence rather than a sudden check to his policy. He had for several months been virtually convinced that he could achieve nothing of value in a government of which MacDonald was Head, and he had come increasingly to believe that the Prime Minister was not just hostile to the raising of the leaving age, but generally incapable of exercising the political initiative which he felt to be necessary before the government could pursue his conception of a socialist programme.

(Barker, 1972, p. 63)

Trevelyan, disillusioned by the leadership of his Party, devoted his energies to his own estate and local political activities. He accepted the Lord Lieutenancy of Northumberland and continued as a member of the Labour Party Executive until 1934, acquiring the reputation of being on the left wing of the Party. The Party learned the lesson of trying to govern without a majority, especially with a House of Lords hostile to its programme. In August 1931 the loss of an Education Bill was overshadowed by the financial crisis and then by MacDonald's formation of the 'National' government.

Educational developments in the 1930s

The National Government, after the 1931 election, still faced an economic crisis. It reverted to the policy of 1922 that had produced 'the Geddes axe': a select committee on national expenditure was set up. Its report recommended drastic cuts in education and other services. Herwald Ramsbottom, the Conservative Under-Secretary for Education, and Secretary to the Select Committee, welcomed the cuts on the grounds that it would avoid the nation becoming 'an educational soup kitchen'.

By 1936, however, the economic situation had improved to some extent and the government responded to pressure by introducing a Bill to raise the school leaving age to 15 (with ample exemptions) with effect from 1 September 1939. This was far short of Labour's demand for secondary education for all, and it was not to be implemented in 1939: by 1 September World War II was too close to allow any government energy being expended on education. One year earlier, another report had been published that remained influential for at least the next twenty years. The Report of the Consultative Committee on Secondary Education (Spens Report) in 1938 recommended three different kinds of school for three different types of children.

The Spens Report (1938) and secondary education

The Spens Report was limited to a consideration of grammar schools and technical schools. It failed to give a lead on the kind of curriculum that would be suitable for the majority of pupils 11–16. By recommending separate grammar schools, technical schools and secondary modern schools on the basis of detailed psychological evidence, it took the debate on secondary education on a path that misled later committees such as Norwood (1943) that will be discussed in Chapter 3.

It should perhaps be stressed that the Spens Report was intended to be an interim report of the Spens Committee, but the committee was disbanded in 1939. Even so, the board (in the form of M.G. Holmes) felt it necessary to say that the Board of Education could not be committed to its recommendations. Lady (Sheena) Simon was a member of the Spens Committee, but at that time had not been convinced of arguments in favour of comprehensive schools. There were other 'progressive' educationists on the committee, for example, Mansbridge and J.H. Simpson, but their influence is difficult to find in the recommendations.

It is clear from the Hadow Report (1926), the Spens Report (1938) and the Norwood Report (1943) that the policy of the Board of Education was to develop a tripartite system of secondary education: separate grammar, technical and modern schools with different curricula for different types of children. The way that the Spens Report was drafted, with an historical introduction and a set of appendices at the end (including one by Cyril Burt whose work was later discredited) was the work of the Secretary, R.F. Young, supervised by M.G. Holmes who was also Secretary to the Hadow Committee and produced the Report of 1926. The intention of the Board of Education was not only to preserve the grammar schools, but also to limit provision of that kind of education to 15 per cent of the population; the board saw the problem of secondary education in some parts of the country as 'over provision' of grammar places.

By 1938, however, the Labour Party, or at least sections within it, were advocating multilateral or comprehensive schools for all children after the age of 11. The Advisory Committee for Education signalled its support for this idea in a report to the National Executive Committee in June 1939. But complete agreement inside the Labour Party on this issue was still lacking. We will return to this question in Chapter 3.

Despite the lack of much significant progress in the 1930s, some ideas were gaining ground. In 1930 the National Association of Labour Teachers (the NALT had broken away from the Labour Teachers' League in 1927) had made a major contribution to the education debate in a pamphlet, *Education: A Policy*. It proposed common schools for all children after age 11. Although the common school idea was not new, this was the first time that it featured as a potential policy that could distinguish the Labour Party from Liberal and Conservative views on education. It was a policy guaranteed to provoke fierce reactions, not only from other political Parties but also from some within the Labour Party who felt that grammar schools had worked well in the past and should be preserved. It would be a long debate.

The National Association of Labour Teachers' (NALT) proposal should be seen in the context of wider discussions that had been taking place since the end of World War I. Grammar schools in the twentieth century had generally been dominated by the curricula and ethos of public schools. Although grammar schools were much admired (as we shall see in Chapter 4) in Labour circles both by those who had experienced them (like Ellen Wilkinson) and those who had not (like George Tomlinson) it was clear by the 1930s that neither the public schools nor the grammar schools could be an appropriate model for the whole secondary system. The fact that so many public school teachers had attempted to break away and establish something better was significant. For example, W.A.C. Stewart (1968) discusses the establishment of radical or progressive independent schools such as Abbotsholm, Bedales, Dartington and several others. Mrs Beatrice Ensor whose evidence was sometimes regarded as suspect on account of her association with theosophical organisations, was critical of the practices of public as well as elementary schools. Her evidence as an Inspector of Schools for Glamorgan and later as an HMI was important. Another HMI, Edmond Holmes, agreed with many of her criticisms; his book *What Is And What Might Be* (1911) had also condemned elementary schools, and suggested an improved approach to education for all kinds of schools. At this time there was a correlation between left-wing politics and progressive ideas in education. Some looked forward to the day when public schools, grammar schools and elementary schools would all adopt better methods of educating the young of all classes and abilities.

Grammar schools, like most public schools, were narrowly academic, valuing the classics more than science, technology and the arts. Perhaps more importantly, their mode of discipline tended to brutalise the young. Grammar schools also only catered for a small percentage of young people, and unless reformed could not possibly provide a curriculum or a school organisation suitable for the majority. A grammar school curriculum for all was seen by many as undesirable, but no alternative curriculum was offered. Even Tawney, who was the pre-eminent Labour theorist on education at this time, had not turned his mind to the curriculum. And the Spens Report was allowed to take the argument in a very dubious direction based on psychological evidence which was, as we shall see, completely unscientific.

Conclusion

There was a series of problems to be solved: first, what kind of structure for all secondary schools would be desirable; second, how to reform the curriculum so that it had less emphasis on academic subjects, especially the classics; and finally, if common schools became the policy, what kind of differentiation within the curriculum would be acceptable? These were extremely complex issues, and many in the Labour Party, if they were conscious of them, felt that until they had a government with a working majority it would be unrealistic to develop a secondary education policy so much in advance of popular thinking. Others, including the NALT, were pressing for a long-term policy that would be not only different from the plans of other parties, but would be truly socialist in the sense of rejecting such capitalist values as greed and competition, and putting forward a programme based on co-operation with a vision of a better society.

It was probably quite unrealistic to expect solutions to the above questions in the 1930s, but more constructive thinking – more than simply raising the school leaving age – might have been expected. There was little evidence of any long-term planning in education apart from that of the NALT, which went a little way in the direction of a reformed curriculum. In Chapter 4, we can examine what happened after 1945 when Labour, for the first time, had a comfortable majority in the Commons. Meanwhile, Chapter 3 will trace the development of the ideas that led from the Spens and Norwood Reports to the 1944 Education Act and its implementation.

3   World War II 1939–45

The social solidarity of the whole nation is more important than any of the
defects to which a comprehensive high school may be subject.
(Godfrey Thomson, *A Modern Philosophy of Education*, 1929, p. 274)

There recently appeared a Report, namely that of the Norwood Committee on
Curriculum and Examinations in Secondary Schools . . . this Report is not a very
satisfactory piece of work. It has been received by teachers without enthusiasm.
It fails either to give a lead or to examine in a philosophic way the bases of the
curriculum and the principles which should guide the curriculum designer.
(*The Content of Education*, Interim Report of the Council for Curriculum
Reform, 1945, p. 7)

The costs of war 1939–45

Having pursued a policy of appeasing Hitler for a number of years that had
allowed him to occupy Austria and Czechoslovakia, Neville Chamberlain, the
Conservative Prime Minister, took a stand together with France on the independence of Poland. Germany invaded Poland on 1 September 1939, and when
the Anglo-French ultimatum ran out on 3 September, war was declared. After a
short period of inactivity (the 'phoney war'), in May 1940 the German army
swept through the Low Countries and France, the British army retreated to
Dunkirk and other ports, and some managed to get back to England. France
had collapsed and was divided into two parts: the regions occupied by Germany
in the north and west; and Vichy France, in the south and east, a supposedly
independent government with Marshal Petain as President. Britain refused to
negotiate with Hitler who began a campaign of intensive bombing from October
1940 to May 1941.

The USA did not immediately join in the war against Germany and Italy, but
in March 1941 began a programme of 'lend–lease' which provided Britain with
military supplies and equipment on the understanding that repayments would be
made in full after the war. This agreement was important, as we shall see in
Chapter 4, because it meant that the Labour government from 1945 onwards

would have to retain a regime of austerity, partly in order to repay our debts to the USA. Post-war reconstruction would have to be done on the cheap.

In June 1941 Germany invaded the USSR, but the USA did not become fully engaged in the war until December 1941, when the Japanese bombed Pearl Harbor. Germany then declared war on the USA. The war in the East further weakened Britain financially (and from the point of view of prestige) when the Japanese captured valuable parts of the Empire, especially Hong Kong, Malaya and Burma, adding to post-war financial problems. By the end of 1942, however, the Allies were gaining the upper hand over the Axis powers. Progress continued in 1943, and a significant turning point was the Anglo-American invasion of France on 6 June 1944 (D-Day). The Germans surrendered on 7 May 1945; the Japanese accepted defeat in September of the same year after atomic bombs had been dropped on Hiroshima and Nagasaki. The cost of the war in lives and money was enormous, and Britain began the period of peace and reconstruction with a massive national debt.

British politics 1939–45

When war began the Conservative government under Chamberlain had a very comfortable majority: 432 seats against 154 Labour and only 20 Liberals. This did not prevent the government from embarking on a system of controls over social and economic activities which in theory were contrary to Conservative ideology. This set of controls, including food rationing and conscription, was intensified when Churchill replaced Chamberlain as Prime Minister. In May 1940 Churchill formed a coalition government, giving a share of the seats in the Cabinet to Labour MPs. Clement Attlee, Leader of the Labour Party, became Deputy Prime Minister, and Ernest Bevin, a prominent trade unionist, as Minister of Labour, took on the delicate task of the direction of labour.

There were no general elections during the war, but by-elections were necessary from time to time. In order to avoid open hostility between the parties, it was agreed that seats becoming vacant would not be contested: the party of the MP whose seat had been vacated simply nominated his successor. However, in 1942, some politicians of the moderate left who disagreed with the policy of not having political contests during the war, and perhaps remembering the National Government of 1931, formed the Commonwealth Party to encourage prospective MPs to stand for election in vacant seats on a programme of active participative democracy, and common ownership. Commonwealth won three seats from 1943 to 1945, all from Conservatives, and enlivened political discussions. The Labour Party refused an application from Commonwealth to affiliate, and in 1945 the Commonwealth Party put up 23 candidates only one of whom was elected. He joined the Labour ranks in Parliament and Commonwealth was dissolved.

The success of Labour ministers during the war, as well as the general spirit of co-operation of trade unions, enhanced the credibility of Labour for the 1945 election. It has also been suggested that the swing to Labour in 1945 was partly caused by the success of planning during the war and the greater feeling of social solidarity that developed as an aspect of war-time national spirit. For whatever reasons, the Labour Party was more popular in 1945 than ever before. There was also some feeling that education should help to protect the young from the false ideologies of fascism and other totalitarian regimes. It was generally agreed that education should be a priority in a programme of post-war reconstruction. Other social priorities were acknowledged in the Beveridge Report (1942), which specified 'ignorance' as one of the major areas for reform in a welfare state. Although the report was not directly concerned with education policy, Beveridge took it for granted that post-war education would be a high priority. The equality of women in terms of pay and employment also took several steps forward.

Education 1939–45

As we saw in Chapter 2, the 1936 Education Act had promised that the school leaving age would be raised to 15 (with exemptions) on 1 September 1939. It would have been impractical to attempt to carry out this during war-time, and the implementation of the Act was abandoned. The Spens Committee was also disbanded, having produced only an interim report on secondary education in 1938. To add to the educational confusion, it was thought necessary to evacuate schools from those areas likely to be bombed. Evacuation plans had been drawn up in advance by the Board of Education in conjunction with the Ministries of Health, Transport and Home Security. The transfer of children to safer regions began on 1 September. Within a few days well over a million children and adults were moved, to lodge with strangers and to find new teaching premises, which were often very unsatisfactory. Evacuation was only a limited success, but one of its effects was to raise the awareness of relatively affluent people in the countryside to the poverty, the poor physical conditions, and the low educational standards of many children from urban areas.

Soon after the war started, the Board of Education officials began to make plans for a better education service after the war. Harold Dent (1948) showed that there was considerable discussion of the future of the education service, not least in the *Times Educational Supplement* from early in 1940. Like the Education Act 1918, the Butler Education Act, 1944 was planned during the war and was passed before the war was over. Unlike the 1918 Act, however, the 1944 reforms had lasting results, and the Act was not completely superseded until the 1996 Education Act. Throughout the war there was much talk in Labour circles about planning education for a new world; and Arthur Greenwood was given Cabinet responsibility for 'reconstruction'. The Advisory Committee on Education of the Labour Party began discussions on post-war education policies in mid-1941. By then there were several vocal supporters of multilateral or common schools on the committee, but some influential members, including Tawney, were doubtful. Other outstanding issues for Labour were the raising of the school leaving age and the abolition of fees, on both of which there was general agreement. On the question of Public Schools, how-ever, no practical solution had been proposed.

The Green Book 1941

Planning by the Board of Education proceeded with a cautious but promising discussion document in June 1941: the 'Green Book' was prepared by the board's officials with little political input at this stage. The Conservative president of the board, Herwald Ramsbotham, in autumn 1940 had given his officials a free hand to set up a planning committee. The Green Book was marked 'confi-dential' but was widely reported on and discussed in educational circles, so much so that the next president of the board, R.A. Butler, who took over in 1941, in answer to questions in the House of Commons, agreed to publish a summary of the proposals under discussion. The topics covered included: raising the school leaving age, definitions of primary and secondary education, school fees, the physical well-being of young people, nursery schools, the youth service, the teaching profession, the dual system, and a unified system for linking schools to universities. There were three specific proposals: raising the school leaving age to 15, establishing day continuation schools 15–18, and ensuring that every child after age 11 could be guaranteed a place in a post-primary school of a suitable type. Butler wanted wider discussion of the Green Book but was overruled by Winston Churchill and Attlee (Wallace, 1981, p. 287). Various Labour MPs succeeded in getting copies of the Green Book but there was no major discussion within the Labour Party.

Brian Simon (1974) quotes Fred Clarke's view that a characteristic English way of thinking was 'the habit of thinking in terms of concrete precedent rather than in terms of abstract principle (with all that this means for the preservation of continuity)'. Simon suggests that this described Board of Educa-tion thinking which was 'deeply conservative'. It is, however, important to acknowledge that later research (by Wallace, 1981) suggests that the board's officials were divided among themselves. Wallace identified two major players: G.G. Williams, Head of Secondary Branch, who supported retention of grammar schools (with more restrictive access), and William Cleary, Head of Elementary Branch, who had been converted to the multilateral secondary school idea. A third official who was involved in discussion of the Education Bill, but who was less influential, was H.B. Wallace, Head of Teaching Branch. Unfortunately, the most forceful of the three civil servants was Williams who was influential in the Norwood Report (see below). Williams favoured not only the retention of grammar schools but also public schools and he was a frequent visitor at the Headmasters' Conference (HMC). He also served as assessor to the Fleming Committee on public schools and influ-enced the drafting of the Fleming Report and the 1944 Act. When there were important decisions at stake, the Permanent Secretary, Maurice Holmes, decided in favour of the more conservative options.

Simon (1974) suggested, however, that the war brought about a change in thinking on expenditure: many things that were too costly in the 1930s became possible during a war-time regime of high taxes and high spending. There was still a long way to go for the Tories to accept good education as a human right for all, but a small move in that direction had been taken (pp. 295–6).

Discussions of the Green Book stimulated a good deal of interaction between ministers and officials of the Board of Education, LEAs, churches, professional associations and trade unions. The TUC response to the Green Paper included a demand for common schools; and the London Labour Party was of the same view. The Party was, however, still divided on this issue in May 1942, but the executive presented a resolution to conference that papered over the cracks, asking, first, for all schools for pupils over age 11 to be covered by the same regulations and having the same standards of finance and teacher qualifications; and, second, calling for a policy on the kind of multilateral schools that would provide different curricula suited to children 'of all normal types'. Rodney Barker (1972) quotes an interesting passage from the speech by Harold Clay, Chairman of the Education Sub-Committee who proposed the resolution:

> We believe it is sound that every child in the State should go to the same kind of school. The curriculum will be different and will provide for varying aptitudes for varying types of children. We have been somewhat concerned at the suggestion that has been made in regard to the grammar school, the technical high school, and the modern school, the suggestion being that there is a difference between certain types of children of a character that we do not quite appreciate.
>
> (Labour Party Annual Conference Report, p. 142, quoted by Barker, pp. 77–8)

This was an early example of the contrasting ideas within the Party between those who wanted a comprehensive education system for all and those who saw post-war reforms in terms of a tripartite system based on selection.

Peter Gosden (1996) has drawn attention to the fact that Ernest Bevin was one of the few politicians who immediately involved himself in discussions of the Green Book. As Minister of Labour, Bevin had a legitimate interest in technical education, but was also generally concerned about education reform. According to Simon, Bevin had been involved in educational discussions since the 1920s, and had intervened in a conference debate in 1933, insisting, successfully, that the Labour policy should include a school leaving age of 16 not 15 (Simon, 1974, p. 192). In 1942 Butler was briefed for a meeting with Bevin that included a warning that the Minister of Labour was not enamoured of Day Continuation Schools. Bevin persisted with his preference for a school leaving age of 16. He also wanted co-operation between the Departments of Labour and Education on a scheme for technical education at school that would be followed by 'supervision' up to age 20. Bevin stressed the importance of early legislation on education. The Board's Permanent Secretary, Maurice

Holmes, reacted unsympathetically in an internal paper to the proposed school leaving age of 16, saying that it was '*hardly one which a responsible person with even a nodding acquaintance with educational conditions of to-day could make*' (quoted by Gosden, 1996). Bevin returned to the subject a month later, offering his Ministry's help in finding a solution to such problems as the shortage of teachers and accommodation. Bevin's ideas were not, however, taken up, and the board continued to neglect the whole question of technical education.

Meanwhile, the Party's Advisory Committee on Education was working on post-war education plans – or at least talking about them. The Committee should have been more productive than it was: it started with George Tomlinson as Chairman and Tawney as Vice-Chairman with Barbara Drake as a vigorous Secretary. However, there were frequent changes in membership: Lees-Smith took over as Chairman in August 1941 but was replaced by Harold Clay in November 1941. Both were supporters of the multilateral school. Apart from Bevin, there was little interest in education reform shown by Labour Party leaders.

Public schools were also much criticised during the war. And in the summer of 1942 Butler set up the Fleming Committee which was a successful device for avoiding any further discussion of this subject (Simon, 1974, p. 38). (I shall return to this question later.) Butler also set up another highly political committee which produced the Norwood Report in 1943 (see below).

The White Paper 1943

The informal consultation on the Green Book was followed by a White Paper: *Educational Reconstruction* (July 1943) which ignored the complex issue of multilateral or common schools (with or without common curricula), proposing instead a tripartite policy that had been advocated by the Spens Committee (1938), that is, three different types of school for three different kinds of children – precisely the policy that had been criticised by Harold Clay at the Labour Party Conference in 1942. The Labour Party, however, was generally supportive of the proposals in the White Paper, regarding secondary education for all and the abolition of fees in secondary schools as considerable victories. Since they were divided among themselves on the tripartite issue, they failed to mount an attack on that aspect of the White Paper. As for the public schools question, as we have seen, Butler had already successfully shunted that awkward problem into a siding.

The Norwood Report 1943

The White Paper was debated for two days in the House of Commons, with little opposition to any of the main proposals for reform. However, ten days after the publication of the White Paper, the Norwood Report was published. This committee had been set up by R.A. Butler in 1941 to make recommendations on the curriculum and examinations of secondary schools after the war.

Churchill had warned Butler against any major educational change *during* the war, bearing in mind the religious divisions caused by the 1918 (and earlier) Acts. Butler was cautious, but realised that it would be important to get some legislation started that would prevent more radical reforms being considered. It seemed strange to many that having disbanded the Spens Committee at the beginning of the war, a quite different body should be set up so soon afterwards. Sir Will Spens complained about this procedure by which the consultative committee was replaced by an ad hoc group from the Secondary Schools Examinations Council. The explanation would seem to be that the Spens Committee had been seen as difficult, even radical in some respects, and what was now needed by Butler was a more compliant body. Norwood was an obvious choice as chairman, since he was known to have safe traditional views on secondary education, especially grammar schools and public schools. Norwood produced the kind of recommendations that Butler wanted and any criticisms of the report, of which there were many, were ignored by the board. It was clear that the major issue for the new Act would be the organisation of secondary education – three kinds of school or one. We shall return to this question many times, but at this early stage it was clear that Butler, as well as his board, were on the side of a tripartite solution, and they made the most of Labour's lack of unity on the issue.

The Norwood Report begins with the amazing assertion that it is possible to divide children roughly into three types for the purpose of education. They claimed that the rough groupings had established themselves in general educational experience. That statement was quite incorrect even in 1943 and has been criticised by educationists ever since. The accumulated evidence suggests that it is unsafe to make any such prediction at age 11 and also that the 'rough groupings' are too crude to be much use educationally. Nevertheless, the report continued with a description of the three types of child which are almost beyond belief in their simplistic stereotyping.

> The Spens Committee in 1938 may have had to rely on over-confident psychological evidence; the Norwood Report of 1943 was concerned not with evidence but with assertion. It has less of a basis in discriminating analysis and concern for data than any other modern report on education; it was produced by a narrow committee, and, it has been said the circumstances in which it was published were 'a perfect example of that departmental procedure which to the uninitiated seems like official chicanery'. The Report contained 'obscurities and inconsistencies perhaps not quite unintentional'.
>
> (Lawson and Silver, *A Social History of Education in England*, 1973, p. 422)

This is a serious charge against Norwood and should be examined in the context of the Labour Party (or at least a section of it) attempting to put forward a new view of secondary education when there was a policy within the board, and within the Conservative Party, of preserving as much of the *status quo* as possible.

The 1944 Education Act

Meanwhile, the 1944 Education Act was being drafted. It is often assumed and sometimes stated that the Act specified that secondary education for all should be implemented in the form of a tripartite system. This is completely untrue: the Hadow Report (1926) had suggested a tripartite interpretation of secondary education for all; the Spens Report (1938) bolstered up that view with flawed psychological 'evidence' which was accepted in the 1943 White Paper. The Norwood Report, as we have seen, pushed the tripartite wagon along with great determination, but the 1944 Act left the field clear for Local Education Authorities to interpret secondary education as they wished. However, the Board of Education moved swiftly to fill that gap by producing a document, *The Nation's Schools* (1945), which advised strongly that there should be three types of school. We shall return to that controversy in the next chapter. The Labour Party accepted, even welcomed, the Act, considering it to be in most respects a fulfilment of some of their policies. But it was essentially a Conservative document; by supporting it Labour missed the opportunity of setting out their own socialist policy for post-war education.

Conclusion

During World War II, three aspects of Labour education policy should have been clarified and developed: first, raising the school leaving age to 16; second, the question of how to deal with Public/Independent Schools; and, third, the meaning of 'secondary education for all'. Only the first made progress (and even the implementation of that was delayed for far too long after 1945). The public school question had received much consideration during the early 1940s and should have been considered as part of the policy of secondary education for all, but Labour allowed this crucial issue to be 'shunted into a siding', as Butler himself described it. Finally, despite the common school having been accepted as policy by several annual conferences, it was effectively replaced by the policy of tripartite secondary education favoured by the board – a policy that was, of course, much more acceptable to the Conservative Party. This failure was partly a question of the Labour leadership not giving sufficient priority to education and not thinking through the implementation of educational changes. There were always more important matters on the agenda.

The split in the Labour Party over a policy on secondary education (common schools or a tripartite system) was not simply a question of left and right (although it was sometimes seen as that). The division was much more deep-rooted. In 1900–1906 there were two major ideological groups: on the one hand, the supporters of Webb and those Fabians who favoured an approach to social policy based on economic efficiency and modernisation; on the other hand, they were generally opposed by 'ethical socialists' whose guiding principles were social justice, equality of opportunity and social solidarity. The ethical socialists were not revolutionary but their vision of a better society involved radical change, including the abolition of class privileges, rather than piecemeal improvements to an essentially conservative education system. The ethical socialists favoured comprehensive schools, not a tripartite system which was a development of nineteenth-century social attitudes that had motivated the three kinds of schools recommended by the Taunton Committee, dividing post-elementary pupils according to social class and occupational destination. That kind of social segregation was now to be replaced by the Webbs' vision of a ladder of opportunity. Ethical socialists, however, saw 11+ testing and divisions according to IQ as another device to divide society rather than to build on the greater social solidarity that had developed during World War II.

The Butler 1944 Act was essentially a Conservative reform, making the existing system more efficient without disturbing the public school privileges and without encouraging people to think of education in a genuinely democratic way. Socialists have criticised the Labour Party's acceptance of the 1944 Act as though it were their own education agenda; they did so for the same reasons as they criticised the acceptance of the Beveridge Report (1942). It must have been very tempting for Labour to welcome the Beveridge Report which received so much good publicity at the time, but it was not a set of socialist policies. As A.J.P. Taylor pointed out (1965, p. 567), Beveridge 'finally rejected the socialist doctrine of social security provided by society'. The 1944 Education Act was a step forward but it was also a missed opportunity to envisage something much better.

4 The Attlee governments 1945–51
Missed opportunities in education

The gravest weakness of British Labour is . . . its lack of a creed. The Labour Party is hesitant in action because divided in mind. It does not achieve what it could, because it does not know what it wants.

(Tawney, 1934)

One might have supposed that an avowedly socialist party would look askance at plans for separate types of secondary school which offered courses of different length and scope to children judged superior or inferior in mental ability: schools which were, therefore, likely to vary greatly in social prestige. But Labour was not an egalitarian party, though it included some egalitarians in its ranks. Although it had . . . several teacher MPs and the sympathy of many professors and administrators, few of the leading figures had the knowledge which would have enabled them effectively to answer the arguments of Ministry officials. Still more important, most saw no need to do so. Much of Labour's thinking was a generation out of date.

(Robin Pedley, 1963, p. 38)

The post-war world

In 1945 the world was slowly recovering from war. Much of Europe was devastated. The war itself had stimulated industrial and economic changes of various kinds. Trade unions were more powerful, and at first there was full employment, even a shortage of labour. Women's position in the labour market had changed irreversibly: having shown their capability in replacing men, the demand for equality was difficult to resist for ever. Attitudes and ideologies had also changed significantly: for example, views about the Empire and imperialism. The war had also changed public opinion on collectivism and the corporate state.

The time was ripe for technological, economic, social and political change. On the other hand, war-time austerity, including rationing, had to continue. The lend–lease arrangement from the USA ended abruptly and Britain was forced to seek a loan from the USA. Some thought that the terms negotiated by Keynes at Bretton Woods and the convertibility strings attached were far from generous. Britain had to rebuild houses, schools and industrial plant, as well as embarking on a programme to reconstruct society, partly with borrowed money. Shortages continued but without the war-time spirit to sustain morale indefinitely.

In February 1945, when the end of the war in Europe was in sight, a summit conference between Stalin, Roosevelt and Churchill took place at Yalta, making plans for spheres of influence in post-war Europe. In May the German forces surrendered unconditionally, but Japan continued the war in the East until atomic bombs were dropped in Hiroshima and Nagasaki in August 1945. By then another summit conference had been started in July, at Potsdam, between Stalin, Truman and Churchill (until he was replaced by Attlee after the General Election).

The political situation in Britain: post-war consensus?

When Chamberlain had lost the support of many of his own party in May 1940, the Labour Party agreed to support Churchill and become part of a coalition government under his leadership. But Churchill, even during the war, had shown that he would not be an acceptable peace-time leader; he had indicated his disapproval of the Beveridge Report (1942), for example, and continued his opposition to Britain's withdrawal from India and other parts of the Empire. Churchill offered to carry on with a coalition government in 1945, but Attlee refused, preferring a general election as soon as possible. For a short time there was a Conservative government once again until a general election could be held in July 1945. The result was that the electorate rejected Churchill and the Conservative Party: the landslide victory gave Labour 393 seats, a comfortable overall majority over the 212 Conservatives, 20 Liberals and 9 others. Churchill continued as leader of the Conservative Party, taking little interest in home affairs, preferring to play the part of a world statesman. In that role in March 1946 he made a speech in Fulton, Missouri, in which he used the phrase 'iron curtain' between Eastern Europe and the West. This probably contributed to the 'cold war' that developed, and eventually to the rearmament policy in Britain which added to Labour's financial problems.

Attlee proved himself to be a successful Prime Minister, even if he was often criticised for some of his policies, including rearmament, support for NATO in 1949, participation in the war in Korea (1950), and for agreeing with Bevin that Britain should fund the construction of an independent nuclear deterrent. All of these added to Britain's financial problems. Attlee did, however, achieve a great deal in the establishment of a welfare society, including a National Health Service and other social benefits. But it is now clear that he should have given higher priority to education. In that respect other Labour leaders must, as we shall see, share the blame for failing to appreciate the key position of education in a post-war socialist society.

Labour and education 1945–51

For a Labour government with a big majority there were two possible approaches to education policy in 1945: education could take its place in the queue for reform along with health, housing etc.; or it might have been seen as not only a benefit in itself but also as a key strategy for reforming attitudes and changing society. Few of the Labour leaders shared that vision of education.

More than any other Prime Minister, Attlee took great care in the selection of his Cabinet and team of ministers. In 1932, long before he became Prime Minister, he had begun to theorise about running a government, and had written down his conclusions in the form of a memorandum (reproduced in full as appendix III of Kenneth Harris's book, *Attlee*, 1982). Attlee later elaborated his memorandum into *The Labour Party in Perspective* (1949). Part of his planning was a set of guidelines for a Prime Minister making appointments. He set himself the task of making careful decisions about three crucial factors: identifying the 'key' posts; the 'fitness' of individuals for specific Ministries; and the status of potential Ministers within the Party. It was not a simple question of rewarding the virtuous or even the best qualified, but a very complex balancing act. Given that kind of self-preparation, it is highly likely that Attlee's choice for the delicate but not very prestigious post of Minister of Education would have been given extremely careful consideration.

It was widely believed that Attlee would give the post of Minister of Education to Chuter Ede, who had served as Butler's Junior Education Minister during the war and had contributed to the planning of the 1944 Education Act. Chuter Ede also very much wanted the job (Harris, 1982, p. 402; see also Kevin Jefferys' discussion of Chuter Ede's diaries); not only was Ede very experienced, he was also an ex-teacher, on good terms with LEAs, and backed by the National Union of Teachers. Could it be that in Attlee's calculating mind those qualities made Ede *less* desirable as a Minister of Education? Is it possible that Attlee preferred cautious implementation of the 1944 Butler Act to more radical changes in education and society, including the public schools? What is the evidence? Chuter Ede was given the prestigious but probably less controversial position of Home Secretary (a more senior post than he himself expected). Attlee's choice for Minister of Education was Ellen Wilkinson, who had been regarded as left-wing in her younger days but had moved to the right, especially since her amorous liaison with Herbert Morrison. Betty Vernon's sympathetic biography (1982) of Ellen Wilkinson declares that 'it was a surprising appointment because Ellen had so few positive ideas about education' (p. 202). Vernon also shows that, unlike Chuter Ede, Ellen Wilkinson had little contact with socialist educationists, not even the National Association of Labour Teachers (p. 204). She was also tired and ill throughout her period in office (1945–7) and was very reliant on her civil servants who included the formidable John Maud as permanent secretary: 'she learnt rather than led' (Vernon, 1982, p. 205).

Attlee must have been aware of the potential conflict in education: annual conferences had repeatedly called for multilateral schools (later renamed comprehensive schools), but the 1945 Party manifesto, *Let Us Face the Future*, made no clear promise about comprehensives. Vernon claims that there was a general lack of interest in education in Parliament and that 'even at Labour Party and TUC conferences, motions on education were usually relegated to the end of the agenda' (p. 202). Attlee himself did not support comprehensive schools and did not want public schools abolished (Brookshire, 1995, p. 77; see also Beckett, 1988, *Clem Attlee*) It may have suited Attlee well to have a weak minister who would not make ambitious claims for the education service. The Minister, Ellen Wilkinson, regarded the 1944 Act as a great achievement, accepting that it was her job to follow its guidance. Her top priority was raising the school leaving age (which was delayed for two years but which she achieved in 1947 despite considerable Cabinet opposition). She did not attempt to rethink the purpose of education or the organisation of secondary schooling. Like some other Labour products of grammar schools, she was reluctant to destroy the kind of school that had served some working-class children well, although there is some evidence that by the end of her life she was moving towards a more favourable view of comprehensive schools (Dean, 1986).

There was also a 'traditional bias within the Ministry towards the tripartite system' (Vernon, 1982, p. 218). There were many bureaucratic reasons for this preference: it would be cheaper; it would cause less disruption; it would be less likely to provoke Tory opposition and even the possible reversal of policy with a change of government. The Minister was clearly led in the direction of a tripartite policy by her officials, especially Maurice Holmes and G.G. Williams. She had to put up with a good deal of Labour and teacher criticism as a result. She was also kept busy with other educational problems: the Emergency Training Scheme for Teachers, supporting the establishment of UNESCO, funding school meals and milk, and raising the school leaving age. All these took a good deal of time and energy. Nevertheless, she faced criticism over her performance, especially the fact that she had not withdrawn a ministry pamphlet (issued by the Conservative administration) that recommended a tripartite implementation of the 1944 Act. She was given a very hard time at the Party conference, and in the House of Commons during 1946.

Ellen Wilkinson died suddenly in 1947, and was replaced by George Tomlinson whose views on education were similar to hers, but he was even less a potential danger to Attlee's preference for a non-controversial education programme. 'In comparison . . . with his predecessor Tomlinson was seen not only as a less significant figure, but in many ways more approachable and less touchy . . . Many among Labour's own supporters became less than enthusiastic about Tomlinson's role by the end of his term of office' (Dean, 1986, p. 98). Tomlinson suffered from the fact that he came to the Ministry of Education at a time when the economic situation was deteriorating; there was also a terribly severe winter in 1947 which caused industrial disruption and further financial problems. He also had to deal with a change of Chancellor of the Exchequer: Dalton, who had consistently favoured education, was replaced by Cripps who was uniformly austere. Robin Pedley (1963) looked back sadly at the missed opportunities of 1945–51: 'Ministry officials took steps to ensure that a divided form of secondary education should prevail' (p. 39).

Both Ministers also avoided any serious consideration of the public school question. We observed in Chapter 3 that Butler had successfully shunted that awkward question out of sight by means of the well-tried method of setting up a departmental committee to delay any possible action (the Fleming Committee). Whether Ellen Wilkinson preferred a tripartite structure for secondary education or another solution, it should have been clear that in a truly democratic society the existence of a superior system catering for a 7 per cent social elite should not have been allowed to continue.

By 1945 the Fleming Committee had reported: it recommended that public schools should extend their association with the state secondary system. Public schools should be progressively integrated by taking pupils from maintained schools who would be given state grants. Starting with 25 per cent of public school places, the scheme would eventually extend so that all places would be open to pupils with state grants. This was not an acceptable total solution, but it could have been a useful starting point for negotiating some kind of scheme that would have drawn the good public schools into the state system. It would not have been easy but, given the post-war spirit of national unity, it might have been possible. Simply to ignore the problem, and later to close some grammar schools in the process of comprehensivisation was an error. The Workers' Educational Association (WEA) had summed up the socialist case in its evidence to the Fleming Committee in 1943: 'the position of the Public Schools is anomalous in a modern democratic society' (WEA, 1943). This was also the view of the TUC (see Griggs, 2002).

It is a pity that post-war Ministers of Education and their senior colleagues ignored the advice given by R.H. Tawney who questioned whether 'the existence of a group of schools reserved for the children of the comparatively prosperous is or is not . . . in the best interests of the nation. It cannot be decided by the venerable device of describing privileges as liberties' (*The Radical Tradition*, 1943, p. 72).

Attlee and his government have been criticised for the missed opportunities of 1945–51. Some of the blame falls on Attlee himself, but in the case of education, some other ministers must share the responsibility. The time was ripe for more radical moves in education, particularly concerning public schools and comprehensive schools. Much has been written about Attlee's personality and his direction of the post-war governments. In some respects his life is a useful case-study of the attraction of the Labour Party for some kinds of middle-class politicians. Attlee was an idealist: no sensible commentator would accuse him of entering politics for his own self-interest. He could have pursued a profitable career as a lawyer, but instead opted for voluntary social work in the east end of

London. He called himself a socialist, and by most definitions he qualified for the title. His achievements were many, including holding the Party together and establishing the welfare state 1945–51. Yet in education his record is disappointing: his vision was limited and his performance as Prime Minister probably prevented more imaginative educational policies. He under-estimated the importance of education as a crucial issue in a socialist society, seeing education policy in much the same way as the Conservative, Rab Butler. He wanted to extend working-class opportunities, and he hated the injustices of the pre-war system, but he failed to see that radical change was necessary, including grasping the nettle of independent schooling and understanding the meaning of secondary education for all. There were always items on the government agenda that were more pressing: the economic situation, foreign affairs, the end of the empire and others. We can understand Attlee's limitations without entirely excusing them. He described himself as a Victorian: in the field of education this was a serious limitation.

Part of Attlee's success was that he was acceptable to the whole Party – left and right, ethical socialists as well as Fabian modernisers and centralist nationalisers. But his ability to avoid trouble was not always an advantage. Harris (1982) said that civil servants liked and trusted him: some even thought him 'oddly apolitical' (p. 408). But was this really a virtue? In the case of education, to accept the apolitical *status quo* was to tolerate inefficiency and injustice, especially in terms of secondary schools and public schools. Attlee's well-known affection for his own public school, Haileybury, as well as its products, should not be regarded as unimportant. It is strange that Attlee was either blind or reactionary on both questions. One interpretation might be that by 1945 Attlee was less 'socialist', or that he had never applied his socialist beliefs to the crucial area of education. Harris's very positive biography concludes with the ex-Prime Minister becoming 'Earl Attlee' with Harris apologetically explaining 'he had always approved of Honours' (p. 560).

Attlee was not the only one to blame for this neglect of educational issues, however: nearly all his senior colleagues were guilty of placing education at a lower level of priority than other pressing problems. For example, Hugh Dalton, although regarded as left-wing, and as Chancellor of the Exchequer supported education spending, had almost nothing to say about education policy. And as for Attlee himself, he was simply not interested in education: he devoted only one short paragraph of his autobiography to the 1944 Education Act. He was more interested in social work and public services. A major purpose of this book is to argue that education is not just another priority but that it must be central to thinking and planning in the development of a more socialist society. Very few Labour leaders showed an understanding of that principle in 1945, by which time R.H. Tawney, the Party's major educational theorist, was losing influence on Labour thinking. It is also important to note that the much discussed Attlee consensus existed only at the surface level: by 1951 some of the old ideological conflicts were beginning to re-emerge.

Conclusion

For a short time after World War II the Labour Party could have benefited from war-time social solidarity left over from 1939–45 to develop real secondary education for all and integrating the independent schools into the comprehensive secondary system. But by about 1949 the goodwill was evaporating and the right-wing media was hostile to most Labour policies, with the exception of foreign policy (which were very right-wing). The opportunity had been lost.

The tripartite system suited those who preferred a segregated society. The public schools retained their exclusive position whilst other secondary schools generally reflected the divisive social structure that returned after the war. The ethical socialist vision of a broad highway lost out to the ghost of Webb's economic efficiency model which was backed up by a crude eugenicist notion of ability. According to that view, the efficient society would select a suitable proportion of the 11-year-old population for a superior grammar school education whilst the majority would have a cheaper, shorter secondary education. This model was justified theoretically by pseudo-psychological ideas about IQ that were morally and intellectually indefensible. Webb and other early Fabians, including George Bernard Shaw, were convinced that a truly modern society must select 'scientifically' the future leaders of society. A strange doctrine to be advocated by socialists.

5 Labour in opposition 1951–64

A chance to theorise and revise

[Gaitskell] detested both selection at 'this frankly absurdly early age of 11+', and the segregation of middle-class from working-class schoolchildren; but he was always against Labour becoming the open enemy of the grammar schools. He thought that would be both unwise in itself and would lose some very useful support, and had therefore argued in 1954 for 'toning down the commitments'.

(Williams, 1979, p. 466)

The problem for the Labour movement, which it has never solved down to the present, is not only that the basic structure of society has remained unchanged, but that capitalism, as a dynamically evolving system, constantly breeds new types of inequality and new categories of the poor; and all state welfare schemes ought regularly to be adjusted to take account of such changes.

(Saville, 1988, p. 108)

A changing political scenario 1951–64

From 1945 to 1951 the Labour Party had pursued a foreign policy of a bipartisan nature, as far as possible avoiding conflict with the Tories. Policies were based on the assumption that Britain was still a great power and that the Empire should be converted into a Commonwealth by gradually granting independence to suitable countries. After the election in 1951 this assumption was maintained by the Conservatives, despite Churchill's misgivings about giving away the Empire. The only major disagreement between the parties on foreign policy occurred in 1956 with the Suez fiasco. Even Churchill had had few quarrels with the policies pursued by the Labour Foreign Ministers, Bevin, and for a shorter period by Morrison. The Labour Ministers had pursued a consistent anti-Soviet line, and had supported the Americans in the war in Korea. The launch of Sputnik in 1958 was interpreted by some as an indication of Russian scientific, military and educational superiority: in the USA this encouraged the spending of public money on curriculum development programmes, especially in mathematics and science. In 1963 a nuclear test ban treaty signed by Britain, the USA and Russia was generally welcomed.

Those who expected a 'cavalier' government under Churchill were disappointed: the Conservatives settled for a mixed economy compromise. When Eden took over as Prime Minister in April 1955, the policy of consensus continued. Both parties were accused of 'Butskellism', policies of the centre which were neither faithful to socialist principles nor to Conservative traditions. At best this complaint was only half true: there were always differences between the parties on domestic issues, and Butler and Gaitskell were never as similar as their critics sometimes alleged, but the Labour and Conservative Parties were still centralist. Few Labour voices were raised in protest when the expensive royal yacht *Britannia* was launched in 1953. *Look Back in Anger* by John Osborne was first performed in 1956: 'angry young men' were said to be frustrated by the lack of causes to fight for or even parties worth supporting. The 'anger' may also have been connected with the failure to achieve the 'classless society' promised after the war.

Eden resigned following the Suez debacle and Harold Macmillan became Prime Minister in 1957. The Empire continued to diminish: the Gold Coast became independent Ghana in 1957, and in the same year the West Indian Federation was established; other African countries followed on the route to independence throughout this period. In 1958 both parties were concerned by the race riots that took place in Notting Hill Gate in London, as well as rumblings of discontent in other areas. The Conservatives under Macmillan won the general election in 1959 – the Labour Party appeared to lack unity after Attlee had resigned the leadership in 1955. Meanwhile, having told the British people that they had 'never had it so good', Macmillan went on to praise the 'wind of change' in Africa and elsewhere in 1959. He was succeeded by Sir Alec Douglas Hume in 1963. In the same year the sudden death of the leader of the Labour Party, Hugh Gaitskell, and his replacement by Harold Wilson was seen, for a time, to be an opportunity to unite the Party, but the left–right struggle continued. Wilson's general election victory in 1964 came with only a small majority, despite the fact that the public appeared to be tired of the Tories after Suez and the Profumo scandal. The UK was also refused entry to the European Common Market, and there had been other difficulties, not least the continuing economic problems.

Education 1951–64

The Conservatives were sufficiently astute to realise that the welfare state was popular and should not be openly attacked. Conservative policies on education were to continue the reforms necessary to implement the ideas of the 1944 Education Act. Brian Simon (1991) has pointed out (p. 150) that the general interpretation of the 1944 Act as a tripartite system of grammar, technical and secondary modern schools had ensured that there was, by 1951, no increase in educational opportunity for working-class children as measured by access to selective schools, higher education and the professions. There was, however, much greater demand for grammar school places, and therefore many frustrated parents. This situation of supply and demand had the effect of distorting the curriculum and pedagogy of primary schools, many of which introduced rigid streaming, and even coached children for the intelligence test which was usually part of the selection process at age 11. The teaching of English and arithmetic also tended to be distorted by the demands of the tests.

Throughout the 1950s, criticisms of the 11+ and the unfairness associated with it increased. The policy of 'parity of esteem' became less and less credible. (Olive Banks was later (1955) to publish her research that indicated the virtual impossibility of schools being regarded equally within a society which accorded differential prestige to the products of those schools.) The result was that the work of secondary modern schools as well as primary schools was damaged. Parents and pupils often saw secondary modern schools as institutions for those who had failed and were destined for further failure. Sociologists talked of 'socialisation' for boring and dead-end jobs as the function of secondary modern schools. All of this was, however, ignored by a *Political Quarterly* issue soon after the 1951 general election: an editorial was very critical of the Labour Party pamphlet, *A Policy for Secondary Education*, that had been produced as a result of the Labour Party 1950 conference resolution calling for a policy of comprehensive education. This pamphlet represented the views of the humanitarian, ethical socialists in the Party, which, once again, was in conflict with the 'Fabian element' that Simon observed 'had always been determinedly meritocratic' (1991, p. 155).

The debate continued between the meritocrats and the ethical socialists within the Labour Party, with many others outside joining in. The debate was complex and confusing: some wanted grammar schools to continue educating a small intellectual elite; others disliked large schools. On the other hand, the arguments in favour of comprehensives were both educational and social. The educational argument disputed current views of intelligence and ability; the social exponents hoped that schools catering for all abilities and social classes would bind society together more successfully. Within each group, views might be more or less extreme.

In the 1951 Conservative government, R.A. Butler was not given charge of education, as many had expected, but the responsibility instead passed to the even less exciting Florence Horsbrugh who was content to pursue a minimalist policy, encouraged by Butler, now Chancellor of the Exchequer, not to demand too much money for education. It was even suggested that the school leaving age might be reduced to age 14, and that the starting age be raised to 6. Both proposals were eventually rejected, but serve to remind us of Conservative views current in the 1950s. There was a veto on any new school building for three months so that steel could be diverted into the arms industry. Horsbrugh also embarked on a 'frills-cutting' campaign to save 5 per cent (or £14 million) of the grant to LEAs. Churchill complained about her bad timing in announcing these cuts just before Christmas. Many Labour voices, including Tawney and the TUC were raised in protest against the cuts, especially those affecting adult education.

Fewer protested against the continuing tripartite policy, but Margaret Cole who had been active in formulating the Labour London County Council comprehensive plan complained about the Conservative ministry's unhelpful – even hostile – attitude to necessary changes. The issue was now becoming a party political dispute (although there was still a lack of complete unanimity within the Labour Party). Gaitskell, before and after he became Leader of the Labour Party in 1955, claimed to be a strong supporter of the comprehensive school but at the same time, was anxious to reassure supporters of selection that the grammar school tradition would not be destroyed (Williams, 1979, p. 466). This desire to have it both ways was either naive or not completely honest – perhaps Gaitskell did not realise that so long as grammar schools remained in existence, there could be no real comprehensive schools operating in the same area. One of his motives was a fear of losing middle-class voters.

In the House of Commons, Herbert Morrison took up the battle against the Minister of Education for obstructing the development of comprehensive schools and encouraging parents to campaign against them. Kidbrooke School became a comprehensive without the benefit of a grammar school intake because Horsbrugh refused permission for the London County Council to close Eltham Grammar School.

Meanwhile, the National Association of Labour Teachers at annual conferences and elsewhere were leading the campaign to abolish selection at age 11. These views were gaining ground within the Labour Party, although some continued to argue along meritocratic, efficiency lines. At the same time, the Horsbrugh stance began to be seen as unpopular: she was dropped in 1954 and replaced by the more charismatic David Eccles. Eccles increased spending on education and gave support to technical education. But he did not wish to advance the cause of comprehensive schools, preferring the traditional grammar school route, segregated from inferior education in secondary modern schools.

In 1955 Churchill resigned as Prime Minister and Eden took over. Eccles continued at Education, but Butler was now even more concerned about the cost of social services when he was trying to find money to pay for the Korean war (which did not end until 1954). Eccles resisted pressure to cut education. In 1956 the Suez crisis pushed education out of the news for a while, but in the following year the Russian success in launching Sputnik produced a more favourable environment for educational expansion. Eccles had already published a White Paper on *Technical Education* (1956) calling for more scientific and technical manpower; this eventually stimulated the development of colleges of advanced technology.

Official reports on education: *Early Leaving* (1954) and 15–18 (Crowther) (1959)

In 1954 the Gurney-Dixon Committee (Central Advisory Council for Education) produced the *Early Leaving Report* which confirmed the view that simply increasing working-class access to grammar schools was not a sufficient step in the direction of greater equality of opportunity. This view was confirmed when, in 1959, the Central Advisory Council for Education reported on the education of 15–18 year olds (the Crowther Report). This included research evidence to show that the higher the father's occupational status, the greater the child's chance of attending a grammar school, even when ability was held constant. It was argued that this 'wastage' of talent could not be afforded. There was also some support in the report for comprehensive experiments but on the assumption that the tripartite system would continue for most children. The Crowther Report recommended a broader curriculum for the 15–18 age group, and was particularly concerned that there was insufficient capacity in higher education to accept all the 18 year olds who had good enough 'A' level results and wanted to go to university. Once more, the detailed evidence showed that working-class students were unlikely to proceed to higher education, however able the tests showed them to be. Later, the Robbins Report (1963) would confirm that evidence, and recommended increasing the number of places available, but the problem of equality of opportunity remained unsolved.

Meanwhile, Eccles had been replaced by Hailsham in 1957 and, later in the same year, Geoffrey Lloyd took over Education. The Conservative policy was that LEAs might wish to have a comprehensive school in a rural area, but were discouraging about this solution in urban areas where grammar schools already existed. The LEAs sometimes disagreed with Tory policy, and the number of comprehensive schools increased steadily during the Tory years. Most children were, however, still put through the tripartite system, despite the mounting evidence against the fairness of the selection process. Professor P.E. Vernon, who had devoted much of his career trying to improve intelligence tests, came to the conclusion (in *Secondary School Selection*, 1957) that tests would always be unfair to quite a high percentage of pupils; the psychologists who contributed to Vernon's book rejected the view that intelligence was unchanging and unaffected by environmental factors. Simon (1991) later showed that regional and gender differences also contributed to the injustice: 'the opportunity to reach full-time higher education for a middle class boy living in Cardiganshire was roughly 160 times as great as that for a working class girl living in West Ham' (p. 215). Similar views appeared in the Robbins Report (1963) which quoted Vernon who contested the view that there exists in the population a fixed distribution or 'pool' of intelligence which limits either the numbers of individuals capable of higher education, or the educational standards that can be achieved by groups of pupils of given IQ level. Vernon added 'I wish to state categorically that this reasoning is unsound, and that no calculations of the numbers of eligible students can be based on tests of intelligence or other aptitudes' (quoted by Simon, p. 235). This effectively demolished the 'more means worse' thesis but did not prevent it being popularised by Kingsley Amis and others throughout the 1960s. The Robbins Committee concluded that there was an enormous pool of untapped ability, much of it working class. The report stopped short, however, of recommending a policy of comprehensive education since it was outside their remit.

Towards the end of this period of Conservative government, it was clear that the 11+ selection process was unpopular and difficult to justify. Eccles, as Education Secretary, feared that it would become a political liability. The Labour Party was by now more united in its opposition to testing at age 11, even if they still lacked a coherent secondary education policy. As we shall see, Crosland was converted to the comprehensive view, perceiving the non-selective school as the best means of moving towards egalitarianism in a mixed economy, even though he gave higher priority to 'freedom of choice'.

1963: The year of two more reports: Newsom and Robbins

Report of CACE: Half Our Future (the Newsom Report 1963)

The work of the Central Advisory Council on Education (CACE) on this topic began in March 1961 with Lord Amory as chair until he resigned in June 1961 when John Newsom, a former Chief Education Officer for Hertfordshire, took over. The terms of reference were: 'To consider the education between the ages of 13 and 16 of pupils of average or less than average ability who are or will be following full-time courses either at schools or in Further Education'.

This task was in some ways a continuation of the work of the Crowther Report (CACE 1959) which was more concerned with those of above average ability. Both Reports strongly supported raising the school leaving age to 16. The Newsom Report also supported the Crowther recommendation that there should be a more demanding programme for the 13–16 age group, including a longer school day. Those who had suspected that secondary modern schools were below average in terms of buildings, equipment and teachers, had their opinion confirmed by the detailed surveys conducted for the report, although it was clear that standards were gradually rising.

The report also recommended that schools should take 'a proper account of vocational interests'. Reference to 'vocational' had in the past aroused suspicions within the Labour Party and the TUC that 'vocational' might be interpreted as training for jobs rather than good general education. It remained to be demonstrated that that was not necessarily the case, although the temptation for working-class boys and girls to be fobbed off with something inferior was still there. Perhaps conscious of that danger, the council recommended that the 'extra year' should be in schools not further education. Unfortunately, the opportunity to re-think the whole secondary school curriculum was missed, although some sensible detailed suggestions were made.

The most important educational idea to emerge in the Newsom Report was the conviction that secondary education for *all*, together with raising the school leaving age, meant that new thinking on the curriculum was necessary (even if they failed to do it). Extending access to secondary education was progress, but access to *what* in terms of content? The idea of grammar school education for all that was beginning to be used as an unofficial Labour slogan (by both Gaitskell and Wilson, for example) was a misleading over-simplification for two reasons. First, because the grammar school curriculum was itself overdue for improvement (as the Crowther Report had pointed out); second, it would not be sensible to expect a narrowly academic curriculum to be suitable for all pupils. What was required was a new formula for a curriculum *for all*, which would be neither inferior to nor a watered-down version of a grammar school programme that was in some respects obsolete. The danger was that secondary modern pupils, and similar pupils in comprehensive schools, would be offered a curriculum that was 'practical', 'relevant' and avoiding anything too difficult. Lawrence Stenhouse in his Humanities Curriculum Project saw the danger and avoided it in his Schools Council Project. He said he wanted to make available to all 14–16 year old students the kind of educational experience he had enjoyed at Manchester Grammar School in the form of General Studies. Unfortunately others were less clear in their aims and various kinds of low-level, simplified courses were prepared for 'the Newsom child', itself an over-simplified conception of the curriculum problem.

The Newsom Report was criticised for some examples of misconceived educational planning, but like many official reports it was a mixture of good and indifferent ideas. The Labour Party was moving towards a unified policy on comprehensive schools (rather than the tripartite system) but had not yet given adequate attention to the problem of a curriculum for comprehensive secondary education.

Report of the Committee on Higher Education Appointed by the Prime Minister (the Robbins Report 1963)

Harold Macmillan set up this committee in early 1961, partly in response to complaints (expressed in the Crowther Report, 1959 and elsewhere) that universities were not expanding sufficiently to meet the growth in demand for higher education and the increasing number of 18 year olds who were achieving good 'A' level results. The Minister of Education, David Eccles, although not then responsible for universities, was also pressing for an enquiry. An immediate cause for the committee was the motion in the House of Lords put by Lord Simon of Wythenshawe in 1960. (He was a Labour peer, Shena Simon's husband, and Professor Brian Simon's father.) His views on the topic of higher education expansion received all-party support, but was very much in keeping with the extension of the Labour Party's desire for greater access to educational opportunity being shifted upwards from the secondary school and into higher education. An interesting idea that emerged from the report was the 'Robbins principle' that courses 'should be available for all those who are qualified by ability and attainment to pursue them and wish to do so.' This principle was strongly supported by the Labour Party.

Several important recommendations were made. University first degree courses should be broadened and increased in length to four years. (This was never implemented generally). Another was that there should be more provision for research and advanced courses. The status of teacher education and training was to be raised by re-naming 'Teacher Training Colleges' as 'Colleges of Education' which would have closer links with universities, and their students would become graduates. Colleges of Advanced Technology were to be granted charters as universities, and the report recommended setting up six new universities and promoting ten other colleges to university status.

The report was immediately accepted by the Conservative government, which made £650 million available for capital expenditure. The policy was generally a success: between 1965 and 1975 university numbers doubled and Polytechnic places increased by almost 50 per cent. Expansion continued into the 1980s and 1990s. The Labour Party supported the idea of expansion but, as we shall see in the next chapter, became involved in a strangely unsocialist policy of a 'binary system of higher education'.

Crosland and *The Future of Socialism* (1956)

A major problem for Labour during the 'thirteen wasted years' was that it did not possess a clear educational alternative to the Conservative logic of the 1944 Act, and was not even united, as we saw in Chapter 4, about how that Act, especially 'secondary education for all', should be implemented. Much has been made of the ideas of Tony Crosland who had ambitions to theorise, or re-theorise, about socialism. He wrote *The Future of Socialism*, published in 1956, which included a chapter on education. The book caused a good deal of discussion which I will not attempt to summarise here. There will only be space to focus on the twenty pages on education, together with other re-thinking which impinged, directly or indirectly, on educational policies.

Crosland set out to reinterpret socialism in Britain in the light of social change, especially since 1939. Before that there were three objectives of socialism: the abolition of poverty and the creation of a social service state; a greater equalisation of wealth; and economic planning for full employment and stability. There was no great work of theory to support those objectives, either Marxist or Fabian (Crosland, p. 19). Since 1939 the position of socialism had, according to Crosland, been dramatically changed by a number of factors: nationalisation; the reduction of capitalist power; the transfer of power from management to labour; the altered role of profit, and the changed political power of private industry. At the same time there was a decline in poverty and inequality, together with a rise in employment and stability. Such were the conditions that encouraged Crosland to ask 'Is this still capitalism?' His somewhat surprising answer was 'no' and this encouraged him in 1956 to modify his view of the socialist alternative. In most respects, including education, Crosland was a revisionist who was firmly within the Gaitskell inner circle.

Crosland's aim in part two of his book was to address the problem that he thought the Labour Party had not answered after the 1951 defeat: 'what is socialism now about?' He questions the meaning of 'going back to first principles', citing Tawney: 'Socialism is a word the connotation of which varies, not only from generation to generation, but from decade to decade' (p. 80).

He also draws on the authority of G.D.H. Cole (1937) writing about British socialism, 'a Socialism almost without doctrines . . . so undefined in its doctrinal base as to make recruits readily among persons of quite different types'. Crosland then attempts a review of those socialist doctrines, including: the philosophy of natural law, Owenism, the labour theory of value, Christian socialism, Marxism, William Morris and anti-commercialism, Fabianism, the ILP tradition (a broad movement on behalf of the bottom dog based on the brotherhood of man, fellowship, service and altruism), syndicalism and guild socialism, and finally, the doctrine of planning. Crosland noted, perhaps unnecessarily, that some of those twelve doctrines contradicted one or more of the others – for example, some were reformist, others were anti-reformist or revolutionary.

At this stage the reader might suspect that a list of incompatibles has been provided as a prelude to another list, which, sure enough, comes in the form of five overlapping themes: the appropriation of property incomes; co-operation in place of competition (Tawney's 'basic element of socialism'); workers' control; social welfare; and full employment.

Crosland's argument seems to be that since the worst excesses of capitalism have been reduced, then the socialist alternative must also be re-stated. At the start of the twenty-first century his arguments might seem less convincing than they did in 1956, although many quarrelled with them at the time. Crosland derides those who want to go back to the earlier socialist ideas (he is good at knocking down straw men), but surely there is a difference between harking back to the conditions of the early twentieth century and discarding the principles that motivated socialists then and continue to be relevant now. Nevertheless, it is worth examining what Crosland considered to be a re-statement of the meaning of socialism. He seems happier criticising the opponents of revisionism than in making a positive 're-statement' himself. To my mind, Crosland wastes a good deal of space trying to achieve a satisfactory definition of socialism that would match the world of 1956, when he might have settled for a list of *principles* that would endure for much longer. Unless he was an extreme relativist that should have been a possible and useful task. However, only two concepts remain after Crosland's critique of various kinds of socialism: he calls them 'the Welfare and Equality aspirations'. He approves of both of them, but is concerned about the costs (including the cost of education). It is interesting that he considers the cost of the education service in terms of the 1956 system – not the cost of a completely reformed socialist education service.

He concludes that more welfare and equality would be 'a good thing' but he is unsure about how much equality we should aim for. He agrees, however, with those who claim that to benefit from such privileges as private education is 'unjust'. But he ends his chapter on social equality thus: 'I do not myself want to see *all* private education disappear: nor the Prime Minister denied an official car . . . nor the Queen riding a bicycle: nor the House of Lords instantly abolished' (p. 217). A strange conclusion for what has been regarded by some as the most important book on socialism in the twentieth century.

Against that general background, it may now be appropriate to examine his chapter on 'The Influence of Education' (p. 258 ff.). It begins well: 'The school system in Britain remains the most divisive, unjust, and wasteful of all the aspects of social inequality.' He then rightly complains that the 1944 Education Act failed to produce equality of opportunity, and accepts that the continued existence of public schools and grammar schools is partly to blame. He objects to the tripartite system for several reasons, including the undesirability of segregating pupils at age 11, but he would not wish to impose a comprehensive plan on the whole country. His analysis of the education problems is followed by a short section (pp. 274–7) on 'A Labour Education Policy' – at last! Unfortunately to say that this 'policy' is superficial would be an understatement:

> Thus even within the state sector there can be no question of suddenly closing down the grammar schools and converting the secondary moderns into comprehensive schools. These latter require a quite exceptional calibre of headmaster [*sic*], of which the supply is severely limited: a high quality staff for sixth form teaching – again a factor in limited supply: and buildings of an adequate scale and scope – and most secondary modern buildings . . . are quite unsuitable.
>
> (pp. 274–5)

(This contrasts with his later feelings when as Secretary of State for Education, 1965–67, he said that 'If it's the last thing I do, I'm going to destroy every fucking grammar school in England' (Susan Crosland, 1982, p. 148). Crosland's thinking on education was not only extremely superficial but often inconsistent. On this he was not alone among Labour Party intellectuals: Hugh Gaitskell, for example, also seemed to want the impossible – comprehensive schools nationally, without upsetting either LEAs or middle-class voters. They also failed to realise that it is impossible to have, in the same area, both grammar schools and truly comprehensive schools.

After some approving comments about the Fleming Report (1944) which recommended that public schools should operate a system of free places, Crosland hopes that they, like grammar schools, will gradually become less important. He concludes his chapter on education with another pious hope:

> The system will increasingly, if the Labour Party does its job, be built around the comprehensive school. But even in the large non-comprehensive sector, all schools will more and more be socially mixed; all will provide routes to the universities and to every type of occupation . . . and it will cease to occur to employers to ask what school job-applicants have been to. Then, very slowly, Britain may cease to be the most class-ridden country in the world.
>
> (p. 277)

This is disappointing not least because it might have been expected that a book about socialism would include a socialist theory of education, including some ideas about a curriculum that would be appropriate for 'secondary education for all'. There is no such attempt made, and its absence may account for Crosland's limited success as Education Secretary (1965–67). This will be discussed in the next chapter.

Crosland continued to think of himself as a socialist, unlike some of his friends and colleagues, such as Roy Jenkins who became embarrassed by the word (Crosland, 1982, p. 229). Crosland's socialist ideals and values included egalitarianism and individual liberty: sometimes these two values were in tension, even in conflict (as in the case of public schools). Gaitskell was worried by the same problem. Although he would have liked to have abolished public schools because he felt they were 'a source of snobbery and social evil' (Williams, 1979, p. 388) he thought that it would be politically impossible and contrary to the principle of individual liberty to deny parents the right to spend their money on the education of their children. I shall return to this question in Chapter 12: it may be that a test for a socialist is which of the two values takes priority – social justice or a narrow definition of individual liberty.

Perhaps Crosland leaned too far away from equality to be a good socialist. This shows in his writing about education. But that was not his main fault as a socialist theorist: the greatest disappointment for educationists reading *The Future of Socialism* is the lack of knowledge of maintained schools (despite his sending his step-daughters to a comprehensive school) and, even more seriously, a lack of ideas in the field of education theory. For example, his section on education in *The Future of Socialism* is entirely concerned with school organisation and structure (tripartitism versus comprehensive schools) when the major concern should have been the content of education, that is, what kind of curriculum should be planned in the implementation of secondary education for all. He also showed little interest in Further Education, Adult Education and Higher Education (including the remarkably successful Open University). He was, unfortunately, not alone in the Labour Party on those issues. Like Crosland, many other Labour politicians were more concerned with power than with abstract ideas.

A.H. Halsey's autobiography includes some thoughtful comments on Crosland for whom he worked as an education adviser from 1965 to 1967. Halsey approved of some aspects of *The Future of Socialism*, as well as some of Crosland's decisions, but the partnership between Crosland, the politician, and Halsey, the social theorist, was much less productive than it should have been. Significantly, Halsey was disappointed by Crosland's lack of knowledge about education as well as his ambiguous attitudes to many crucial educational issues:

> I could never quite make out where Tony Crosland stood on education . . .
> It was obvious to me that he was not especially well-informed, which is not
> in the least surprising since he had been reared in the private sector and at

Trinity College, Oxford . . . To outward appearances at least, immediately
before the Second War, Crosland was a clever playboy.

(Halsey 1996, pp. 126–7)

The school curriculum

On several occasions in this book I have complained that Labour politicians and
educationists have neglected to go beyond traditional demands for greater
access to education by examining the nature and quality of the content of
education – the curriculum. Almost no mention was made about curriculum
in the 1944 Education Act; Labour Education Ministers expressly refused to
have anything to do with it, preferring to regard the curriculum as the responsibility of LEAs, or even of teachers themselves. This view became almost a
doctrine of teachers' professional organisations, especially the National Union
of Teachers (NUT), but it should have been clear that the curriculum was a
central political and educational issue that sooner or later had to be grasped.

The first serious (post-1944) attempt to lay down some guidelines on the
school curriculum was made by a left-leaning group of academics and others,
the Council for Curriculum Reform, who produced *The Content of Education*
(1945). The Council was then chaired by Professor Joseph Lauwerys, University
of London, Institute of Education, and included a number of well-known
educationists. The report itself contains specialist sections by non-members,
for example, 'Education as a Social Function' by Julian Huxley. The report is
critical of the Norwood Report (1943) and established an alternative view of
the primary and secondary curricula.

The Council's origin was a meeting in Oxford, in 1940, called to discuss
the reconstruction of the curriculum by two individuals, Mrs. E.M. Hubback
(Association for Education in Citizenship) and Paul Volkow (New Education
Fellowship). Out of a meeting of about thirty representatives a smaller committee for curriculum reform was established, initially chaired by J.P. Meredith,
later replaced by H.G. Stead until his death in 1943 when he was succeeded
by Lauwerys. Their work was inadequately financed (mainly £50 from the Institute of Education with an additional sum of £25 from the London Co-operative
Society) – the nearest the council came to backing from the Labour movement.
The report is described as 'interim', but no final report was ever published, and
the council seems to have disintegrated after 1945 largely because funding was
lacking. This was a great pity: even as an interim report, the ideas on curriculum
were far in advance of anything else at the time, and remained so for many years
during which time very little attention was paid to the report. From 1945 to the
early 1960s the school curriculum was rarely discussed as a political question by
either the Labour Party or the Conservatives. The Labour Party was constrained
to some extent by its links with the NUT which remained hostile to what they
regarded as potential government interference in professional matters.

The Schools Council for Curriculum and Examinations

A change took place in the early 1960s. This was part of a bigger move away from an almost bipartisan policy on education. Consensus was at an end and in 1960 David Eccles, Conservative Minister of Education, during a debate on the Crowther Report in the House of Commons, said that he regretted that parliamentary discussions on education were so much devoted to bricks, mortar and organisation rather than the content of the curriculum. He said that it was his intention to 'make the Ministry's voice heard rather more often and positively and no doubt controversially'. He wanted to encourage the Ministry to undertake more educational research. It was at this time that Eccles used the phrase 'secret garden of the curriculum'. Soon afterwards he established the Curriculum Study Group (1962). Teachers and LEAs were alarmed, probably unnecessarily (Kogan, 1978). Professional teachers' associations and Local Education Authorities remained hostile to the study group, and in 1963 the new Minister of Education, Sir Edward Boyle, replaced it by an organisation intended to be more acceptable to the teaching professionals. A committee was set up under John Lockwood which was to be called the Schools Council for Curriculum and Examinations. The Schools Council is important to the history of educational ideas for at least two reasons. First, it was an important stage in the growth of central control over education in general and the curriculum in particular; second, the Schools Council financed a number of significant curriculum projects which themselves produced new ideas in curriculum and pedagogy: for example, Stenhouse's work on the Humanities Curriculum Project. More will be said about the Schools Council in later chapters: it remained important until it was abolished by Sir Keith Joseph in 1982. By then a number of educational ideas had been developed, especially in the field of curriculum.

Conclusion

The years 1951 to 1964 have been seen by some as 'thirteen wasted years' in education, and by others as a period of expansion and improvement, especially after the Crowther Report (CACE 1959) and the acceptance of the Robbins principle (1963). As far as the Labour Party was concerned, the years were squandered in as much as too little re-thinking about education had taken place. Little happened to develop any kind of theory of education apart from Crosland's *The Future of Socialism* (1956), and I have indicated that this was a puny contribution to educational ideas. More will be said on that topic in Chapter 6 when Crosland's performance as Education Secretary will be considered.

6　The Wilson governments 1964–70

We are restating our socialism in terms of the scientific revolution. The Britain that is going to be forged in the white heat of this technological revolution will be no place for restrictive practices or outdated methods on either side of industry.

(Harold Wilson at Labour Party Conference, October 1963)

Labour has never passed any major piece of educational legislation, but has worked within the blueprints provided by other governments. This is unfortunate because Education Acts passed by other governments have been complex compromises, notably between the central government and the secondary school teachers, the private schools and the church interests; but also between different sections of the political parties, between the Minister and his civil servants, and between the central and local administrations. As a result the major Education Acts (1870, 1902, and 1944) have all appeared late on the scene to legitimate changes which were already substantially under way and to shore up the existing creaking and out of date structures, but scarcely to promote change.

(Marsden, 1971, *Politicians, Equality and Comprehensives*, Fabian Tract 411)

From optimism to disillusion 1964–70

Harold Wilson became leader of the Labour Party after the death of Hugh Gaitskell in 1963. In October of the following year he led the Party to victory at the general election, but with an overall majority of only 4. (317 seats against 304 Conservatives and 9 Liberals). Nevertheless, there was a general feeling of optimism in 1964. By means of a well-timed general election in March 1966 Wilson improved his majority considerably (363 Labour against 253 Conservatives, 12 Liberals and 2 others). Throughout this 6-year period, the Labour government was plagued by international and commonwealth problems: for example, in Southern Rhodesia, whose Prime Minister, Ian Smith, made a unilateral declaration of independence in 1965, after the collapse in 1963 of the Central African Federation (that had been set up by the Conservative government in 1953). The Labour government was faced with a difficult situation, and appeared to vacillate between imposing sanctions on the white settler regime and attempting, unsuccessfully, to negotiate with its leader. This was seen as weakness, as was the stance taken by Wilson and his government to the Vietnam War: Wilson supported the USA military intervention in what became a very unpopular war – especially the indiscriminate bombing of peasants.

In his sympathetic biography of Wilson, Ben Pimlott (1992) stressed Wilson's radical background:

> Harold Wilson was an egalitarian by instinct and conviction, as well as by birthright. His was a Lib–Lab, Nonconformist, free-thinking egalitarianism, fertilized by the hardships suffered by his family in the 1930s, by irritation at the social snobberies of Oxford and Whitehall, by the cold rationalism of Sir William Beveridge, and by the experience of administering fairness as President of the Board of Trade. Greater social and economic equality had been the theme of Wilson's Gollancz-inspired book, *The War on World Poverty*, and of many of his 'white heat' speeches in 1963–4. The theme was not distinct from his modernization doctrine. On the contrary, it was one of his most heartfelt arguments that a more equal society would be a more efficient and economically successful one. It is not surprising, therefore, that the pursuit of equality and fairness should have provided the motif for the most important domestic policies of the 1964–70 administration.
>
> (Pimlott, 1992, *Harold Wilson*, p. 510)

By the late 1960s, however, Wilson had become unpopular with the left wing of his Party, as well as with students and others. Student disaffection, not only about Vietnam but also about the universities themselves, reached a peak in 1968 – in Britain, France, the USA and elsewhere. The major expansion of higher education that had taken place in the UK since the Robbins Report (1963) was criticised, and Wilson's plans for further development of higher education were made more difficult. That expansion was also hampered by the ever-recurring economic problems of post-war Britain. In 1967 the Wilson government was forced to devalue the pound, whereupon the Chancellor of the Exchequer, Jim Callaghan, resigned. Public expenditure was reduced, making reforms – including education – difficult to implement. It was also a period of 'permissiveness', later referred to as the 'swinging sixties'. As we shall see, those who disliked the alleged permissiveness tended to blame schools and universities for low standards.

Education 1964–70

Wilson appointed Michael Stewart as Secretary of State for Education in 1964. This was regarded as a wise appointment, but Stewart did not have long to demonstrate his competence: an early re-shuffle in 1965 sent him to the Foreign Office in place of Patrick Gordon Walker who had twice failed to gain a seat in

Parliament. Tony Crosland became Secretary of State for Education until 1967. Jenny Lee was an imaginative appointment as Minister for the Arts, and she also had responsibility for the new, and very successful, Open University (which Wilson himself initiated and always supported).

Michael Stewart, Education Secretary 1964–65

Stewart began well: in November 1964 he reaffirmed that it was the government's policy to reorganise secondary education along comprehensive lines. The exact pattern would vary from area to area, but all LEAs would need a plan. The election manifesto had referred to 'grammar school education for all' and that certainly needed clarification. He said that one aim of the education policy was to preserve what was valued in grammar school education and to make it available to more children. This must have been a deliberate ambiguity, intended to look conciliatory and moderate. But as Brian Simon (1991) pointed out, it was 'a far cry from the objectives some held of a fundamental transformation of the system in line with democratic objectives' (pp. 276–7).

In any case, the 'moderation' was not going to work: the Conservatives in a Commons debate on education embarked on a campaign deploring the 'wholesale abolition' of direct grant and grammar schools. Stewart responded by showing that LEAs of all political colours were already planning comprehensive reorganisation, and said that he was only going to do what the ex-Minister, Edward Boyle, would have done from within the Conservative Party. Stewart was still trying to promote comprehensive secondary schooling as national policy, but it was increasingly difficult to do so.

It would be a mistake to see 1964 as the beginning of a dispute between the two parties about comprehensive secondary education. Both Knight (1990) and Chitty (1989) have shown that Tory opposition to the way that education was developing began much earlier. I shall return to that issue later; meanwhile, Stewart's attempt to be conciliatory had a mixed reception in the press. Quintin Hogg (Lord Hailsham) also attacked comprehensive planning on the grounds that it offended against the 1944 Education Act and the spirit of partnership between central government, LEAs and schools. Stewart responded by stressing the idea of willing co-operation between the partners. In the House of Lords opposition to Labour policy was stronger. Unfortunately, the government case was presented by C.P. Snow who, when challenged by David Eccles, had to admit that his own son was at Eton.

Crosland as Education Secretary 1965–67

Soon after these debates Michael Stewart was replaced by Tony Crosland, an appointment that was generally welcomed in the world of education at the time. It was an era of growth in higher education: seven new universities were in existence by 1966, and other universities were expanding rapidly. Science and technology were, in theory, the priorities, and some progress was made in that direction; but in practice it was the arts and social science subjects which attracted large numbers of students. Crosland was, at age 46, the youngest member of the Cabinet, and was expected to make his mark in education. Despite the financial difficulties, he succeeded in increasing the money available to education. His order of priorities were secondary school reorganisation, teacher supply and higher education – but he admitted to his wife that he was 'not frightfully interested in universities' (Crosland, 1982, p. 143). Before Crosland took over the Education Department, a decision had been taken not to introduce legislation on comprehensive reorganisation. It was felt that reasonable progress was being made on a voluntary basis. Crosland used the circular, 10/65, drafted by Stewart, as a basis for consultation with LEAs, teachers and others. He decided not to 'require' LEAs to submit plans for comprehensive reorganisation but to use the gentler word 'request'. (His Junior Minister, Reg Prentice, wanted to go for the tougher word but Crosland insisted.) He issued circular 10/65, agreeing with the earlier decision that legislation was undesirable. It was a weak form of encouragement rather than a requirement.

Crosland also realised that something should be done about public schools, but was not sure how to proceed. In *The Conservative Enemy* (1962) he had stated that public schools should be assimilated into the state system, allocating *most* of their places as free places – a token number would not be acceptable. He wanted either radical reform or none at all. If necessary he would recommend legislation, not to prohibit all private fee-paying, 'which would be an intolerable restriction of personal liberty, but, by regulating the conditions under which education is bought and sold, to secure a more equitable distribution of educational resources between different classes of the nation' (Crosland, 1982, p. 148). This would have been a compromise position for Crosland to adopt. But unfortunately he had not thought out how such a plan might work: instead of action he set up the Public Schools Commission chaired by John Newsom. It delivered its first report in 1968, making recommendations along the Crosland lines, but it was never acted upon. Butler's Tory plan to avoid any serious interference with the private sector was still allowed to continue.

Teacher supply improved during Crosland's term of office but this was more the result of the Robbins Report (1963) reforms rather than any policy put forward by Crosland who took little interest in this subject. As for higher education, Crosland became associated with the 'binary policy' which he introduced in his Woolwich Polytechnic speech in 1965. This policy, initially planned by a deputy secretary at the Department of Education and Science (DES), Toby Weaver, was concerned with a new kind of non-university higher education. In 1966 Crosland published a White Paper, A *Plan for Polytechnics and Other Colleges* (Weaver Report). The plan was to create or upgrade a number of LEA Colleges to higher education standard, but not to simply copy the work of universities. Thirty polytechnics would be established over a 6-year period. The plan was accepted somewhat uncritically by Crosland, but others objected to it for two reasons: first, it was said to be 'Higher Education on the cheap' without adequate research provision and other facilities; second, for creating a lower tier, or inferior form of higher education, for those who could not manage 'real' university work. Both criticisms were, to some extent, valid. In a hierarchical society like Britain it was almost inevitable that polytechnics would not be seen as a different kind of institution, but as second best. And it soon became clear that many polytechnics tried to compete with universities, acquiring a higher status by shedding as much of their sub-degree work in science and technology as possible, but developing courses in arts, humanities and social sciences that were never intended to be introduced on that side of the binary line. In the long run, polytechnics proved their value but not in the way that Crosland had intended. It was hardly a socialist policy for higher education. (Eventually, in 1992, a Conservative government would take polytechnics away from LEA control to be developed as part of the national higher education system, and then allowed to change their names to incorporate into their titles the magic word 'university'. See Chapter 10.)

The real contribution to higher education ideas at this time was the establishment of the Open University (OU). This initiative originally referred to as 'The University of the Air' was very much a Prime Ministerial project that owed very little to any of his Education Ministers and nothing to Tony Crosland who was not sympathetic to the idea. Wilson had to work against the Secretary of State for Education and his senior officials who felt that the amount of money spent to launch the Open University would have been better used for conventional higher education. Harold Wilson claimed that he had worked out the basic ideas for the OU in the early 60s as part of his thinking on social justice and education: the OU was intended to provide an opportunity for genuine higher education for those who had missed the chance of going to a conventional university but who would like to pursue university-standard courses on a part-time basis making use not only of correspondence courses but also the advantages offered by radio and television. One of the features of the Open University has always been the very high quality of materials produced for students and the high standard of course planning and assessment. The early day-to-day negotiations for this initiative were handled by Jenny Lee working independently within the DES, as Minister for the Arts.

> She threw her radical energy into the task. But it was Wilson who made the running. The Open University became his pet scheme, almost a hobby. Callaghan recalls the frequency, and the insistence, with which the Prime Minister pressed him to rescue it from proposed Treasury cuts, and to ensure that it was properly funded. On occasion, Wilson had to fight his own Education Minister, as well as the mandarins.
>
> (Pimlott, 1992, p. 514)

This is a very rare example of socialist ideas of equality and community being applied to the elitist world of higher education. Wilson has not always been given sufficient credit for this initiative which has not only been a great success in the UK but has been copied throughout the world. Wilson should also be given credit for attempting to stimulate science and technology in education. This was by no means a new idea, but Wilson tried to convert the idea into action. He did not succeed completely, partly for financial reasons, and partly because he was unable to overcome the traditional culture of higher education.

During his short time (two and a half years) in Education, Crosland certainly worked hard and made progress. His limited success might be explained in terms of inadequate theoretical knowledge about education. Some might think that this is an unfair accusation: in order to provide some evidence for my point of view I embarked upon a little textual analysis of *The Future of Socialism* (1956) by examining all the books mentioned and other references and classifying them under subject matter headings. It goes without saying that Crosland is well read in economics and politics. He also refers to quite a wide range of books on sociology, social policy and the social services. But he makes very little reference to works on education policy or educational theory – a serious gap in his own education. The breakdown of books and other references in *The Future of Socialism* is as follows:

Economics: 98 references
Politics: (including political biography): 72
Sociology, social policy, social services: 51
Psychology: 11
Education: 8
Others, including history and literature: 14

Since the education references are so few it may be of interest to list them:

A.H. Halsey and L. Gardner, 'Social mobility and achievement in four grammar schools', *British Journal of Sociology*, March 1953.
Early Leaving Report, 1954.
P. Jay, *Better Schools Now*, 1953.
H.D. Hughes, *A Socialist Education Policy*, 1955, Fabian Society. Fleming Report, 1944.
E. James, *Education and Leadership*, 1951.
R. Pedley, *Comprehensive Schools Today*, 1955.
'Can Our Teachers Read and Write?', *Harper's Magazine*, November 1954.

So, his only references to education consisted of three books, one pamphlet, two government reports and two articles (one from Harper's Magazine which might be criticised as lacking authority, even in a student's essay).

It was noted in Chapter 5 that there is only one chapter in *The Future of Socialism* that touches on education, and significantly it is called 'The Influence of Education' (Chapter 12). It consists of twenty pages and makes no contribution to our understanding of educational theory, with only three pages devoted to 'a Labour Education Policy'. Clearly, Crosland did not share the views of socialists such as William Morris who saw education as central to socialism. Crosland's discussion of education is superficial in the extreme, relying on anecdote and assertion rather than the kind of scrutiny and analysis that he would apply to an economic judgement. For example, in his discussion of 'testing and differentiation designed to produce homogeneous classes of more or less similar standards of attainment' in comprehensive schools, he suggests that streaming

> has shocked some comprehensive enthusiasts, who had hoped for a system of social promotion on the American model, with virtually no grading by ability. But both common sense and American experience suggest that this would lead to a really serious levelling-down of standards, and a quite excessive handicap to the clever child. Division into streams, according to ability, remains essential.
>
> (p. 272)

A reader's response to Crosland must be 'What American experience? Where is the evidence?' It would be good to know what Crosland had read about this important and controversial issue in education. Clearly, he had not read Robin Pedley's short book very carefully, although he quoted it in *The Future of Socialism*: there is a section in it that contains a balanced argument quoting some very useful evidence (Pedley, 1955, pp. 87–97). This might have caused Crosland to be less sweeping in his statement about streaming. Would Crosland rely on 'common sense' in an argument about economic policy? He also tends to sneer (on p. 273) at those who disagree with him for having 'an excessive attachment to Deweyism'. We might suspect that Crosland had not read Dewey and if he had he might have treated his views with greater respect. This is a great pity. Chapter 12 of *The Future of Socialism* and other sections of the book that touch on education are frankly not up to the quality of the rest of Crosland's book which has in recent years been criticised more generally, including the economic arguments (see, for example, Saville, 1988). But we must concentrate on Crosland's educational ideas which were not only superficial but occasionally contrary to socialist principles. For example, in *The Politics of Education* (Kogan, 1971), a very interesting set of conversations with Maurice Kogan, Crosland made a very strange statement about the work of the Central Advisory Council: 'The reports got longer and longer, and more and more monumental, and took up more and more of the time of already hard-worked officials. Some of the reports were very good; others like Newsom, could have been sharper – though the "Newsom child" has been a most important and influential concept' (Kogan, 1971, p. 174).

This not only shows Crosland's somewhat contemptuous attitude to expert opinion in education, but also, perhaps more significantly, his naive acceptance of the concept of the 'Newsom child' which even then was regarded as politically and educationally unsound.

The Plowden Report (1967) and the philosophy of primary education

What was to be the final task of the Central Advisory Committee for Education was an examination of primary education which had not been officially considered since the two Hadow Reports in the 1930s (*The Primary School*, 1931, and *Infant and Nursery Schools*, 1933). The committee, chaired by Lady Bridget Plowden, was charged to 'consider primary education in all its aspects, and the transition to secondary education'. Two very interesting educational ideas were developed within the report, both of which became contentious issues when the anti-progressive backlash in education became powerful in later years. The first was 'positive discrimination', the second was 'educational priority areas'. The title of the report, *Children and Their Primary Schools*, is itself an indication of the child-centred philosophy that prevailed in the primary school world at that time, a particular version of progressive education that was itself a reaction against the harsher regimes of the nineteenth century. Apart from the title, the report is progressive in other ways: for example, the case against the fixed, genetic view of intelligence is carefully argued in a section on heredity and environment (pp. 13ff.). The link between social class and educational performance is also explored with greater sensitivity than is usually the case in official documents. The important role of parents for the education of primary age pupils is stressed, as is the need for better home–school relations within the community. Out of those discussions emerged the notion of educational priority areas: the fact that many inner-city areas had been neglected for generations so that schools had poor buildings and equipment, matching the poor quality of housing, with large numbers of immigrant families, teachers who did not stay very long, and often with low morale. The committee recommended 'A new distribution of educational resources' – that is, 'positive discrimination' for areas that were deprived. This was an important step, going beyond the traditional Labour Party demand for equality, recognising that in some contexts equal treatment would be neither fair nor sufficient.

Educational Priority Areas (EPAs)

One direct outcome of the Plowden Report was an allocation of money (£16 million) negotiated by Crosland to set up action research in five 'deprived areas'. These EPAs and their intervention programmes were carefully researched (separately funded), but the immediate enthusiasm for the Plowden view of primary education was not sustained; as we shall see in later chapters, there was a right-wing backlash in the 1970s. As for the EPAs, despite promising results, their funding did not continue long after Margaret Thatcher became Education Secretary in 1970. The idea of positive discrimination was attacked by the right and inadequately defended by Labour. To be really successful EPAs would have needed long-term funding throughout the 1970s and into the 1980s. This was not to be: the 1970s saw the beginning of a series of right-wing anti-educational campaigns that succeeded in casting doubt on such ideas as 'positive discrimination', and even equality of opportunity as well as many other progressive practices. What did survive, however, was the acceptance of nursery education as a very important factor in many children's development: the number of pupils gaining pre-school places continued to rise steadily into the twenty-first century.

Patrick Gordon-Walker, Education Secretary 1967–68

In 1967 Crosland was replaced by Patrick Gordon-Walker who was by then regarded as a very lame duck. This appointment may have shown that Wilson allowed kindness to prevail over judgement when he appointed Gordon-Walker. Wilson failed to realise the importance of having a person of real ability in charge of education at this time. Halsey, who was Crosland's Education Adviser, made the following perceptive comment: 'I might go further and declare the whole experience of Crosland politics applied to education as a disaster were it not for three things' (Halsey, 1996). The three things were: first, that Crosland was honest when he applied his mind to education; second, that although Crosland was a libertarian socialist he still recognised the evil of inequality in education; and, third, his successors, including Patrick Gordon-Walker were much worse.

There is little more to say about Gordon-Walker, as Education Secretary, except that he seemed to be attracted to the idea of fees for nursery education although it had been dismissed by the Plowden Committee. Perhaps even worse, was the fact that in 1968 he did not oppose the Cabinet decision to postpone, once again, raising the school leaving age to 16. He even voted for the postponement in Cabinet on that decision which caused Frank Pakenham (Lord Longford) to resign from the Cabinet at this betrayal of Labour promises. Roy Jenkins's arguments in favour of cutting public expenditure won the day, despite many protests from the Labour movement, especially the TUC (see Griggs, 2002, p. 260).

Edward Short, Education Secretary 1968–70

Ted Short was certainly a considerable improvement on Gordon-Walker. As a teacher and headteacher Short started with the support of the teaching profession and he earned the respect of his civil servants. He was not an original thinker on education, but showed a dogged determination to implement the Labour Party's policy on comprehensive education. He encouraged those authorities who wished to integrate grammar schools into comprehensive schemes and by 1969 produced a Bill that would have compelled those recalcitrant LEAs to produce plans for fully comprehensive secondary education. This Bill reached a second reading in 1970 but was not enacted before the 1970 general election when the Wilson government lost control.

It is to Short's credit that he realised that what the Labour Party needed in the field of education was a long-term plan for the whole of the education service. He put this proposal forward in 1969 but did not get any further with the writing of a new 25-year plan for education. Short is probably remembered most for his reaction to the first Black Paper in 1969. Instead of replying in measured tones and producing convincing counter arguments, he condemned the Black Paper in somewhat emotional terms, adding to its media publicity rather than defeating it intellectually. During his period in office, the Newsom Report on public schools was published, but Short took no action; had he attempted to do so it is probable that there would have been little support from the rest of the Cabinet, except from Tony Benn. (See the Diaries of Barbara Castle and Tony Benn for the lack of interest shown when the report was very briefly discussed in Cabinet, CACE, 1959.)

The New Left

The New Left in the UK has been given various dates of origin going back at least as far as the 1950s, but some of the ideas took time to make an impact. It has been suggested that there were at least two, very different, causes. The first was disappointment with Labour Party achievements, especially among the young on the left of the Party. Second, was a loss of faith by British communists and fellow travellers, after the death of Stalin in 1953 and the consequent revelations about his regime. This kind of disillusionment was aggravated by such events as the Hungarian uprising in 1956. Some on the left also felt a need to find a vision better than Crosland's *Future of Socialism* which was in danger of becoming almost a sacred text for the right wing of the Labour Party.

Another aspect of the New Left, especially after Bevan's acceptance of a nuclear defence policy in 1957, was the Campaign for Nuclear Disarmament (CND). At the 1960 Labour Party conference a unilaterist motion had been passed, with a small majority, which prompted the 'fight and fight again' outburst from Gaitskell, intensifying the left–right split within the Party. Another, more academic, feature of the New Left was the *New Left Review* which was attractive to those looking for modern theories of socialism, often with a strongly Marxist flavour.

The New Left and education

The New Left is of some significance to the history of educational ideas for related but different reasons. The New Left in education developed out of dissatisfaction with traditional sociology of education. Sociological studies of education in England had, since the 1920s and 1930s, concentrated on problems of inequality of access to secondary education. After 1944 this tradition had continued within the context of a system, albeit imperfect, of secondary education for all. Official Reports (Early Leaving, 1954, Crowther, 1959, Newsom and

Robbins, 1963), as well as numerous sociological academic studies (e.g. Ford, 1969) all showed that, although standards appeared to be rising, the gap between working-class and middle-class children continued to be very wide. During the later 1960s one important development was the suggestion that it was time to have a paradigm shift in the sociology of education: instead of accepting the 'commonsense' world of schooling, all aspects of institutions, especially the curriculum, assessment and pedagogy, should be called into question rather than taken for granted.

These ideas became important for two reasons: first, they questioned not only traditional sociology of education but also criticised some established Labour Party views on schooling; second, they provoked various kinds of right-wing backlash in education which became important in the 1970s and 1980s. These points will be taken up in later chapters.

Conclusion

The year 1970 when the Labour government was defeated by Heath was something of an anti-climax to Wilson's 1963 conference slogan about a technological revolution which headed this chapter. The Labour defeat at the general election was, to some extent, an expression of public disappointment about the gap between rhetoric and reality. In terms of education a gap was caused by a lack of interest in education by senior Labour politicians and a lack of educational vision by those who were responsible for education policy. The only exception to this was the establishment of the Open University which was not only radical but a considerable success almost immediately.

The period covered by this chapter, that is, 1964–70, also witnessed the beginning of another set of political ideas, 'The New Left'. Some of these challenges to traditional Labourism would later have important implications for educational theory and practice.

7 Heath and a taste of Thatcher 1970–74

Freedom for the pike is death for the minnows.

(R.H. Tawney, 1931, *Equality*)

Heath's four years of power: the background

These were difficult years for the new Prime Minister, Edward Heath, who won the June general election despite the predictions of nearly all the polls. He had 330 Tory seats, against 287 Labour, 6 Liberals and 7 others. The international situation was far from peaceful. The civil war in Nigeria came to an end but left a feeling that all was far from well in post-colonial Africa. In 1972 there was a military coup in Ghana, and other problems followed. Of more direct political importance was the US bombing in Vietnam which continued until 1973, and in April 1970 had spread to Cambodia. In Pakistan there was a civil war resulting in many deaths and Bangladesh (East Pakistan) becoming independent. Even more important to the UK was the Middle-East situation where Israel fought Arabs on several fronts, managing to defeat Egypt in the Yom Kippur war (October 1973). The oil states then increased the price of oil by 70 per cent, which caused the dramatic deterioration of the UK's balance of payments, and rapidly rising inflation. De Gaulle died in 1970, and in the following year the EEC agreed terms on which the UK could be admitted.

At home, Heath inherited the Northern Ireland problems, and in 1972 paratroopers fired on Derry marchers – Bloody Sunday. The troubles steadily deteriorated over the period of Heath's premiership, and attempts at power-sharing failed. Heath's most serious problem was, however, the failure to control or negotiate with trade unions: strikes proliferated, including action by dockers, postal workers, local authority workers, newspaper workers, railway workers, ship workers and the mine workers. Working days lost by strikes rose to the highest figure since the General Strike of 1926. Worse still, in December 1973 the Heath government introduced a three-day working week in an attempt to overcome the shortage of power, partly caused by industrial action. Having failed to persuade the mineworkers to end their strike, Heath called an election.

His campaign relied on the slogan 'Who Rules Britain – The Government or the Miners?' Heath lost and on 6 March Harold Wilson returned to power.

Education 1970–74

Heath appointed Margaret Thatcher as Secretary of State for Education. The education expansion that had started in the later 1960s continued into the early 1970s, and, at first, morale was generally high at all levels of education. But the cuts in public expenditure inevitably hit education. Nevertheless, the language of expansion continued, and in December 1972 Thatcher even produced a White Paper, *Education: A Framework for Expansion*. However, that was mostly rhetoric: the reality was to become a programme of closures of Colleges of Education and a tight control over education spending generally.

In their 1970 election manifesto the Conservatives had promised to withdraw circular 10/65 which had requested LEAs to put forward plans for comprehensive secondary education. Soon after the election, Thatcher published circular 10/70 saying that it would be wrong to impose a uniform pattern of secondary schools on all LEAs; it was a 'steadying' document rather than an invitation for LEAs to go back on any plans that appeared to be working. Even so, the Conservative Party, and Margaret Thatcher in particular, faced much criticism from the world of education, from the TUC and others for taking a backward step. There was also unfavourable comment from within the Conservative Party: for example, the moderate Bow Group said that the withdrawal of 10/65 was bad for education and bad for the Conservative Party. The implication was that Edward Boyle would have behaved differently had he been Secretary of State. At the Party Conference Thatcher said that the Conservative priority was now primary education; this was popular but failed to prevent a rift between left and right on education, mostly about comprehensive schools. The right wingers focused their campaign on saving the grammar schools.

One of the best known ironies of education at this time was that Margaret Thatcher, however unwillingly, approved more comprehensive schemes than any other Education Secretary. The pressure from parents, including those in Conservative-controlled LEAs, was strongly against the selection process at 11+. Thatcher tried to slow down the pace of comprehensivation, and succeeded to some extent. But public opinion was strongly against her: teacher unions, including the National Association of Headteachers, were also in favour of comprehensives. Nevertheless, the Secretary of State refused permission to several LEAs where their proposals involved the closure of existing grammar schools. One of her tactics was to give priority to new building for primary schools rather than secondary, when most comprehensive schools necessarily involved some new building. Ted Short, the Labour Shadow Education Secretary, saw through this manoeuvre and publicly condemned the thinly disguised reactionary intention. This was overshadowed, however, by the general cuts in public expenditure after the 1973 oil crisis, forcing a good deal of education replanning.

A framework for expansion?

The proposals in the White Paper, A *Framework for Expansion* (1972), including developing nursery education and polytechnics, looked less and less plausible. In the same year, the James Committee that had been set up to look into education and training, issued its report – *Teacher Education and Training* (1972). The committee was originally established because standards of reading in schools were considered to be poor, and that many teachers had been inadequately trained in methods of teaching reading. This view was reinforced by some contributors to the Black Papers (Cox and Dyson, 1969) which will be considered below. Short had, in 1970, invited the Area Training Organisations to carry out their own enquiry into teacher education. The Conservatives promised, in 1970, to set up a committee, if they won the election, to look into the whole question of teacher education and training. The Conservatives kept their promise and set up a small committee under the chairmanship of Eric James, known to be right-wing and critical of teacher education. The committee reported in December 1971 with two members of the committee (Professor J.R. Webster and James Porter) writing a 'Note of extension' (see below).

The James Report proposed a complete reorganisation of teacher education into three cycles: the first, general higher education; the second, professional training; and the third cycle, in-service training. The committee put forward two alternatives for the first cycle. For some teachers the first cycle would be in a university or polytechnic, taking a first degree; for others the first cycle would be in a College of Education and would lead to a new Diploma in Higher Education, taken at the end of two years. The first cycle might contain some education but would be general in character, and professional training would follow as a consecutive (second) cycle rather than the familiar College of Education pattern of general education and professional training being pursued concurrently.

The James Committee considered that the most important innovation would be to introduce far greater priority for in-service education for teachers: every teacher should be released with pay for the equivalent of one term every seven years (to be raised to one term every five years as soon as possible). In order to cope with the validation of the new qualifications offered at each stage, it was recommended that a National Council for Teacher Education be set up with the power (previously a monopoly of universities) to award the degrees of BA(Ed.) and MA (Ed.). The note of extension signed by Webster and Porter argued in favour of closer ties between colleges and universities, (including the possibility of some colleges merging with universities). In that case, universities could validate the Dip.HE for many colleges and some colleges would be encouraged to do three-year degree work, together with four-year honours degrees (to include education as a course of study). Needless to say, the report was extremely controversial, one particular bone of contention being the principle of concurrent education and training. Other criticisms included the acceptability of the Dip.HE, the validating bodies and the credibility of the BA (Ed.). The National Union of Teachers, suspecting a downgrading of teacher qualifications, were particularly hostile to the proposals (apart from the in-service education reforms).

It soon became apparent, however, that the 'Framework for Expansion' was hardly an appropriate title. Two other developments caused the policy of expansion to become one of contraction. First, the declining size of school populations meant that fewer teachers would be needed. Second, there was an overriding need to reduce spending on education. The result was a massive programme of colleges of education being reorganised, either closing down or merging with polytechnics and universities. Very large numbers of redundancies in the colleges followed, cushioned by the strangely generous 'Crombie' scheme. The recommendations of the James Committee were watered down or ignored. The plan to reduce class size was virtually abandoned, especially after the notorious Barber budget (December 1973) made even more cuts to public expenditure – £1200 million, including much of the school building programme. The Heath record on education ended in a very negative way.

Labour views on education 1970–74

What of the Labour Party during the Heath years 1970–74? Labour was very good at criticising Thatcher and the Conservatives for having no real education policy; they made little progress in finding one themselves. Strangely, even in opposition, the Labour Party was, to some extent on the defensive, not least in reaction to the three Black Papers which continued to be discussed and used as anti-Labour propaganda during these four years. The nearest thing to an official Labour Party vision for the future came from the Fabian Society: *Planning for Education in 1980* (February 1970, Research Series 282) edited by Howard Glennerster (LSE) on behalf of a group that included H.E. Hughes (Ruskin College), Caroline Benn and Tessa Blackstone. The pamphlet included several ideas worthy of note: first, a plea for holistic planning in education (reacting against the series of CACE reports on limited aspects of secondary and primary education). Second, they wanted educational planning to take place in the context of social and technological change. Third, they demonstrated their practical realism by costing and prioritising their recommendations. Unfortunately, when Labour returned to power in 1974, insufficient notice was taken of this interesting exercise in educational planning. Although it was not a new vision of education, and by no means a complete solution to Labour Party needs, it could have taken the Labour Party several steps forward. The pamphlet was extremely well written but published in a very unattractive format compared with the Black Papers that had by now succeeded in reaching a much wider readership despite noticeably inferior arguments and ideas.

Education theories and political ideas 1970–74

One of the purposes of this book is to bring together the separate strands of Labour history and the development of educational ideas in the twentieth century. One aspect of that relationship has been touched on in earlier chapters: individual members of the Labour movement have occasionally, but not very frequently or in any systematic way, voiced their disquiet about the kind of education being provided for the working classes. Whilst the mainstream Labour policy has been to press for more and more schooling, a few have been concerned that the state system was either sub-standard or, worse still, likely to socialise the working classes into an acceptance of their place in an unjust capitalist society, rather than helping them to be liberated from it. Brian Simon (1960) who generally supported the mainstream Labour policy of extending access to schooling, nevertheless quoted with some concern the views of Thomas Hodgskin in the nineteenth century who, talking of the control of Mechanics' Institutes, said that if they were under the control of the rulers they would be worse than useless. I also pointed out, in Chapter 1, that H.G. Wells was highly critical of the 1870 Education Act, for similar reasons. Working-class opposition to state education was not simply about its quality but also about its purpose and direction.

These were minority views within Labour, however; the usual policy was that schooling had been a privilege of the upper and middle classes and that something like it should be made available by the state for working-class children – the more, the better. From time to time, opposition from right and left was voiced against the kind of education that had been provided. For example, D.H. Lawrence (1885–1930), himself an unsuccessful teacher, thought it unsuitable in the early part of the twentieth century, as did Geoffrey Bantock, a right-wing Professor of Education, in the 1960s. They were often dismissed as reactionary views, perpetuating the social class gap in educational achievement. But there were left-wing writers who were equally unhappy.

In the 1970s the disenchantment with the *status quo* in education was on the increase and a series of publications and events brought this issue to a head. I will deal with them under the following five headings: Ivan Illich and the de-schoolers; Paulo Freire; James Coleman; the new sociology of education; and the Black Papers and the new right.

Ivan Illich

It is important to stress that Illich was criticising modern society as a whole, from an international perspective, not simply modern education. His argument consists of a number of different but related strands. From a history of ideas point of view it may also be important to say that he was not the first 'de-schooler'. In the USA Paul Goodman had, a decade earlier, produced *Compulsory Miseducation* (1962) which condemned schools in capitalist USA for misleading the young. Goodman, however, never hit the headlines in the way that Illich did, and he died in 1972 before the de-schooling debate reached its peak. Illich, in *De-Schooling Society* (1971) argued that the overall effect of state schooling was harmful, because as part of an over-bureaucratic society, schools confused teaching with learning, and passing grades with genuine education. Schooling was for Illich in the same category as other modern institutions: for example, medical treatment had been confused with health care, social work with improving the quality of life in a community. Illich condemned many modern institutions, including education for being 'manipulative' rather than 'convivial'. He said that schools had become de-humanised, manipulative institutions like prisons and hospitals. Illich also argued that schooling actually increased inequality in society and served to divide society rather than unify it, using such terms as 'academic' and 'vocational'. He likened 'mass education' to a modern religion, separating the saved from the damned. This analogy runs through a good deal of his writing: Illich seemed to be suggesting that just as the Reformation took place in the sixteenth century and destroyed the monopolistic power of the church, so it would become necessary in modern society to destroy the power and monopoly of mass education that indulged in 'people-processing', socialising the young into a corrupt, unjust capitalist society.

It is easy to see that this de-schooling idea might have an attraction for some on the left, including teachers and other educationists. The diagnosis was, however, more convincing than the cure. Schools certainly needed to change, but it was by no means clear that the young in modern society would be better off without them. Despite their imperfections, for many young people a good school represented a friendly and humane environment in a hostile world. Nevertheless, Illich's criticisms of mass education were powerful and deserved to be taken seriously. They became part of the educational debate in the 1970s and later.

Paulo Freire

Another educationist from the other side of the Atlantic whose work began to be discussed in the UK at this time was Freire, whose book *Pedagogy of the Oppressed* (1970) was just as critical of capitalist society and the way that the young were mis-educated. This offered a more constructive solution to the problem of educational reform. Freire was not a de-schooler and towards the end of his life he actually accepted the challenge of running the Sao Paolo school system. What Freire showed was that traditional curriculum and pedagogy did not and could not work with some groups in South America whose early experience of life was quite different from that of more privileged groups.

In one respect, Freire's message was similar to Illich's complaint that education often confused the outward manifestation of teaching for genuine learning of something worthwhile. In Freire's terms, it was the 'banking' concept of schooling that he objected to:

In the banking concept of education, knowledge is a gift bestowed by those who considered themselves knowledgeable upon those they consider to know nothing. Projecting an absolute ignorance onto others, a character-istic of the ideology of oppression, negates education and knowledge as processes of enquiry. The teacher presents himself to his students as their necessary opposite; by considering their ignorance absolute, he justifies his own existence. The students, alienated like the slave in the Hegelian dialectic accept their ignorance as justifying the teacher's existence – but, unlike the slave, they never discover that they educate the teacher. The raison d'etre of libertarian education, on the other hand, lies in its drive towards reconciliation. Education must begin with the solution of the teacher–student contradiction, by reconciling the poles of the contra-diction so that both are simultaneously teachers and students.

(Freire, 1970, pp. 46–7)

There was a good deal of wisdom in Freire's writing – wisdom based on practical experience. But it did not claim to prescribe a complete solution for modern schooling. It was less negative than Illich; his criticism of capitalist society included elements of remedial action. But, above all, in the 1970s, it was seen as a critique of the educational *status quo*.

J.S. Coleman

The importance of the US sociologist, J.S. Coleman was that he did a good deal of research that seemed to indicate that schooling had very little statistical significance in terms of changing working class life-chances. This view was later challenged, using more sophisticated statistics, but in the early 1970s it was interpreted as indicating that 'schools made no difference'. Coleman's work gave rise to at least two important ideas in education: first, the effective school and second, school improvement. After the Coleman Report (1966) the pessimistic interpretation of the statistics was that schools make little or no difference to pupil achievement – social class was the major determining factor. That view was gradually transformed after a number of studies in the USA, the UK and elsewhere that showed that the performance of children from similar social backgrounds was different according to what came to be referred to as 'the culture of the school'. An effective school's culture had a number of positive features: for example, collaborative planning, co-operative commitment to goals, staff stability, maximum use of learning time and other cultural features. New studies in the 1970s stressed, however, that the individual factors correlated with effectiveness could not be treated in isolation: effective-ness was a holistic idea representing a more enlightened school culture. Despite that warning, some school effectiveness projects have become very mechan-istic, focusing on effectiveness criteria on an individual basis. In the hands of more enlightened researchers the school effectiveness concept has been a useful professional tool in the process of school self-evaluation and school improvement.

Like school effectiveness, school improvement has become a movement concerned with improving the achievement and quality of primary and secondary schools. Good studies have been broader than typical studies of effectiveness, concentrating on overall quality of the schooling experience rather than narrow measures of performance. Both concepts have been much used and abused since the 1960s. They have altered the way that administrators look at schools (for better or worse). On the one hand, both school effectiveness and school improvement have encouraged atomistic thinking and reductionism – looking at parts not wholes; on the other hand, they have encouraged teachers themselves to get more involved in educational planning and evaluation. In that sense both ideas can be related to socialist replanning of education.

The sociology of education

The fourth group which influenced the debate on education in England in the 1970s was related to the New Left in politics, and became known, somewhat misleadingly, as the new sociology of education. The key text was *Knowledge and Control* (1971) edited by M.F.D. Young. We must start with the 'old' sociology. This was a tradition that, as we have seen, had existed as an academic pursuit since the 1920s. It was concerned with demographic aspects of educational opportunity, particularly in pre-1944 studies of working-class limited access to grammar schools. It provided useful maps of inequality of educational opportunity. This tradition continued with studies already mentioned in earlier chapters: Early Leaving Report (1954), Crowther Report (1959), Newsom and Robbins (1963) and Plowden (1967). All these reports produced similar findings: despite general improvements in standards and access to education, the gap between middle-class and working-class pupils remained wide. The contribution of the new sociologists was that it questioned the premises of the educational *status quo*. Young and his colleagues suggested that instead of accepting the rules of the educational game and then wondering why the working classes always seemed to lose the race, we should question the suitability of the rules and even the desirability of the game itself: the new sociologists advocated 'making' new research questions rather than simply 'taking', that is, accepting, the research questions established by earlier sociologists who were, they claimed, too inclined to accept the values and traditions of a very imperfect education system in a capitalist society. In other words, they asked why sociologists should simply accept such matters as examinations as a test of true ability. Why accept the traditional curriculum as suitable for secondary education for all? Like Freire, some called into question traditional pedagogy and even the school itself as a desirable institution. These were radical questions which were bound to provoke hostile responses from both right-wing and left-wing traditionalists. And they did.

The Black Papers, the New Right and the end of optimism

Despite the general success of comprehensive education, the Tories were making capital out of the problems existing in some of the new schools, especially in the inner cities. The reactionary views of the Black Papers were written in a populist style that reached a wide readership. The first two Black Papers, *Fight for Education* and *Crisis in Education* were written in 1969; the third more personally entitled *Good-bye Mr. Short!* was published in 1970. They attacked modern teaching methods, the so-called Plowden philosophy; they advocated the retention of selection for secondary education and the provision of superior schools for the gifted. Contributors consisted of academics, teachers, writers and politicians holding right-wing views, including G.H. Bantock, Rhodes Boyson, Kingsley Amis and Cyril Burt. They were edited by C.B. Cox and A.E. Dyson. The obvious feature of the Black Paper debate was that the first three appeared when Labour was in office as a direct criticism of progressive education policies and included in that group, comprehensive education. None were written during the Heath government, but they started up again in 1975. The right-wing polemics distracted the Labour Party from developing their own policies, because they were wasting time and energy on countering all kinds of accusations about progressivism. They would have been better employed developing a real education policy based on socialist principles. It is also significant that Keith Joseph and Margaret Thatcher saw the need for a set of right-wing policies, and accordingly established, in 1974, the Centre for Policy Studies, as a kind of right-wing think tank specialising in social policies, including education.

Although the Black Papers were essentially backward looking, the authors were careful not to look back too far and be accused of being socially reactionary rather than critical of modern educational methods and structures. Central to many of the Black Paper ideas was the concept of intelligence and IQ. Although they did not use the word, their thinking was 'meritocratic'.

The emphasis on grammar schools and selection by ability was a change in Tory thinking from social elitism (superiority by social status) towards intellectual elitism (superiority by IQ). This change of Tory attitude was neither complete nor a simple switch from social to intellectual elitism: the old Tory view of social superiority included an assumption of intellectual superiority corresponding with social status. One complaint about early Labour party leaders was that they were too deferential and half believed in the superior intellectual abilities of their social betters. (There are many examples of early Labour MPs being thrilled by having a conversation with a lord, and Ramsay MacDonald's liking for upper-class company was notorious.) This deferential attitude has still not disappeared and represents a danger to Labour education policies. Since 1997 meritocracy has been revived and is openly referred to as a respectable policy, presumably forgetting that the term invented by Michael Young in *The Rise of the Meritocracy* (1958) was a fable intended to show that a society based on meritocracy would be a truly nightmare world.

Men as different as Robert Morant and Sidney Webb saw the need to educate and train the future leaders of society and agreed on the crucial importance of the selective secondary grammar school as part of the 'ladder of opportunity' in an efficient modern society. An essential feature of democratic education, however, is to open up opportunities for all young people, and any structure or set of practices which prevents that process by premature selection into categories such as intellectual/practical, academic/vocational is essentially undemocratic. It took the Labour Party a long time to realise that selection at age 11 should be avoided partly for that reason. Unfortunately, when the controversy about grammar school selection was revived from 1969 onwards, the Labour Party often focused their criticisms on the difficulty (or even impossibility) of devising fair tests at age 11 rather than on the principle of selection itself. We shall return to this point in later chapters.

Conclusion

Despite the right-wing backlash and four years of Margaret Thatcher as Education Secretary, the number of comprehensive schools doubled between 1970 and 1974, so that more than half of secondary school pupils were then attending comprehensive schools (see *Half Way There* by Caroline Benn and Brian Simons, 1970).

Since 1945 the Labour Party had seen as its major task in education to push forward the implementation of the 1944 Education Act as quickly as possible. After 1974 they had to face the reality of a change in Tory attitudes: from then onwards, part of the task was to prevent the pendulum swinging back to pre-war attitudes and practices. How the Labour Party coped with that problem will be taken up in Chapter 8.

8   Wilson and Callaghan 1974–79

All I can say is – my prayers.
>   (Harold Wilson on hearing the results of the first 1974 general election
>   6.3.1974)

Bernard Donoughue, whom Callaghan inherited as his Senior Policy Adviser, drafted an important memorandum suggesting, among other things, that it would be appropriate, given the widespread interest in the subject, for the Prime Minister to make educational standards an important feature in his new administration. In Donoughue's view, this was an area where the Prime Minister might well reveal his personal concern and commitment.
>   (Chitty, 1989, *Towards a New Education System*)

The international background

On 6 March 1974 Harold Wilson became Prime Minister for his third term of office, but without a majority in the House of Commons. Edward Heath had, before resigning as Prime Minister, unsuccessfully attempted to form a coalition government with Liberal support and a Cabinet seat for Jeremy Thorpe, the Liberal leader. The world scene was still troubled: in Israel the Labour Prime Minister, Golda Meir, resigned, and there were problems with both Syrian and Palestinian raids (as well as, later on, war with Egypt). In Greece the military rule of the colonels came to an end, and a peace deal in Cyprus was signed by the Foreign Minister, James Callaghan, in May 1974. But peace was short lived: in August Turkish troops landed and stayed, creating a problem of partition that remained into the twenty-first century. In Vietnam, a series of Communist victories in 1975 signalled the beginning of the end of US intervention; Cambodia also fell to the Communist Khmer Rouge. Later in 1975 attention returned to Africa where a bloody civil war started in Angola between the Marxist MPLA supported by Russia and Cuba who were pitted against two anti-Marxist groups supported by the USA. In 1977 there were more problems in India and Pakistan where the Prime Minister was overthrown in a military coup. In 1979 the Shah of Iran was exiled; but in the same year a peace treaty was arranged between Egypt and Israel. Later in 1979 the USSR and USA signed a hopeful arms limitation treaty. But the oil crisis dominated the economic scene after 1973.

UK domestic politics

Harold Wilson, PM 1974–76

Wilson's term of office, 1974–76 was more difficult than his period as Prime Minister from 1964 to 1970:

> In 1964 the manifesto had been the product of thirteen years reassessment. In 1974 it was, at best, a shopping list, at worst a collection of slogans. The Labour Party in Opposition had been too preoccupied with its factional quarrel to develop a new set of ideas that carried conviction.
>
> (Pimlott, 1992, *Harold Wilson*, p. 618)

One of Harold Wilson's first acts as Prime Minister was to bring the miners' strike to an end by giving them most of their pay demands. Callaghan became Foreign Secretary, and Denis Healey won the difficult post of Chancellor of the Exchequer. Healey was soon faced with the economic effects of the dramatic rise in OPEC oil prices: he reacted with half-hearted cuts in public expenditure, including education. Soon after the election, Sir Keith Joseph, Shadow Home Secretary, deviated from the official Conservative Party line by embracing monetarism, advocating tight control of money supply. In October 1974, Wilson called another general election, hoping to secure a good majority: he gained enough seats to give him an overall majority – of three. Not quite the answer to his prayers that he wanted; nevertheless, he said that it was good enough. It was a blow to Heath who in February 1975 was to lose the Tory leadership: Margaret Thatcher, who had been supported by the right wing of the Party, replaced him.

In March 1975 a future problem for the Labour Party was signalled by a lack of unity about the Common Market: the Cabinet was split 16 to 7 on advising voters in the referendum about remaining inside the Common Market. Soon after this, Labour was also faced with the problems of rising unemployment as well as high wage claims; there was a run on the pound, high inflation, followed by an attempted pay freeze. As soon as this situation appeared to have settled down, Wilson, to the surprise of some of his Party, announced his resignation. 'Asked about the most important achievements of his decade at the top, he [Wilson] listed three: getting the economy right, the Open University, and "despite the Common Market issue, keeping the Party united without once going off course"' (Pimlott, 1992, p. 601).

James Callaghan, PM 1976–79

In April 1976, Callaghan was elected leader. Soon he was faced with greater than usual financial difficulties, and an appeal was made to the International Monetary Fund for a loan of £2.3 billion: they insisted on some unsocialist policies, including cutting public expenditure, much to the concern of Tony Benn and others on the left of the Party. Relations with the trade unions were far from harmonious, and in July 1977 the 'social contract' was abandoned. In 1978 the TUC voted against a 5 per cent limit on pay increases. In 1978–79 the 'winter of discontent' meant that unofficial strikes throughout Britain led to considerable disruption. The problem seemed to be patched up by a long-term pact with the unions; but Callaghan lost the general election in May 1979. Tony Crosland had died in 1977, and not long after, his vision of an improving welfare state based on constant economic expansion also faded.

Education 1974–79

There were three Education Secretaries during these 5 years: Reg Prentice from March 1974 to July 1975; Fred Mulley from July 1975 to September 1976; and finally, Shirley Williams, the longest serving Secretary of State during this period, from September 1976 to March 1979.

Reg Prentice, Education Secretary 1974–75

There was an interesting reason for the appointment of Reg Prentice. During the final part of the Heath government, Roy Hattersley was Shadow Education Secretary. He had a considerable interest in education, and despite the fact that he was then seen as right of centre in the Party, he believed that it was time for some action to be taken about public schools. In a speech to the headteachers of some independent schools, in 1973, he reminded them that it was Labour Party policy to remove charitable status from independent schools and that he hoped to be able to introduce legislation in the next Labour government. Hattersley also engaged in a lively television debate on the same subject with the Tory spokesman Norman St John Stevas. This caused a considerable flurry of excitement, and for that reason, Wilson told Hattersley that he wanted a safe pair of hands in charge of education: after the election, he appointed Prentice, who, three years later, joined the Conservative Party.

This episode reinforces the point of view that I have been developing throughout this book: namely, that the Labour leadership up to and including Wilson, regarded education as less important than other problems, such as, economic policy and appealing to middle-class voters. Wilson did not want to rock the bigger political boat with any proposal that might be controversial at this time. They wanted the impossible – a non-political stance on education that would not threaten any section of the community – even unfair privileges.

In December 1975 the Houghton Committee recommended a 29 per cent pay award for teachers, costing £432 million. However, Prentice refused to restore the Tory education cuts imposed as a result of the Barber budget; he also refused to honour Roy Hattersley's promise, as Shadow Education Secretary, to bring all classes down to below 30 pupils. He failed to resist the Chancellor's demand for further cuts in education covering the next four years. In addition, Prentice was responsible for a reduction in university funding, and for replacing their sensible five-year planning programmes by annual grants. In so far as Prentice had a policy, it was to 'protect' schools 5–16, and to let the cuts fall on further education, youth service and adult education. Hardly a socialist policy.

Fred Mulley, Education Secretary 1975–76

Under Mulley education was no better off. By 1976 the financial situation had deteriorated still further, and education took more than its share of the overall cuts in public expenditure. Cash limits were also imposed. It fell to Mulley to implement some of the negative aspects of Thatcher's 'framework for expansion': the supply of teachers was cut back drastically. Tony Crosland, by now Chancellor of the Exchequer, surprised some by remarking that 'Cuts could be a blessing in disguise.'

The 1976 Act required LEAs to submit comprehensive schemes. Unlike the previous circulars, this requirement had the force of law. But it made little difference. Meanwhile, the Bullock Committee, that had been set up by the Tories, had produced a report on the teaching of English, *A Language for Life* (1975), which was somewhat critical of the teaching of reading and other aspects of English: better resources and in-service education for teachers were recommended. In the same year, the problems of the William Tyndale Schools in Islington had resulted in the ILEA setting up a Committee of Enquiry, chaired by Robin Auld, QC. The Auld Report (1975) painted a very bleak picture of one primary school and its associated infant department which was used by right-wing Conservatives as a stick to beat the Labour Party and the 'educational establishment'. They criticised unstreamed classes as well as the 'Plowden philosophy'. There had always been a small number of extremists in education who had more in common with the anarchist movement than the Labour Party. London had more than its fair share of them. Nevertheless, the Labour Party must take some blame for not having a coherent policy on education theory and practice by which the schools might have been judged. Simply to believe in equality of access to schools was not enough. The Tyndale scandal certainly damaged the Labour Party, not least because the Inner London Education Authority (ILEA) was a Labour-controlled authority which had failed to act until it was almost too late.

Callaghan, the Yellow Book and his Ruskin College speech 1976

Callaghan's speech has rightly been regarded as a highly significant event. Its background is complex. At one level the speech can be interpreted as a demand for better 'value for money' in education; Callaghan was attempting to convince education spenders not to expect ever-increasing expansion of resources – they must spend more wisely. Quality in education rather than quantity was one of his adviser's maxims (Clyde Chitty, 1989, p. 59, reporting on his interview with Bernard Donoughue). Callaghan was also reacting to the criticisms of some employers, views that were shared to some extent by the TUC (Chitty, pp. 60–3). Chitty pointed out that the Ruskin speech had been preceded by a growing media 'campaign' against education in general and comprehensive schools in particular. Journalists seemed to be ever on the alert to pick up problems and difficulties in schools and magnify them. They made much of the William Tyndale scandal and the Auld Report (1975) that had complained of poor arrangements for accountability of schools. Television joined in with some biased, or at least unbalanced, presentations of chaotic classrooms.

It has been alleged by critics of Callaghan that he decided, expediently, to 'walk away with the Tories' clothes'. He attacked permissiveness and the inadequate performance of some teachers as well as 'standards' in schools. On the other hand, Callaghan did care about education and, conscious of his own lack of university education, his attitude to schools as a whole was traditional, even old-fashioned. On education and other social issues Callaghan was unashamedly right of centre. Soon after becoming Prime Minister, Callaghan had an informal but probing meeting with Fred Mulley, the then Education Secretary. He asked about four areas of concern. Was the Education Secretary satisfied with the basic teaching of the three Rs? Was the curriculum sufficiently relevant and penetrating for older children in comprehensive schools, especially in science and mathematics? How good was the examination system? And what was available for the further education of 16–19 year olds? (Chitty, p. 73). Mulley presumably did not know the answers to these hard questions and went away to have a memorandum written by his officials. This became the Yellow Book which was passed on to the Prime Minister in July 1976. The Yellow Book was secret but widely leaked. It was critical of many aspects of the education service. In October 1976 Callaghan used the occasion when opening a hall of residence at Ruskin College, Oxford, to make a speech that was sharply critical of schools and teachers for failing to produce a well-educated labour force. The Prime Minister took a highly technocratic view of the purpose of education rather than a socialist position. He blamed schools for not producing the kind of human resources needed by British industry. Chitty (1989) and others have regarded the Ruskin speech as a turning point in Labour education policy – even as a 'betrayal'.

Shirley Williams, 1976–79

Shirley Williams, who had become Secretary of State for Education in September 1976, a short time before the Ruskin speech, was given the job of following up the Yellow Book and Callaghan's speech with a Great Debate on Education. The agenda, set by the Department for Education and Science, included the curriculum (aims and content); standards and the performance of the schooling system as a whole (including examinations and assessment); teacher education and training; schools and working life. According to Max Morris and Clive Griggs (1988, p. 8) there was an additional item on a hidden agenda: at a private DES meeting in 1975, chaired by John Hudson, the civil servants had decided that it was time to 'kill off' the Schools Council. This was without the complicity of Labour politicians who appeared to have no views, or policy on the council. They should have had.

The Schools Council for Curriculum and Examinations had existed since 1964 to promote research and development in the fields of curriculum and examinations. It began with very distinguished leadership: Sir John Maud, retired Permanent Secretary of the Education Department, and Derek Morrell, a very respected civil servant who had enlightened views about teacher professionalism. The history of the Schools Council from 1964 to 1975 was mixed, with some failures and mediocre work, but it had funded a number of excellent projects and had made sensible recommendations about school assessment and examinations, including reform of the sixth form curriculum. However, it was clearly a rival, in some respects, to the DES itself which, in 1976, had been criticised in an OECD Report for failing to have any consistent policies on education, and for being content to act simply as a central agency for distributing educational resources. Part of the DES agenda for its own self-improvement was to take over curriculum responsibilities from the Schools Council. In the Yellow Book written for the Prime Minister, they had, therefore, taken the opportunity to criticise the Schools Council, and were now poised to abolish it and take over some of its responsibilities. The Council, strongly supported by teachers, and to a lesser extent by LEAs, responded to DES hostility by embarking on its own review of its committee structure, with a view to streamlining, greater efficiency and general reform of its procedures.

One of the Council's recommendations in 1970 had been a single system of examining at 16+, combining the GCE 'O' level examination, taken by about 20 per cent of students at 16, and the Certificate of Secondary Education (CSE), which was taken by about 40 per cent of pupils at a less academic level (the other 40 per cent were at this time considered to be 'unexaminable'!). The 1970 Schools Council recommendation was generally accepted, and the Council embarked on a series of feasibility studies in conjunction with examining boards. In 1976, on the basis of favourable results, it recommended that a common examination at 16 should be put into operation nationally for all secondary schools. This recommendation was clear, based on good evidence, and should have been welcomed by a socialist Education Secretary as a step in a democratic direction. The new examination had passed the feasibility tests and was ripe for implementation. Shirley Williams, however, well known for her inability to make up her mind on matters educational, was persuaded by her DES officials to set up yet another committee, outside the Schools Council, to undertake a study of 'outstanding problems'. The committee, chaired by James Waddell, spent another two years going over the ground already covered by the Schools Council before giving a positive recommendation in 1978 for a single system at 16+. (Courses eventually started in 1986, giving schools and examination boards time to reorganise. The first examinations took place in 1988.) Apart from causing the unnecessary delay, Shirley Williams and her colleagues were guilty of failing to see the political importance of a reform which was part of the logic of a comprehensive system 11–16. Fortunately, the Conservatives, when they came into office in 1979, did not yield to the temptation of abandoning the whole reform.

The Green Paper, July 1977

Shirley Williams was no more decisive in other aspects of education policy. Following the Great Debate, which was criticised as 'showbiz publicity' she published a Green Paper, *Education in Schools: A Consultative Document* (1977). One of her conclusions was that there should not be a national curriculum, but instead the DES would carry out a questionnaire survey to judge what kind of curriculum planning the LEAs were already engaged in. This was another missed opportunity by a Labour politician who had the chance to make some real progress in the field of education planning. Nothing was achieved. Even a very modest scheme for maintenance allowances for 16+ students still at school died with the government in May 1979. And this was not taken up by her Conservative successors. The Great Debate was a very poor substitute for a coherent policy on education. Shirley Williams had allowed the Great Debate and the ensuing Green Paper to be 'captured' by her DES officials. The result was a strengthening of bureaucratic control of education and especially the curriculum, but the language of partnership was preserved so that LEAs would be required to collect data on curriculum. It was a rather feeble compromise that missed the opportunity of setting some national guidelines on a common curriculum. As such it left the way clear for the Tories in 1988 to impose a very different over-detailed and prescriptive national curriculum on schools whether they liked it or not.

Education theories and political ideas

Meanwhile, the academic debate about education continued to develop and to interact with a variety of political ideas. Throughout the second half of the decade sociologists debated among themselves, and occasionally with the rest of the world. As we saw in Chapter 7 the 'new sociologists of education' had wanted to move their discipline away from traditional demographic mapping exercises concerned with working-class 'under-achievement' to more theory-based explorations of the nature of education as an institution in modern capitalist society. It should not, however, be assumed that the new sociologists spoke with a single voice: some of them even objected to being included within that group. They also disagreed among themselves on at least two major parameters: sociological and educational theories, and the appropriateness of various social science methodologies, both of which influenced some aspects of educational research.

Social theories

Some of the sociologists were influenced by Marxism or neo-Marxism. One group, for example, agreed with the French structuralist Marxist, Louis Althusser, who had argued that schooling was a powerful aspect of the Ideological State Apparatus (ISA). The theory here was that whereas in earlier times the state had exercised control by means of such forces as the army and the police (the state apparatus), in modern states more subtle control was needed and took the form of religion and, more recently, education – the *ideological* state apparatus. Supporters of Althusser would have agreed with Engels's description of teachers as 'the hired lackeys of the bourgeoisie'. Others would have seen the development of education as a much more complex phenomenon: whilst accepting the idea of ISA they might also want to acknowledge that there were other motives behind mass education that developed in the nineteenth century, even genuine philanthropic and religious motives. They would, however, criticise the emphasis or even the dominance of the human resource planning aspects of education in a capitalist society. The word 'contradiction' was often used: for example, the idea that, consciously or unconsciously, those who advocated better education for the workers were also aware that education might enlighten them about their exploitation and increase their desire for greater social justice. A careful balance had to be preserved to avoid the contradiction becoming a disaster. Although they disputed among themselves, the new sociologists tended to agree about the failings of capitalism and wanted to change the function of education within capitalist society, or even to replace it. The link between education and politics was very strong.

One particular concern in the 1970s was the whole question of knowledge and the curriculum. Previously, knowledge had been 'taken for granted' as 'commonsense', but now some sociologists put forward the view that knowledge was 'socially constructed' and, consequently, different societies had different views of knowledge. Arguments raged about the extent to which a society might construct knowledge. Even the less extreme versions of 'knowledge and the curriculum' called the traditional curriculum into question, and made it a problem. They suggested that middle-class children's 'superior' performance at school could be partly accounted for by arbitrary definitions of knowledge.

As well as the curriculum, traditional pedagogy was also called into question during this period. Critics on the right interpreted such sociological discussions as a deliberate subversive attack on 'authority'; others worried that blame for working-class under-achievement was being transferred from the pupils themselves and their parents to teachers and schools. Such discussions within education were often blamed for disaffection in schools, and specifically for the mismanagement of William Tyndale School mentioned earlier.

Disputes about methodology

There were two main camps, with many sub-divisions. Positivism or at least positivistic methods were very much under attack, but individuals, and groups, differed about how much might be retained. Many early sociologists including Comte and Durkheim had hoped to generate social science methodology as productive as the scientific procedures followed by chemists and physicists. It would not be fair to suggest that early sociologists copied the methods of physical scientists but Comte's 'positive philosophy' was certainly guided by the scientific method that had been so successful. The result was that the nineteenth-century social scientists looked for methods that were similar but not identical to those of the physical sciences. The major difference was, of course, that human beings are very different from atoms and molecules; not only were they more complex but they also changed under observation – human consciousness was a problematic complicating factor.

By the 1970s some sociologists, the positivists, were trying to remain as close as possible to classical scientific method; on the other hand, others wanted to develop a quite different methodology. In the 1970s such esoteric terms as 'grounded theory', 'ethnomethodology' and many others were used, sometimes influenced by social anthropology rather than the physical sciences. The methodology issue was less obviously relevant to politics and education, but in the 1980s the Conservative government (in particular, the Education Secretary, Keith Joseph) would criticise sociology and refuse to accept its scientific pretensions, partly because he regarded 'social science' as a misnomer. He felt sufficiently strongly about this issue to insist on the Social Science Research Council being re-named the Economics and Social Research Council (ESRC). This was symptomatic of a political attitude to both education research and the methods used and argued about throughout the 1970s.

Other educational ideas and controversies

Education Act 1976

I have already made reference to this Act in the context of the Labour Party's policy of requiring LEAs to develop plans for comprehensive secondary reorganisation. The definition of 'comprehensive', was wide enough to cover most schemes, excluding only those that involved selection at age 11+ for a grammar school education. There were two other major issues mentioned briefly in the 1976 legislation. The first was a reference to private schools, tightening up the possibility of LEAs paying the fees for certain categories of pupils to attend such schools. The second, was the encouragement of LEAs to make more use of normal primary and secondary schools for the education of children with special educational needs. (This encouragement, as we shall see, anticipated the recommendations of the Warnock Committee which was still sitting.)

The Warnock Report 1978

In 1973 a Committee of Enquiry had been set up on the Education of Handicapped Children and Young People. It was chaired by Mary Warnock, Senior Research Fellow at St Hughes College, Oxford. She was originally a philosopher who later became an expert on 'special educational needs' and ethical questions relating to this area. The Warnock Report was published in 1978 but, as we saw above, the 1976 Education Act anticipated some of its recommendations, especially the question of 'integration' of children with special educational needs into primary and secondary schools. The idea of integration was not an invention of the Warnock Committee, but the Warnock Report received a good deal of publicity and favourable comment resulting in replacing such words as 'handicapped' by the more acceptable concept of 'special needs'. One interpretation of 'special needs' was that all young people and adults have some kind of special educational needs and that it is not only wrong to give some categories of children undesirable labels, but also wrong to isolate them from normal educational institutions. The concept of integration became important in educational and Labour Party circles and led to other educational developments such as the policy of 'inclusion' which we will return to in later chapters.

Conclusion

Much of Labour's education failure 1974–79 can be blamed on the three underachieving Secretaries of State. But they had been appointed by Wilson and Callaghan who must, therefore, share some of the guilt. Wilson seemed to be uninterested in the details of school education; Callaghan was interested, but adopted a technicist, unsocialist stance, neglecting to consider the importance of education for society as a whole rather than simply concentrating on the needs of industry.

Callaghan became Prime Minister in April 1976. By then it had become fashionable for the popular press to criticise standards in schools and the competence of some teachers. Callaghan, possibly prompted by his daughter's threat to send her children to independent schools, took the politician's way out, asking his officials and advisers for information on the schooling system as it existed rather than how it might be reconsidered in a democratic society. We saw in Chapter 7, and earlier in this chapter, that there were many important educational ideas being discussed in the 1970s, including fundamental re-thinking of the purpose of mass education in a democratic rather than a capitalist society. All of this was ignored by Wilson and Callaghan, their Education Secretaries and advisers. Instead, the debate on education moved to the right, focusing narrowly on the question of 'servicing the labour market' rather than on wider purposes of education. This left the way clear for truly reactionary policies after 1979.

9 Thatcherism 1979–90

Where there is discord may we bring harmony; where there is despair may we bring hope.

(Margaret Thatcher, 4.2.79 on hearing the general election result)

We believed that levelling in schools had to stop and that excellence (discrimination) had to return. Our key perception was differentiation. We equated the stretching of children, at all levels of ability, with caring.

(Keith Joseph in an interview with Christopher Knight, 1990, *The Making of Tory Education Policy in Post-War Britain 1950–1986*, p. 152)

Background events 1979–90

During these eleven years, there were four themes dominating the world scene: dramatic changes within communist regimes; improving co-operation between East and West; instability, especially in Africa and Asia; and problems in the Middle East.

Communist regimes

In 1979 Pope John Paul II visited his native Poland and was given the kind of welcome that must have disturbed the communist rulers in Poland and elsewhere. By 1990, not only had Poland elected a non-communist government, but East Germany had got rid of the Honnecker regime, demolished the Berlin wall and formed a reunited nation with Western Germany. In 1989 Hungary, Czechoslavakia and Romania also turned against their communist leaders and elected democratic governments. Russia itself embraced Gorbachev's proposals for *perestroika* and *glasnost*, and eventually went beyond them, abandoning the Marxist-Leninist regime. Even China, without renouncing communism moved towards a market economy and other features of capitalism.

East–West co-operation

All of the above encouraged greater efforts to avoid conflict between the world's great powers, especially the USA and Russia. A series of arms limitation agreements and other treaties took place at meetings during the 1980s. Eventually the Soviet Union realised that their attempt to control Afghanistan was unrealistic, and in 1989 withdrew all their forces. The cold war was virtually over.

Africa and Asia

Instability continued in Ghana, Nigeria and elsewhere in Africa, not least in Zimbabwe. And in Asia, Pakistan ceased to have a democratic government, after getting into the habit of having military coups. There was a lingering problem of hostility between India and Pakistan. The USA was sometimes concerned by their unpopularity in the region: for example, in 1979 when their embassy in Islamabad was stormed.

Middle East

A change in the balance of power developed in 1981 when Israel announced its nuclear capability. Conflict between Palestinian Arabs and Israelis continued throughout and beyond this period. After a long war with Iran, Iraq picked on an easier target – Kuwait – and rapidly took over the whole country and its oil. The USA and UK eventually drove them out again in 'the Gulf War', 1991, without solving the problem.

All of these events, directly or indirectly, had lasting effects on the UK's military resources and finances.

Politics in the UK 1979–90

In May 1979 Margaret Thatcher won a convincing victory in the general election: 339 seats against Labour 269, Liberals 11 and others 16. In June, Jeremy Thorpe, former leader of the Liberals, was found not guilty on a charge of conspiracy to murder his ex-lover. The British public apparently found this more interesting than the first direct elections for the European Parliament – only 32 per cent bothered to vote. Later, in May 1980, Margaret Thatcher demanded, and obtained, big reductions in the UK contributions to the European Community. Unemployment continued to rise, especially in manufacturing, and by the end of August exceeded 2 million.

On 15 October 1980, Callaghan resigned the Labour leadership, leaving a left–right struggle between Foot and Healey. Michael Foot, aged 69, won 139:129. He was faced with the difficult task of re-uniting the party. In February 1981 the 'Gang of Four' (Roy Jenkins, Shirley Williams, David Owen and William Rodgers) left Labour to form their own Social Democratic Party.

Meanwhile, Thatcher was pressing ahead with privatisation. In April 1981, serious riots took place in Brixton among disaffected black youths. More riots followed later in the year in Liverpool, Birmingham, Wolverhampton, Luton and Preston: unemployment and poor housing were blamed. Lord Scarman's Report (November 1981) confirmed that 'racial disadvantage', including education, was a serious problem. By January 1982, unemployment had risen to more than 3 million: some Tory 'wets', including Heath, called for government action. But attention was diverted by the Falklands War when Margaret Thatcher told the British to 'rejoice' at the collapse of the Argentine resistance. Later in the year (December 1982) 20,000 women demonstrated against Cruise missiles at Greenham Common, and established a peace camp.

In June 1983 Margaret Thatcher won her second general election: Tories 397; Labour 209; Liberal Social Democrat Alliance 23; others 21. The biggest overall majority since 1945. In June 1983 Neil Kinnock replaced Foot as leader of the Labour Party with Roy Hattersley as Deputy Leader. In May 1984 there were scenes of considerable violence at Orgreave Colliery, Yorkshire, between striking miners and police in full riot gear. Kinnock, anxious to modernise the Labour Party, was faced with a dilemma: to what extent should he support a strike that had been called without a ballot of its members? In October the Conservative Party Conference at Brighton was shattered by an IRA bomb blast in the Grand Hotel. One MP was killed and several people injured. In February 1985 the pound fell to its lowest level ever against the dollar. In October there was another race riot – in Tottenham, North London – where a policeman was hacked to death by a mob. In December Thatcher followed Ronald Reagan's example and withdrew the UK from UNESCO.

The year 1986 began well: Mrs Thatcher and President Mitterrand agreed to co-operate on the Channel Tunnel. But at home she faced a Cabinet row: both Michael Heseltine and Leon Brittan resigned over the Westland contract dispute. In December Harold Macmillan, who had accused Thatcher of 'selling off the family silver' died aged 92.

In June 1987 Margaret Thatcher won her third general election: Tories 375: Labour 229; Alliance 22; others 24. The date 19 October 1987 was a bad day for capitalism: £50 billion, or 10 per cent of value, was wiped away in one 'Black Monday' at the Stock Exchange. There were similar losses worldwide. In January 1988 David Steel, who had been leader of the Liberals for twelve years, decided not to stand for the leadership, despite the possibility of a complete merger with the Social Democrats. Later in the year (November), inflation rose to 6.8 per cent. In 1989 Thatcher celebrated her tenth year as Prime Minister; she also said 'We are a grandmother.' In June, Labour did well in the European elections. In October a dispute between Thatcher and her Chancellor of the Exchequer, Nigel Lawson, led to his resignation and replacement by John Major. In November, Thatcher faced a leadership challenge from Sir Anthony Meyer, a self-confessed stalking horse. By March 1990 Margaret Thatcher was losing popularity and ignored advice about the poll tax. There was a riot in London. In the May local elections the Tories lost about 300 seats. In June,

Thatcher opposed the European Community plans for greater economic and monetary union. By September 1990 inflation had risen to 10 per cent and in October, the UK joined the European Exchange Rate Mechanism. In November, Sir Geoffrey Howe delivered a resignation speech strongly critical of the Prime Minister's policies and style. On the following day Heseltine announced his bid for the leadership; having failed to get an overall majority on the first round, Margaret Thatcher withdrew from the contest. In a three-horse race (Major, Hurd and Heseltine) Major won with 185 votes to 56 and 131. Thatcherism was over – or was it? The Labour Party under Kinnock was still far from united but his attempts at modernisation and eliminating the extreme left were making progress.

Education 1979–90

The Thatcher years witnessed an unprecedented volume of educational legislation, and, more importantly, a significant change of ideology in education. Margaret Thatcher's four years as Secretary of State for Education (1970–74) had led her to believe that education was not only too costly but was in the hands of the 'producers' rather than the 'consumers'. This distinction was, of course, itself an expression of a market view of education rather than seeing it as a service provided for the public good. Parents in the 1980s would be encouraged to exercise choice – a key word for the new ideology.

During her eleven years as Prime Minister, Thatcher appointed five Secretaries of State for Education: Mark Carlisle; Keith Joseph; Kenneth Baker; John MacGregor and Kenneth Clarke who was appointed by Margaret Thatcher just before she resigned, but continued in Education under Major until 1992. They were 'shadowed' by Neil Kinnock, Giles Radice, Jack Straw, and Anne Taylor.

Mark Carlisle, Education Secretary 1979–81; shadowed by Neil Kinnock

Mark Carlisle was a moderate; Margaret Thatcher liked him as a person but said in her autobiography (1993) that he had only performed 'moderately' and had to go. Soon after the general election he steered through the Education Act 1979 which simply cancelled the obligation of LEAs, under the 1976 Act, to have plans for comprehensive secondary education. This was expected, and Labour almost automatically opposed the legislation as reactionary and contrary to the views of most parents who disliked the whole process of selection at age 11. In the following year the 1980 Education Act was a clear signal of a change of policy: the Act included provision for the Assisted Places Scheme, by which 'able' pupils from maintained schools could be selected to attend independent schools, either for reduced fees or no fees at all, according to parental income. This was strongly opposed by Labour on the grounds that it indicated a belief that comprehensive schools were not suitable for 'able' pupils, and also because it would tend to strip comprehensive schools of potentially high-performing pupils and lower the overall achievement of some schools. The gap between the Labour and Conservative Parties on education was growing: Labour was the Party of comprehensive education for all; the Conservatives wanted parents to exercise choice. This right to choose was enshrined in the Act itself, as was the right of parents to be represented on governing bodies of all schools. To assist in the process of choice LEAs and governing bodies were required to provide parents with information about the school, including examination results. The power of LEAs to restrict the admission of pupils from outside their authority was also limited. The Labour Party argued that choice could often have undesirable consequences, such as the tendency for some schools to become 'sink' schools. Carlisle's final Education Act (1981) was less controversial, but was given an ideological spin. The Act followed the general acceptance of the Warnock Report (1978) on the education of children with special needs: LEAs were made responsible for implementing the recommendations, but parents were given the right to be consulted as well as the right to appeal against LEA decisions affecting their children's placement or treatment.

Sir Keith Joseph, Education Secretary 1981–7; shadowed by Neil Kinnock until 1983, then Giles Radice until 1987

In September 1981, Carlisle was replaced by the much more ideological Keith Joseph who was a monetarist believing that public expenditure had to be reduced. He was determined that education should take at least its share of the cuts. He disliked what he called 'statist' education and wanted to reduce the power of local bureaucrats. He succeeded. The 1984 Education Act allowed central government to allocate money to LEAs for specific purposes (earmarked grants), thereby reducing LEA financial autonomy. His first 1986 Education Act had similar intentions – earmarking LEA money for specific government intentions and projects. The 1986 Education (No. 2) Act was, however, more general, returning to the theme of parental choice. Governors were required to publish an annual report for parents and to organise a meeting to discuss it. Governors were also made responsible for sex education syllabuses and were required to ensure that teachers did not indulge in the political indoctrination of their pupils. Governors also became responsible for producing a policy document on curriculum, which could depart from LEA curriculum policy. LEAs were also restricted in the power to find more money for education 'from the rates' – a policy of 'rate capping' was introduced in 1984 to prevent some authorities from thwarting government financial cuts.

The Labour opposition saw that the effect of some of this legislation was to reduce the control of education by locally elected representatives. It was, however, difficult to make this case strongly without appearing to be against the wishes of parents. This was another important difference between the Conservative and Labour views: the Conservatives saw local control in terms of choice; Labour in terms of local planning. Unfortunately, in many areas (but not all) LEAs were not very popular.

Keith Joseph also disliked the Schools Council, partly because it spent money, partly because it was largely controlled by teachers (which in his mind meant teacher unions). He asked Mrs. Trenaman to conduct an enquiry into the Council. Her report was quite favourable; nevertheless, Joseph went ahead with his plans to abolish it, replacing the Council with two smaller (cheaper) committees under the control of the Secretary of State. Again Labour protested at this blow to the education 'partnership' tradition, but the size of the Conservative majority in Parliament ensured that the arguments would come to nothing. Keith Joseph's intention had been to reduce expenditure on education, to limit LEA powers and to encourage parents to take over as much as possible. He would have liked to introduce a voucher system for schools which would have encouraged market forces even more, but, after an experiment in Kent, he was persuaded that any voucher system would be expensive and difficult to operate. In September 1985, Neil Kinnock, who had changed his role from being Shadow Education Secretary to Leader of the Labour Party, made a powerful speech to the British Educational Management and Administration Society, in which he set out his views on 'Choice, Relevance and Standards'. This was a much more considered Labour Party position than that expressed by Callaghan in 1976, but received much less coverage in the press. He made the case for good central planning and local management rather than leaving education to market forces.

In 1987 Keith Joseph was replaced by Kenneth Baker and went to the House of Lords where he later criticised some aspects of Baker's Education Reform Act 1988.

Kenneth Baker, Education Secretary 1987–9; shadowed by Jack Straw

Whereas Joseph was at heart a privatiser who disliked state education, Baker was a Conservative moderniser who wanted a more efficient national education system. Baker did, however, believe or at least said he believed, that there was a conspiracy within the 'education establishment' to block any progress towards market forces in education: he wanted to champion the wishes of parents against the 'vested interests' in education who still advocated 'egalitarianism' in education. As far as he was concerned, Conservative policies should move further away from Labour's 'equality of opportunity' doctrine. He was soon working on a 'Great Education Reform Bill' (Gerbill) which became the Education Reform Act 1988 – the most comprehensive legislation on education since 1944. The ERA advanced the attack on LEAs by creating a new kind of school, City Technology Colleges, completely outside LEA control. There were other plans such as Local Management of Schools that gave school governors and headteachers rather than LEAs the major role in financial budgeting. A key feature of the Act was the National Curriculum which received less opposition from teachers than might have been expected. The national curriculum will be considered in detail later.

At the time, there was little critical comment on the national curriculum, partly because some saw it as a Labour idea rather than being based on any kind of Conservative principle. Labour was, however, much more concerned about the apparent downgrading of the LEA 'partner', and even more so by the clear intention to introduce market principles into a hitherto public service.

John MacGregor, Education Secretary 1989–90; shadowed by Jack Straw

John MacGregor achieved little in his one year in office. But he had to take some of the blame for Baker's National Curriculum which began to be attacked at this time by teachers as well as academic educationists. (See Lawton and Chitty, 1988). It was now becoming clear that the proposed National Curriculum of ten subjects was too detailed and over-prescriptive. The more irksome problem for teachers was, however, the bureaucratic assessment procedures which were attacked by teachers' organisations as well as Labour politicians. But, as we shall see in Chapter 10, the government resisted changes to the Baker master plan until, in 1993, all the teacher unions boycotted the tests and forced some reduction in the detailed testing requirements. The Labour Party was pleased to cheer from the sidelines but were not strong on offering alternatives. *Kenneth Clarke, Education Secretary 1990–92*, will be considered in Chapter 10 since most of his period in office was spent under John Major.

Changes in Labour's political ideas

Throughout this period the Labour Party was engaging in a process of internal debates about beliefs and organisation, especially after Callaghan resigned the leadership in 1980. A more significant watershed was the Labour conference in 1981, which shifted Party structures away from the parliamentary party towards constituency activists and trade unions; Michael Foot had the difficult task of trying to unify both wings of the Party, or at least to prevent them from destroying it. Foot did not succeed, and Neil Kinnock, who had performed well as Shadow Education Secretary, took on the leadership of the Party. There followed a period of re-thinking both the organisation of the Party as well as its values and ideas. Those on the left who had supported corporate socialism of the Herbert Morrison kind with traditional nationalisation as a central policy, yielded to those who accepted rather than tolerated a mixed economy, including market forces. How to regulate the market and control choice within a more moral society based on social justice became a central issue. There was, of course, still plenty to argue about at the level of detail, but the future direction of the Party now seemed clear. The collapse of Soviet Russia helped the swing away from far left economic policies. Unfortunately, too little attention was paid to the central role of education, although Neil Kinnock had given some thought to curriculum matters as well as pressing on with the policy of comprehensive secondary education.

Geoffrey Foote (1997) points out (p.326) that, ironically, it was the communist historian, Eric Hobsbawm, who in 1978 had delivered the lecture 'The Forward March of Labour Halted?' which drew attention to the demographic and economic changes that had taken place in the UK and were continuing to take place; they tended to diminish Labour support because working-class occupations were declining and class consciousness was less important in voting choice. As a possible solution, Hobsbawm had recommended a modern version of the 'popular front' thinking of the 1930s which had united middle- and working-class opposition to fascism. Foote, however, suggests that this analysis led the Party along a path that Hobsbawm had not intended: the Labour Party would attempt to 'adapt its political values to those of the non-socialist sections of the population, hungering after an illusionary security from the frightening world outside' (p. 328).

There was, however, plenty of scope to gain support by criticising some of the new right values of selfish materialism and the disregard for social problems such as unemployment and the homeless. The Labour Party managed to hold on to its moral values whilst not condemning the market economy altogether. The word 'community' began to be used in Labour circles, demonstrating that traditional 'ethical socialist' values had not been abandoned. This contrasted sharply with Thatcher's own stance which denied the existence of society. Kinnock presented the 'moral alternative' to Thatcherism very clearly, even if he was criticised for verbosity and sometimes, by the extreme left, for hypocrisy. Kinnock rejected the Morrisonian economic version of bureaucratic socialism, stressing instead the need for 'an enabling state . . . a servant state' (speech to Labour Party conference, 1985, quoted by Foote, 1997, p. 328).

Foote sees the change in the following way: 'This concentration on values was the subject of a ferment of ideas on the left, seeking to replace the traditional socialist attack on capitalist power with an attack on the selfish materialism which was coming to the fore in Thatcher's Britain' (p. 329). Unfortunately, this attack was not extended very effectively into the field of education.

A number of Labour Party academics were also putting forward views similar to those of Kinnock at this time. For example, Bernard Crick, a former Professor of Politics at Birkbeck College, London (the same College as Hobsbawm, but representing a different political stance) argued 'against both the Marxists and the technocratic pragmatists, that it was values which bound a society together, and that socialists had to reassert the traditional values of liberty, equality and fraternity . . . if they were to recapture their political appeal' (Foote, 1997, p. 329). As we shall see in Chapter 11, Crick was later to combine these political ideas with some very positive educational suggestions in the form of a curriculum for citizenship education.

Another London Professor, Raymond Plant, a member of the Socialist Philosophy Group 'sought to express the precise relationship between the market and socialist values in the terms of political philosophy, a revival of which had been occurring in the Anglo-American Academy since the publication of John Rawls's A *Theory of Justice* in 1972' (pp. 329–30). Rawls's ideas were at the same time being discussed in educational circles, not least in the context of choice in education. Like Crick, Plant linked 'community' to 'citizenship'; he also advocated a market economy with the government directing its operations in the interests of equality (Plant, *Equality, Markets and the State*, 1984). His discussion of 'legitimate inequalities' was, however, considered suspect in some Labour circles.

Another interesting publication was jointly written by David Blunkett (the future Labour Education Secretary) and Bernard Crick, who had taught Blunkett politics some years before at Sheffield University. The main message of *The Labour Party's Aims and Values: An Unofficial Statement* (1988) was that the market has a legitimate place in society, but that moral values of a co-operative community had priority, and they could only be realised in a democratic society which laid down national minimum standards. Blunkett and Crick wanted a careful balance between centralisation and local participative communities.

It is clear that the time spent in opposition was not wasted by the Labour Party. A good deal of writing and re-thinking took place, although most of those involved probably felt that the period 1979 to 1997 was too long. It was a pity that the Labour Party was denied a victory in 1990; by 1997 some of the ideas were perhaps 'over-cooked'. This point, together with a discussion of the relevance to education of other New Labour ideas will be taken up again in Chapter 11.

In August 1990 Claus Moser, Vice-President of the British Association, said that Britain was selling its schoolchildren short. He stated that education in Britain was 'not worthy of a civilised nation' – after ten years of cuts the service was demoralised with under-skilled teachers.

Education ideas, policies and research 1979–90

It was significant that after 1979 there were no more Black Papers: their task was, for the time being, completed. Public opinion had been shifted towards a more critical position on education: comprehensive schools and progressive methods were treated with great suspicion in the press. Consensus was over. When successive Education Secretaries embarked on a series of right-wing policies, especially those encouraging choice and the market in education, a good deal of educational research was building up an evidence-based case against such policies as the assisted places scheme; vouchers in education; the National Curriculum and its assessment; the case against selection and the use of intelligence tests.

Unfortunately, to build a credible research case against the Assisted Places Scheme, for example, took longer to generate than two or three Black Papers. Nevertheless, in 1989 Edwards, Fitz and Whitty published evidence which at least cast serious doubt on the wisdom of spending public money in this way when education in general was suffering from cuts. Two years later Walford and Miller (1991) published the results of their research on City Technology Colleges, a very costly programme that had attempted to involve industry, and private money, in setting up 'independent' CTCs in inner-city areas. The scheme was clearly a failure, but was never condemned in the press on anything like the scale of any individual LEA school that encountered difficulties. More general criticism of the market and choice in education included: Clive Griggs (1985b) *Private Education in Britain*. These were, however, academic publications written by scholars who had been trained not to over-state their case. They did not reach such a wide readership as the Black Papers which were nearly all characterised by exaggeration and poor use of evidence.

Conclusion

The years 1979–90 were difficult for the Labour Party but by the time that Thatcher was on the way out, the Party had been reorganised under the leadership of Neil Kinnock. It presented a moral alternative to Thatcherism that might be acceptable to middle-ground voters frightened by more extreme left policies. In education, however, by the time that Kinnock moved from being Shadow Education Secretary to Leader of the Party, it was clear that simply to press on with a compulsory programme for full comprehensive secondary education would be a step forward but would not in itself be enough. Since the late 1960s, sociologists had published studies that showed that comprehensive schools did not completely solve the problem of working-class under-achievement (for example, Julienne Ford, 1969, showed that some comprehensives were often no more than the tripartite system under one roof). Neil Kinnock realised that democratic education needed more than simply abolishing grammar schools or integrating them into comprehensive plans: he had turned his mind away from questions of how best to legislate to ensure full comprehensive education to more difficult educational issues concerning the organisation of schools and the content of the curriculum inside those schools. Unfortunately, before getting very far into those complex areas, he took over the leadership of the Party and was faced with more immediate problems of unity. His successors as Shadow Education Secretary did not take his thinking much further until John Major became Prime Minister and Ann Taylor took over responsibility for education within the Labour Party. That will be taken up in the next chapter.

10 A Labour education policy found and lost 1990–97

If I am going to be trivial, inconsequential and deceitful, then I might as well be in government.

(Joseph Heller, *Closing Time*, 1994)

Background events 1990–97

The first part of John Major's seven-year rule was dominated by the Gulf War which continued until February 1991. This was followed by civil war in Yugoslavia which also involved the UK militarily and financially. In Russia, Gorbachev lost control and the country moved towards chaos. Clinton became President of the USA in 1992, and in the following year he persuaded Rabin (of Israel) and Arafat (PLO) to shake hands. But peace did not last. The UK gradually became more committed to Europe, signing the Maastricht Treaty that Denmark had voted against: the EC increasingly became the issue that split the Tory Party and, to a lesser extent, the Labour Party.

UK politics 1990–97

The internal problems of the Labour Party continued: Neil Kinnock, after troubles at the Walton by-election, promised a purge of the militants. He moved towards the general election with confidence, but on 10 April 1992, contrary to most of the opinion polls, the Tories won with a majority of 21. Some attributed the Labour defeat to their commitment to raising income tax, but there was little evidence to support that pessimistic view. Kinnock resigned from the leadership of the Party on 13 April and was replaced by John Smith. In May 1993 Major dropped Norman Lamont as Chancellor of the Exchequer. And in December he signed a peace declaration for Northern Ireland; an IRA cease-fire followed in August 1994. Despite these achievements, Major's unpopularity grew, as the number of accusations of sleaze and sexual misdemeanors among some of his colleagues continued to grow. In July 1994 Tony Blair became leader of the Labour Party, after the death of John Smith in May. In April 1995 Blair succeeded where Hugh Gaitskell had failed: scrapping clause 4. He proclaimed a policy of a mixed economy with a thriving public sector. He also said that he would like to achieve peace in Northern Ireland, sort out the NHS, welfare and education, as well as improving our position in Europe. Labour Party pessimists (or realists) feared that Blair was a closet Tory, recalling that he had attended regular *Daily Mail* lunches, and that Sir David English and Lord Rothermere had liked his views on welfare and education (White, *Guardian*, 12.2.02).

Education 1990–97

In general, education under Major continued in much the same direction as before: a mixture of encouraging market forces and struggling to achieve greater efficiency. Major inherited Kenneth Clarke as Education Secretary and kept him in that office until 1992, when he was replaced by John Patten who was not a success by any standards. Finally, Gillian Shephard took over in 1994 and stayed until 1997; she was regarded as someone who knew about education from direct experience of the maintained system. They were shadowed by Jack Straw, Ann Taylor and David Blunkett.

Kenneth Clarke, Education Secretary 1990–92; shadowed by Jack Straw

Clarke was said to be very popular with his civil servants but he was not much loved by teachers and others in the education service. For example, he was irritated by the complexity of the national curriculum and its assessment; he was correct in that judgement but wrong when he dismissed the standard assessment tasks as 'elaborate nonsense', and returned to simple but unreliable paper and pencil exercises. He was respected for his intelligence but he never gave the impression that he was interested in education in its wider sense. Another of his problems was education 16–19. In April 1990, Sir John Cassells had produced a report for the Policy Studies Institute, *Britain's Real Skill Shortage*, recommending a new qualification covering both academic and vocational areas. The debate about 16–19 continued throughout 1991. The Secondary Heads Association recommended five foundation subjects in the first year, followed by choice in the second year. The vice-chancellors also called for a long-term solution, and many industrialists claimed that 'A' level was irrelevant to industry and higher education. However, the Conservative Party was committed to retaining the two separate routes (academic and vocational) and in November 1990 Clarke had promised the House of Commons that 'A' levels would remain the gold standard. In 1991 he said he intended to maintain the two post-16 pathways.

The White Paper, *Education and Training for the Twenty-first Century*, was launched by the Prime Minister in May 1991. It was generally considered to be unsatisfactory: the *Independent* leader (21.5.91) was headed 'Timid Tory Plan for Training'. At this time the Labour Party was in favour of a more radical solution: a broader curriculum, possibly by means of a British baccalaureate (as recommended by the Labour-supporting think tank, the Institute for Public Policy Research (IPPR)), narrowing the gap between the vocational and academic pathways. The Labour Party was critical, at this time, of the Conservative old-fashioned approach to the 16–19 problem. As we shall see, the Labour Party in office after 1997 became less positive.

Kenneth Clarke claimed that his slogan for education was simply 'choice and diversity', which became the title of the White Paper in 1992. The temptation was too great for some critics who re-labelled the policy as 'chaos and perversity'. It was essentially a policy of diverting more money away from LEAs into schools which were encouraged to become more and more market oriented. The White Paper was criticised not only by Labour, but by the press and even by moderate Conservatives for over-emphasising choice, especially in the form of grant maintained schools that were free from local authority interference.

The first Education Act of 1992, the Education (Schools) Act, was little short of disastrous. HM Inspectorate had had a distinguished history, surviving a number of earlier reviews, and passing with flying colours the efficiency tests of Marks & Spencer boss, Derek Raynor. The trouble was, as far as the Conservatives were concerned, that inspectors did not spend enough of their time inspecting. This was the basis of the Clarke solution: he reduced HMI to a small core HQ body (the Office of the Chief Inspector) which would supervise the inspection tasks of a new partially privatised system. Inspectors would be recruited independently and they would tender, as teams, for inspection jobs as they arose. The rump of HMI would act as a kind of quality control within OfSTED. In this way every school would be inspected every four years – whether they needed it or not! The style of inspection became more like an inquisition, so much so that teachers began to dread OfSTED visits, not necessarily because they were unsure about their own competence, but because masses of paperwork were required before, during and after an inspection.

There were criticisms of this innovation in both Houses of Parliament, but OfSTED had come to stay – even after 1997. Labour objected to the possible effects of privatising a particularly sensitive part of the education service, as well as the cost-effectiveness of the proposals which turned out to be extremely expensive in cash terms. OfSTED was also seen as an example of de-professionalising teachers and for making teaching less attractive as a career.

The second Act of the year, the Further and Higher Education Act (1992) was less controversial and more difficult for Labour to attack. The Act had been preceded by a Working Paper, *Higher Education: A New Framework* (May 1991). The main proposal was the abolition of the binary line in higher education (i.e. having two kinds of higher education, universities and others such as polytechnics). This may have been an example of doing the right thing for the wrong reason: it was justified by the Conservatives in terms of competition. They asserted that universities and ex-polytechnics would compete more effectively within the same market. The Universities Funding Council (to be re-named HEFC: Higher Education Funding Council) would distribute research money selectively so that some universities might end up as 'teaching only' institutions. Scotland and Wales would have separate HEFCs. Quality control and quality audit became the orders of the day. Managerialism seemed to be taking over higher education. The Labour Party was broadly in agreement with the idea of abolishing the binary line, but the cost in terms of added bureaucratic controls was questioned. The Council for National Academic Awards (CNAA) was abolished by the Act and the new universities (ex-polytechnics mainly) would be able to award degrees themselves. But the CNAA would be replaced by a complex pattern of control. It was not clear how the new arrangements would cure one of the problems of higher education – that is, how to increase the participation rate. The 1992 Act also removed further education colleges from LEA control, and financed them from central funds (through what became the Further Education Funding Council). This left LEAs with a seriously diminished realm of authority.

John Patten, Education Secretary 1992–94; shadowed by Ann Taylor

By 1993, and yet another Education Act, education had passed into the hands of John Patten. The main objective of the 1993 Act was to secure greater control over curriculum and examinations. In Chapter 9, I described how Keith Joseph had abolished the Schools Council, despite a favourable report on its record. It was then, in 1982, replaced by two separate committees: the School Curriculum Development Committee and the School Examinations Committee; these two committees were, following the ERA (1988), toughened up and re-named the national curriculum Council and the School Examinations and Assessment Council. In 1993 it was decided that curriculum and assessment really belonged together and that the two councils should be merged into a single body – the School Curriculum and Assessment Authority. (That was not the end of the story. In 1997 SCAA was merged with the National Council for Vocational Qualifications to become the Qualifications and Curriculum Authority) It was difficult for Labour to oppose such rational re-planning.

There were, however, other, less acceptable, aspects of the very long 1993 Act. It was decided that 'unsatisfactory schools' should be subject to tighter supervision, and the Act provided the necessary legislation. Ann Taylor and other Labour members criticised this approach to school improvement. Later, after 1997, however, the Labour Party continued to tighten the screw on schools in punitive ways.

In 1994 there was yet another White Paper, *Competitiveness: Helping Business to Win*, intended to encourage what was now seen as the most important, if not the only, purpose of education – servicing the human resource needs of the economy. In the same year the Education Secretary published the results of the Dearing Review of the national curriculum (following an interim report in 1993). Ron Dearing had been asked to review national curriculum and assessment in 1993, following the teachers' boycott of the testing arrangements which were criticised by the Labour Party and others for being managerial and bureaucratic rather than educational and professional. Dearing recommended a slimming down of the detailed specifications of the curriculum and a simplification of testing arrangements. He also recommended that there should be vocational options at key stage 4 (14–16 year olds). Teachers generally welcomed the Dearing proposals, although it was realised that there was a loss of coherence regarding the national curriculum idea: it was almost ceasing to be a 'common curriculum' in the sense that the notion of 'entitlement' was seriously eroded.

Worse was still to come in 1994. The Education Act of that year established the Teacher Training Agency (TTA). Teacher education and training had long been a political issue. I described (in Chapter 7) how the James Report attempted a solution, but its recommendations were virtually ignored. By the early 1980s it was clear that some kind of reorganisation within a national scheme was necessary, and in 1984 the Council for the Accreditation of Teacher Education (CATE) was established 'to advise the Secretaries of State for Education and Science on the approval of initial teacher training courses in England and Wales'. Unless courses were 'approved' they did not carry qualified teacher status. But in order to be recommended for approval by CATE, courses needed to have been recently inspected by HMI and to comply with criteria established by the Secretary of State. The original criteria included rules about the selection of students, the qualifications and experience of staff, the course organisation, minimum amounts of time devoted to subject studies and method, as well as education and professional studies. In 1989 a consultation document was issued proposing new terms of reference for CATE and new criteria to cater for the National Curriculum.

All of this represented a steady increase of central control over teacher education and training, especially initial teacher education. This was achieved with the complicity of HMI, in opposition to the views of the Labour Party in both Houses of Parliament. In principle some central control was not objectionable, but in practice the model that developed out of CATE was wrong. It was essentially a training model rather than an educational model; the CATE criteria were then transformed into narrow objectives or 'competencies' more suitable for plumbers than for teachers whose classroom behaviour had to be sensitive and flexible. The 1994 Education Act replaced CATE by the even more objectionable Teacher Training Agency (TTA): its approach was symbolised by its title – it was now concerned with training not education. This remained the case, until 2001, when, as we shall see, there was an important change to TTA procedures (although the name was unchanged). Meanwhile, Ann Taylor as Shadow Education Secretary had been working with the Labour Party's 'Education Commission', outlining a number of educational reforms, including the abolition of the TTA.

In July 1994, soon after Blair was elected leader of the Labour Party, he indicated his interest in education by making a speech on Labour's education policy that was largely derived from Ann Taylor's review that she had been working on since the 1992 defeat (see later in this chapter). Her review published as

Opening Doors . . . (Labour Party, 1993) included recommendations to abolish League Tables and City Technology Colleges, and replacing 'A' levels with something like the British baccalaureat. Blair's version (1994), however, changed the policy to retaining and broadening 'A' levels; he did not use the term 'gold standard' but that seemed to be his view. Later in 1994 he further distanced himself from Ann Taylor's review by replacing her as Shadow Education Secretary by David Blunkett, who was perceived to be less friendly towards teachers and their unions. In 1994 Blair also indicated his preference for choice rather than equality by sending his son to the Oratory School, a Roman Catholic grant maintained school; the word 'hypocrisy' was used by several Labour MPs and supporters, as well as in *The Observer* (4.12.94).

Gillian Shephard, Education Secretary 1994–97; shadowed by David Blunkett

In 1995 the Department for Education merged with the Employment Department to become the Department for Education and Employment (DfEE) (but not for long: in 2001 it became the Department for Education and Skills (DfES)). The merger was generally welcomed, and it was in line with the current Labour Party thinking that the gap between the worlds of education and training was too great and should be narrowed, the blurring of the distinction between vocational and academic courses was overdue. The Conservatives, however, still maintained that the academic 'A' Level was the gold standard for 16–19, and there were disturbing signs that on this issue, and others, Blair agreed with them: for example, at the 1995 Labour Party conference, David Blunkett made his famous promise 'watch my lips – no selection!' But by 1996 he shifted his position on this issue to accommodate Blair's criticism of unstreamed comprehensive schools.

In 1995 there was also an interim report from Dearing on 16–19 qualifications. He was generally in favour of bringing academic and vocational pathways closer together, but one of his recommendations was counter-productive. He recommended that the GNVQ should be assessed in ways that were closer to, and more comparable with, the well-established 'A' level assessment procedures. The intention was good, but the result was to eliminate precisely those features of GNVQ assessment that had made GNVQ attractive to non-'A' level students.

Claus Moser and a Commission on Education

In Chapter 9 I mentioned the speech by Claus Moser that was critical of the state of education in Britain. One outcome was a recommendation that there should be a royal commission on education. As this was refused by government, the British Association decided to go ahead independently with its own enquiry funded by the Paul Hamlin Trust. In 1993 an excellent report *Learning to Succeed* was published. The report was discussed with political parties and debated in the House of Lords. In 1995 a follow-up report was produced by the National Commission on Education, *Learning to Succeed: The Way Ahead* (1995). Both reports included a number of criticisms of the *status quo* and recommendations for the future that were supported by the Labour Party.

1996: five education Acts

In 1996 there were no fewer than five Education Acts as well as another Dearing Report and a White Paper *Learning to Compete*. The five Acts were:

1   Education (Student Loans) Act;
2   Education (Scotland) Act;
3   Nursery Education and Grant Maintained Schools Act;
4   Education Act (which consolidated earlier legislation or repealed them);
5   School Inspections Act.

All five Acts were very much in the Thatcher–Major tradition of 'efficiency' in the sense of tidying up the system, and emphasising competition, choice and the market. The fourth Act tidied up to such an extent that there was virtually nothing left of the 1944 Education Act which until 1988 had been the key to the post-war education service. The consolidation process continued in the next year with the Education Act (1997), the last before the general election, which by negotiation with the other parties was unopposed in the House of Commons.

It may be important to mention one other event that marked a shift in education policy. Reacting to various criticisms, including those from the Labour Party, that education had become too much concerned with preparation for work, the School Curriculum and Assessment Authority produced an interesting list of social values that they hoped all schools would accept and use. They were accepted by most organisations, including the Archbishop of Canterbury on behalf of the Church of England.

Labour education ideas 1990–97

One important source of ideas was the Institute of Public Policy Research (IPPR) that had been set up in 1989 by a group of Labour intellectuals chaired by Tessa Blackstone, then head of Birkbeck College, with a full-time director, James Cornford, an expert on social science research and formerly the director of the Nuffield Foundation. David Miliband (later to become head of Blair's policy unit and then a junior education minister) was a full-time researcher. IPPR published a number of very important policy and discussion documents on education between 1990 and 1994. One series was the *Education and Training Papers* that were intended to be contributions to the debate from a left-of-centre point of view, written in clear, jargon-free style. These were generally very successful, and I will review a few of them below, together with other IPPR publications on education. The IPPR was, of course, involved in other social research, the publications of which are outside the scope of this book.

A British Baccalaureat: Ending the Division Between Education and Training (1990) by David Finegold *et al.* was the first of the Education and Training Papers. It was a practical proposal to solve two long-standing problems of the 16–19 age group. The first was that the 'A' level examinations had been criticised, from the beginning in 1951, as being too narrow in scope, forcing early specialisation in either 'arts' or 'science', resulting in a curriculum that lacked balance and encouraged arts students to drop the mathematical and scientific aspects of their culture at much too early a stage in their development. The second problem at 16–19 was that the structure encouraged categorising students into the 'academic elite' (hence the use of the term 'gold standard'), who were separated physically and culturally from those following a 'vocational' route, which was often criticised for being too job specific and low level. The paper was much more than a recipe for a new examination. The authors began by looking more deeply into the social and educational problems, one of which was that Britain was an 'early selection, low participation' culture. They advocated replacing it by a 'late selection, high participation' system that would be more appropriate for an advanced democratic society. Stressing that this reform was not just about producing a more skilled workforce, they say:

> Education is not primarily about narrow preparation for work, but rather preparation for adult life, of which work and continuing education are a part. It is vital, therefore, that educational provision – most obviously for children and young people but also for adults – be designed to help people meet social and economic demands.
>
> (p. 7)

The solution proposed was a new examination structure, supported by changes in employment and the creation of a new government Department of Education and Training which would see that appropriate maintenance grants would become available. The examination proposed would have offered all young people 16–19 a mixture of 'academic' and 'vocational' courses, plus a strong element of political and social education as well as community and work experience. These proposals reflected a number of Labour values and principles: for example, avoiding segregation in education; moving 'secondary education for all' further away from the pre-1944 elitist and exclusive assumption that 'academic' was superior. The ideas were generally well received in 1990, but rejected by the Conservative government for the same reasons that the Higginson Report, *Advancing 'A' Levels* (1988), had been dismissed by Thatcher two years earlier: 'A' levels were the gold standard and should be modified rather than abolished. This view was scorned by Labour in 1990, but since 1997 has become Labour practice if not official policy. (In March 2003 an OfSTED enquiry concluded that the AS/A2 modifications had not produced a broader 16–19 curriculum. (*Curriculum 2000: Implementation*, 2003, OfSTED).

Markets, Politics and Education: Beyond the Education Reform Act (1991) by David Miliband can be described more briefly. It is an excellent study putting the case clearly against the market as a policy for education. The market is not dismissed completely, however: it exists. But it must be regulated carefully to avoid the anti-socialist situation of market choice producing 'winners and losers'. A Labour education policy must result in good schools *for all*.

My final example from Education and Training Papers is *A National Curriculum for All: Laying the Foundations for Success* by Philip O'Hear and John White. This is another excellent study by a practising headteacher in conjunction with a philosopher who had written extensively on education and the curriculum. The paper represents the 1988 Labour Party view on the principle of a national curriculum: accepting the notion but rejecting the particular form that the 1988 national curriculum had taken as well as the detailed formula which was both over-prescriptive and badly assessed. This IPPR paper criticised the national curriculum as it had developed 1988–90, and then set out a much better alternative. (Had the Labour Party after 1997 built on a national curriculum along these lines, it would have been much better than the impoverished curriculum that many young people now face. Above all, the idea of 'entitlement' to a broad and balanced curriculum has been lost. I shall return to this in Chapter 11.)

In addition to the Education and Training Papers (only a few of which have been reviewed above), IPPR published a number of longer studies about education. I will mention only two: *Education: A Different Vision* (1993) and *Educational Reform and its Consequences* (Tomlinson, S. 1994). Both were collections of papers resulting from seminars of experts, and they were very skillfully edited. I include the first book because it presents an alternative vision to the 1992 government White Paper, *Choice and Diversity*, that I referred to briefly earlier in this chapter. The starting point of the book was a letter to *The Guardian* written by fourteen professors of education who criticised the White Paper and said they wanted a government 'which treats education as a public service and not as a commodity to be traded in the marketplace' (p. i). the professors were then organised by Ted Wragg (the editor) and Fred Jarvis (formerly NUT General Secretary) into producing 'a different vision': different from the White Paper that resembled a party political pamphlet, and different from the view that 'the market will provide'.

The new vision rests upon different values that are carefully spelt out (pp. 13–23). Only then do we proceed to questions of organisation, accountability and provision. The book is still worth reading for the relations set out between values, principles and practices. The second collection of papers *Educational Reform* (1994) was edited by Professor Sally Tomlinson, who had long been associated not only with IPPR but with Labour Party education policies and the Fabian Society. Although not all the contributors to the book were Labour Party members (some were more committed than others), Sally Tomlinson wrote as a Labour Party 'insider'. Much of what I want to comment on is from her own Introduction.

The starting point of this book was a seminar called in March 1993 to discuss the education 'reforms' since 1988 from the point of view of what had been demonstrated by *research* on such issues as the market, the national curriculum, education 16–19, teacher education, inspection, assessment, and a concluding chapter by Stewart Ransom on 'Towards education for democracy: the learning society' (the learning society became increasingly important as an idea for Labour education). The whole collection, although intended primarily as a critique of Tory policies (or the lack of them) should be read by all concerned with policy-making in education – including Tony Blair and his advisers. Sally Tomlinson's Introduction includes a theme that runs through the book:

> The educational reforms of the 1980s and 1990s have not been notable for their grounding in research findings, and a large Parliamentary majority has enabled government to push through policies whose nature and possible outcomes were unresearched. Indeed, Ministers of Education have been at pains to distance themselves from research, even that which they themselves commissioned, when the results did not accord with ideological preference. The problematic implementation of many of the reforms, notably those relating to curriculum and assessment, parental choice, the impact of market competition on schools and pupils, and the effects of the erosion of local democracy, is largely because research on these issues was not commissioned, or research results were used only in support of preconceived policies.
>
> (p. 2)

One more quotation will make the central point about vision, principles and values:

> The new vision must be built on the notion of genuine democracy and transcend individualism, recognising that individuals can and must come together as a society. They can and must engage in public debate over economic, social and political arrangements if they want to reconstruct the values, beliefs and practices of their society.
>
> (p. 5)

It may be significant that the best IPPR publications on education were concentrated in the years 1990–94.

The importance of IPPR in reviving and re-presenting Labour education ideas should not be under-estimated. Many of the documents included socialist moral values reformulated as 'a new vision' opposed to the Tory market view.

The Labour Party itself was also publishing documents on education policy at this time. Some reflected aspects of the IPPR's new vision, but others were concerned with research on 'effective schools'. Both Jack Straw and David Blunkett were attracted by that line of 'school improvement' research. In addition, great concern was expressed about the need to extend pre-school provision and education and training for the 16+ age group. There were also interesting discussions about the school curriculum and especially curriculum choice 14–16. Before Blair became leader he, as shadow Employment Secretary, with Jack Straw had produced a reasonable paper, *Today's Education and Training: Tomorrow's Skills* (1991), which was close to IPPR thinking.

The 1992 Labour Party election manifesto seemed to be optimistic about education. The vision for a well educated Britain was modest but clear: 'We want every child to get qualifications that count. We need safe, disciplined schools, where professional teachers work closely with parents. Learning must become a lifetime opportunity, with new chances to up-date skills at work' (p. 17). Specific promises included nursery education for 3–4 year olds, higher standards and a modernised national curriculum; and a higher percentage benefiting from higher education.

That was before the 1992 election defeat. Ann Taylor managed to sustain the optimism – but not for long. She was removed from education in 1994 and replaced by David Blunkett, whose contribution will be reviewed later.

Ann Taylor performed well in her Shadow Education role: she was committed to education, trusted by teachers and other educationists. She was the best Shadow Education Secretary since Kinnock, but quieter and less assertive. Her consultation paper, *Opening Doors to a Learning Society* 1993/94, that was written when John Smith was leader, retained ethical socialist values in a modernising context – economic advantages of education are not ignored. The publication merits detailed analysis. It begins with a promising message from John Smith that includes the following:

> We reject the approach of a Conservative Government which is driven by consumerist dogma, by oppressive dictation by the central state, and by a false and inadequate theory of choice. What is more, the uncertainties of constant experimentation and erratic changes of policy have disrupted and demoralised schools throughout the land.
>
> (p. i)

The paper itself begins with a statement of Labour vision:

> Education needs a vision, a framework in which policy can be set out, and values upon which it is based. This Green Paper sets out the values and principles which we believe should guide policy-making in education. It seeks to apply those principles and values to the different sectors of education. At present, Government values look back to the Victorian era. Labour wants to look forward and understand the needs of the 21st century. We must create an education system that will allow us to live as an educated democracy, a learning society. Schools can make a difference.
>
> (p. 1)

This is a clear statement of socialist belief in equality and of inclusion where the present system excludes by unnecessary hurdles. There is, of course, plenty of reference to the economic need to compete by having a better educated work-force, but this is balanced by insistence on education as a benefit in its own right – for the individual and for society:

> The market view of education with each school as an island competing in order to 'defeat' other schools, is not one that will provide the best for each and every child. Quality and equality of opportunity are part of the same aim. We cannot have a quality education system that fails most children. Quality education must not be rationed. It must be the right of all. Our view is that education is not only about learning blocks of facts . . . It is about developing personal skills and the self-confidence and self-esteem to apply them. It is about the spirit of enquiring and of challenging ideas, uncomfortable though that can be for politicians as well as others.
>
> (p. 5)

Specific aims included a revised national curriculum: 'that provides a framework for schools rather than a straitjacket syllabus; the need for appropriate assessment and not simplistic testing for . . . misleading league tables' (p. 5). The paper then proceeds to a discussion of values or principles, including:

> A learning society which requires individuals who participate with self-confidence in decision making; Access (education must open its doors for all); Quality and equity; Continuing education; Accountability (education belongs to the whole community and is for the benefit of everyone); Partnerships (a civilised society cannot operate its education system on the basis of competition alone – quality education depends on partnership).

This is something of a mixed bag, but each principle is justified in terms of values – not just market choice. Then, each stage of education is dealt with in terms of the values and principles: pre-school, 5–16 (with a long section on effective schools); the national curriculum 5–16 (making a good distinction between a curriculum framework and a detailed syllabus); appropriate assessment at all stages (but *not* league tables); special needs. A whole chapter is devoted to the teaching profession, starting with complaints about the Conservatives undermining teachers in recent years. The proposal to replace the Council for the Accreditation of Teacher Education (CATE) by a 'quango' charged with overseeing the de-professionalisation of teaching is a dangerous and retrograde step (p. 45). (Such a quango, the TTA, was established after the 1994 Education Act, and was not abolished by Labour after 1997.)

The paper also discusses, constructively, school examinations, the whole field of further education as well as access to higher education. It would be easy to criticise minor details of the paper, but what is more important is to see the document as a whole, relating each stage or topic to a coherent set of values.

For example, Chapter 8 comments on the current structure of secondary school examinations, pointing out how that system divided young people unnecessarily by segregating the academic from vocational courses. The recommendation was that they could be replaced by a more unified system perhaps called a General Certificate of Further Education, closer to some kinds of baccalaureat structure, but incorporating credit transfer and continuing education and training. (After 1997 much less ambitious reforms were introduced, as we shall see in Chapter 11.)

Unfortunately, it would seem that after Labour's defeat in 1992, there were various moves to the right in education: the Labour policy on selection for schools, and the abolition of grammar schools, was softened; streaming and setting were recommended (despite the evidence). Blair should not get all the blame for this shift to the right in education: others were involved in a readjustment to cater for middle-class voters. But Tony Blair was the leader at this time and began to take a particular interest in education and to interfere with the details of policy-making. David Blunkett had generally been an effective Labour spokesperson on education and it was expected that he would become Education Secretary after the election. He clearly wanted the job and did not openly quarrel with Blair's views on education which were said to come from Blair's right-wing advisers about whom more will be said in Chapter 11. Blunkett was also said to be dismayed when Blair, in a pre-election TV interview (1997), said that he would want Chris Woodhead, the ultra-traditional Chief Inspector for Schools, to continue when Labour came to power. Some Labour supporting educationists became increasingly apprehensive about Blair's willingness to disagree with the views of the majority of the professionals in the education world.

Conclusion

In many respects 1990–94 were good years for Labour educational ideas (despite the electoral defeat in 1992). Labour came very close to producing a framework of education policies that were based on established socialist values and principles in a modernising context. After 1992 and particularly after 1994, education became less central to Labour strategies, despite the Blair slogan 'education, education, education'; compromises and U-turns were considered to be acceptable to what was thought to be the educational prejudices of middle-class voters. This will be discussed more fully in Chapter 11.

I have already suggested, earlier in this chapter, that 1994 was a significant turning point for Labour education: Ann Taylor's Green Paper (1993/4) was a serious and successful attempt to combine Labour Party ethical values and principles with the needs of a modernising society. Later in 1994 she was relieved of her responsibilities in education and replaced by David Blunkett. At the time, many of us failed to realise the significance of this change. David Blunkett was much more pragmatic in his approach to education, and more concerned to link education with economic efficiency. He also found it possible, as we shall see in Chapter 11, to compromise when faced with right-wing ideas from Blair and his advisers. Although Blunkett had a strong sense of social justice and the importance of quality education for all, he was very critical of teachers and shared some Tory suspicions about 'the educational establishment'.

In the years 1994–97 Blunkett began to plan legislation and structures for a Labour government. Some of these plans were seen as a continuation of Conservative ideas, but that would be only partly true. It will be more useful to see what Labour did when in power.

11 Education, education, education or targets, targets, targets?

1997–2001

> Today a new Labour Party is being born. Our task now is nothing less than the rebirth of our nation.
>
> (Tony Blair at the Labour Party Special Conference, 29.4.95, having won the vote to abandon clause 4)

> I shall argue that Blair is turning out to be a distinctive Prime Minister. Commentators have already compared him to Thatcher, Bonaparte, Clinton and even Stalin: the term Presidential has become almost a Pavlovian adjective when his leadership is discussed.
>
> (Dennis Kavanagh, 2001, pp. 3–4)

Introduction

The structure of this chapter will be slightly different from Chapters 1–10. I shall start, as usual, with background events 1997–2001 and then move on to British politics. But after that it will be better to have the following structure: a section simply listing, without much comment, critical or otherwise, the educational events and publications of the first Blair government. This will be followed by an account by Michael Barber on the achievements of the Blair government as well as some hopes for the future. That will be immediately followed by some views and evaluations by educational researchers. Finally, I will write my own evaluation of the four years, detailing the achievements and disappointments. The chapter will end with a discussion of commercialisation, marketisation and privatisation in education since 1997.

Background events

The international scene since 1997 was similar to the years preceding the change of government: discord in the Middle East; threats of war between India and Pakistan; the need to supply troops to keep the peace in Europe. The threat of war between the USA and Iraq was intensified after the election of George W.Bush; famines continued to be a problem in Africa; the Foreign Secretary, Robin Cooke, promised that the government would sign the

European Social Chapter; in December 1999 the UK did not yet join the Euro; by 2001 the UK seemed to be drifting away from Europe in some respects.

Blair's 'socialism' (1994)

On 18 June 1994 Tony Blair made a speech, shortly after becoming Labour leader, which was reprinted as a Fabian Pamphlet (Blair, 1994). This is a fascinating document for a number of reasons: first, it briefly rewrites Labour history in terms of two strands – ethical socialism and Marxism. (From earlier chapters of this book, readers will realise that I would regard this as an over-simplification.) Second, he 'reasserts' his version of ethical 'social-ism'. This is interesting because since 1997 he has usually preferred to avoid the word 'socialist'. Third, there is no mention of the third way, but he stated that he did not want a Tory economy with a bit of compassion added. Fourth, there is very little on education. Fifth, he was clearly using the paper as an attempt to unite the Party: he concludes with a clarion call 'It is time now to rediscover our central mission of social advance and individual achievement. This is a time in which we will make our own history; not power at the expense of principle, but power through principle and for the purpose of the common good' (p. 7). By the end of this chapter we may be in a better position to judge the extent to which Blair lived up to those bold promises.

British politics

The Labour victory at the general election was expected, but not the size of the majority (179). Not only did Labour have a more than comfortable majority in the House of Commons, the Conservatives were demoralised, disunited and, after the departure of John Major, had difficulty in finding a suitable leader. William Hague was intelligent but lacked gravitas and sometimes judgement; Ian Duncan Smith lacked gravitas, judgment and sometimes a voice. In that respect Blair had an easy ride. He also managed to avoid one problem of a large majority: the tendency for an opposition to develop within the Party. Blair was spared that, possibly because the memory of 1979–97 in opposition was still very much alive. In May 1999, elections for the Scottish Parliament and Welsh Assembly gave Labour in Scotland and Wales the largest number of seats but not an overall majority. In July, legislation was passed to establish the Northern Ireland Assembly. At the 1999 Conference, Blair promised to free the UK of 'all kinds of conservatism'. In November 1999 there was a minor revolt of Labour MPs voting against the privatisation of Air Traffic Control. In January 2000, the millennium got off to a poor start: the Dome was not a success. In May, Ken Livingstone won the London mayoral election against Labour's Frank Dobson. At the end of the September 2000 Labour Party conference, Blair admitted errors over the Dome and pensions, but promised to do better. He did not restore the link between pensions and average earnings.

New Labour's achievements

Blair started his first government in 1997 with many advantages: he had been preparing himself and his Party since July 1994 when he had been elected leader; he had a large majority; he had already reorganised the Party to minimise internal disputes; he was popular with the public and with much of the media. On the negative side, his style was criticised for being too close to the cult of personality to be truly democratic; some of his views (including those on education) were suspiciously right-wing, even Thatcherite; and he was said to be something of a 'power freak', demanding his own way, and interfering too much in the policies of his shadow ministers, and, after 1997, his ministers. Above all, he seemed to be obsessed with the task of ensuring the backing of those outside his Party's traditional supporters – the middle-class floating voters. His decision to promise not to increase income-tax above the levels proposed by the Tories was seen by some Labour stalwarts as a serious error of judgement. He also attempted and usually succeeded at dominating the media: he relied heavily on 'spin doctors', notably Alistair Campbell who had been a tabloid journalist. This domination has been achieved at a cost – cynicism on the part of the public.

It may be that Blair will go down in history as a constitutional reformer: the legislation for devolution in Wales, Scotland and Northern Ireland was remarkable. Other successes were in the field of social welfare, but even so, by the end of his first term the gap between rich and poor had widened and Blair refused to apologise for this. Other failures were transport and, to a lesser extent, housing. Education was a strange mixture of successes and failures.

Education 1997–2001

Of the 40-page 1997 election manifesto, three had been devoted to education. Promises included smaller classes, more nursery places, higher standards, access to computers, life-long education (a new University for Industry) and more spending on education. There was a guarantee that the 11+ would not be revived, but there was a warning that:

> We must modernise comprehensive schools. Children are not all of the same ability, nor do they learn at the same speed. That means *setting* children in classes to maximise progress, for the benefit of high-fliers and slower learners alike.
>
> (p. 7)

Other statements included 'Zero tolerance of under-performance' – failing schools unable to improve would be prescribed a fresh start; and also 'every school needs baseline assessment of pupils when they enter the school, and a year-on-year target for improvement'.

1997

In Chapter 10 I described how Labour education planning reached a high point after the 1992 electoral defeat, when Ann Taylor's Commission on Education produced some excellent ideas, resulting in the consultation document, *Opening Doors to a Learning Society*. But in 1994 Blair had replaced Ann Taylor by David Blunkett, and reversed some of the suggested policies between 1994 and 1997. Just before the election, in a television interview, Blair angered many teachers and other educationists by saying that he intended to keep Chris Woodhead on as Chief Inspector of Schools. This was seen as support for right-wing traditional attitudes to education.

As expected, Blair appointed Blunkett as Secretary of State for Education and Employment. One of their first actions was to set up the Standards and Effectiveness Unit, headed by Michael Barber, who had been a Professor at the Institute of Education, University of London. It was not long before Barber had about one hundred people working in his unit.

Excellence in Schools (1997)

The next task was to work on a White Paper: *Excellence in Schools*. It stated that 'standards matter more than structures'. Some complained that this was a misleading distinction. The White Paper also said that intervention would be in inverse proportion to success, and that there would be 'zero tolerance of under-performance': there would be 'unrelenting pressure' on schools, but pressure would be balanced by 'support'. Targets were set for improvements in literacy and numeracy. Baseline tests would be put in place for children starting primary school and a daily literacy hour prescribed (with the promise of a numeracy strategy to follow). There were other pedagogical instructions including the need for whole-class teaching. Targets were set for 2002, and Blunkett promised to resign if they were not met. But in 2001 he had moved on to other kinds of targets at the Home Office. The principle that education must be 'for the many, not for the few' represented an intended change from Conservative education policies.

LEAs and schools would also be required to provide more management data. LEAs would be expected to have development plans prepared, by 1999, in line with instructions from the Department's School Standards and Effectiveness Unit. OfSTED would now be empowered to inspect LEAs on a regular basis. In another section of the paper there was a promise to modernise the comprehensive school system. There was also a new proposal for Education Action Zones: more details will be given later.

By July 1997 an Education Act was passed, abolishing the assisted places scheme. This was welcomed by the Labour Party and most of the education world. One aspect of New Labour policy on education was 'inclusion', an emphasis that education benefits must be for all. Two more demonstrations of this belief were turned into action before the end of 1998. First, a Green Paper, *Excellence for All*, which was a discussion of provision for children with special educational needs. The second was setting up a Social Exclusion Unit within the Cabinet Office. This was intended to promote activities across several departments, including education, concerned with those young people who were in danger of being excluded from normal opportunities.

1998

In July there was another Education Act: *The School Standards and Framework Act*. This was the first major piece of New Labour legislation on education, and it was very long. Much of it dealt with a new structure for classifying schools. There would be three kinds of school: foundation, aided and community – with sub-divisions. Infant class size was limited. There was a duty laid on LEAs to promote high standards, but their powers of intervention were clarified. The financing of maintained schools was specified. The selection of pupils was reviewed – selection by aptitude of up to 10 per cent of intake was permitted. (This was seen as a broken promise.) Another provision in the Schools Standards and Framework Act (1998) was the establishment of Education Action Zones (EAZ) in areas of disadvantage. This had something in common with the idea behind Educational Priority Areas in the 1960s (discussed in Chapter 6). The difference between EPAs and EAZs was that the new scheme seemed to have two intentions: first, to take some schools out of LEA control, and, second, to replace LEAs by the private sector.

In the same month, July 1998, a third Education Act reached the statute book: *Teaching and Higher Education Act*. The long-promised General Teaching Council (GTC) would be established in 2000. This was a reform, welcomed by educationists, although the powers handed over to the GTC fell short of the Scottish equivalent. Nevertheless, it represented a symbol of professionalism at a time when teachers had been under increasing central control in terms of curriculum and pedagogy. Another feature of the Act was the extension of OfSTED functions in the world of Initial Teacher Education and Training. That aspect of the Act has to be seen in conjunction with the Green Paper and DfEE circular later in 1998.

The Green Paper, *Teachers Meeting the Challenge of Change*, was accused of including another broken promise. In 1994 Ann Taylor's consultation paper had indicated that the Teacher Training Agency (TTA) would be abolished, but by 1998 it was decided that Teacher Training Departments in Higher Education would continue to be scrutinised and regulated by the TTA as well as being inspected regularly by OfSTED. The DfEE circular 4/98 set out in considerable detail what amounted to a compulsory curriculum for Initial Teacher Training.

Citizenship education

Meanwhile, September 1998 saw the beginning of the implementation of a significant Labour Party educational idea. The event was the publication of *Education for Citizenship and the Teaching of Democracy in Schools* (the Crick Report). Bernard Crick, Emeritus Professor of Politics at Birkbeck College, London, had for many years been an advocate for the teaching of politics and citizenship at all levels, including primary and secondary schools. His book *The Teaching of Politics* (1969) had made a convincing case:

> As a Professor of Political Studies, I am interested in political education at the secondary level of education because it should be there both in its own right and in the public interest, not as a feeder to the university Moloch. At some stage all young people . . . should gain some awareness of what politics is about. It is more important that all teenagers should learn to read newspapers critically for their political content than that they should have heard of Aristotle or know – may Heaven forgive us all – when the Speaker's Mace is or was over or under the table.
>
> (pp. 3–4)

Unfortunately, these ideas had been slow to reach the level of politicians' thinking, despite Crick's involvement in a Hansard Society curriculum project in the 1970s that resulted in a book, *Political Education and Political Literacy* (1978). At some stage in his own education, David Blunkett had been exposed to Crick's ideas and became convinced of the need to include something on citizenship in the school curriculum. In November 1997 Blunkett, having briefly referred to citizenship in *Excellence in Schools*, with the approval of the Prime Minister, asked Professor Crick to Chair an Advisory Group with the following terms of reference: 'To provide advice on effective education for citizenship in schools – to include the nature and practices of participation in democracy; the duties, responsibilities and rights of individuals as citizens; and the value to individuals and society of community activity' (p. 4).

An interim report on aims and purposes was published in March 1998, and a final report came six months later, meeting the deadline set by the Qualifications and Curriculum Authority for inclusion in the general revision of the National Curriculum from 2000. The Advisory Group must have worked hard because the final report is not only clearly argued but is a polished and diplomatic document with positive recommendations. This was achieved from a large advisory group presumably designed to cover a wide range of views (Kenneth Baker, now Lord Baker, formerly Conservative Secretary of State for Education, was, for example, a member). Citizenship is carefully defined, and examples of good practice from schools are included as part of the Report, together with some good research evidence demonstrating the need for a national programme of some kind. Finally, a set of recommendations proposed a statutory entitlement for all pupils to be added to the National Curriculum in its revised, post-2000, form:

Aim and purpose
The purpose of citizenship education in schools and colleges is to make secure and to increase the knowledge, skills and values relevant to the nature and practices of participative democracy; also to enhance the awareness of rights and duties, and the sense of responsibilities needed for the development of pupils into active citizens; and in so doing to establish the value to individuals, schools and society of involvement in the local and wider community.

(p. 40)

Three strands were spelt out for this ambitious programme: social and moral responsibility, community involvement, and political literacy. The essential elements comprised: key concepts, values and dispositions, skills and aptitudes, knowledge and understanding. They were further sub-divided into social, moral, political, economic and environmental.

1999

All of this progress on political education or citizenship became part of the general review of the national curriculum, May to July 1999. The new national curriculum for 2000 was intended to have a more explicit rationale and be both more inclusive and less prescriptive. The advisory group's recommendations were converted into key stages and published as part of *The Review of the National Curriculum in England: The Secretary of State's Proposals* (1999). This was part of a further consultation exercise, from which the citizenship curriculum emerged unscathed. It was established as the *Citizenship Order* (1999) which David Blunkett described as 'light touch and flexible'.

There were a few more educational events in 1999, but nothing to compare with the importance of citizenship education. One was the publication of *Excellence in Cities* (DfEE, 1999) which began by criticising the low standards in many inner city schools, and proposed an action plan for immediate improvements. The plan involved more Beacon schools and specialist schools in deprived areas, as well as encouraging opportunities for the 'gifted' and 'talented'. The proposal also included special programmes for the top ten per cent of the ability range, new 'world-class' tests, and more setting by ability groups with provision for the less able and disruptive pupils to be segregated in 'learning support centres' (LSCs).

The final education Act of 1999 was the *Further and Higher Education Act* which took account of the recommendations of the Dearing Reports on further and higher education.

2000

There was a comparative lull in educational initiatives in 2000. In the field of teacher education there was a general expectation that there should be some relaxation of control and bureaucratic scrutiny. Perhaps in response to criticisms of the excessively prescriptive national curriculum for ITT (mentioned briefly earlier in this chapter) there was a review of the operation of circular 4/98. The TTA retreated a little from its hitherto controlling stance; this, combined with a review of the OfSTED arrangements of ITT, under the new leadership of the experienced Chief Inspector, Mike Tomlinson, meant that a much more reasonable set of guidelines was produced for consultation. The training year for student teachers was still very crowded and contained little background educational theory, but it was a great improvement, especially when seen as part of the new proposals for Continuous Professional Development for Teachers which aimed at integrating ITT, the induction year, and education and training opportunities for the whole of a teaching career.

2001

From January 2001 the government was preparing for the next general election – in May. There were some important speeches made about policy by the Prime Minister and in February the DfEE published the Green Paper: *Building on Success: Raising Standards, Promoting Diversity, Achieving Results.* It began by re-stating the achievements of New Labour since 1997 together with its plans for the future. A major theme was the need to transform secondary education by modernising the comprehensive principle, and creating more specialist schools. The range of specialist schools was to be extended, by adding engineering, science and business to the existing list of technology, languages, sport, and the arts.

The election manifesto, *Ambitions for Britain*, was also important. It will be treated in some detail in Chapter 12. In the May general election, Labour was, as expected, returned with a good majority.

Michael Barber and New Labour ideas on education

Our next task is to look at an evaluation of New Labour and education 1997–2001 from the point of view of a committed New Labour 'insider' – Professor Michael Barber who became Director of the Standards and Effectiveness Unit and Chief Adviser on School Standards in 1997. His responsibilities included the National Literacy Strategy and the National Numeracy Strategy, as well as dealing with school failure, modernising secondary education in the inner cities and the contracting out of failing LEAs. Before his appointment he had published *The Learning Game* (1997). In so far as New Labour has an 'education theorist', Barber was the education ideas man. His evaluation of New Labour education 1997–2001 was published as 'High expectations and standards for all, no matter what. Creating a world class education service in England' (published in Fielding, *Taking Education Really Seriously: Four Years Hard Labour*, 2001).

Michael Barber begins his paper with 'the vision' – a world class education service. His ambition is to avoid a situation in which more people would pay for private education and become less willing to pay taxes to fund public education. He quotes Richard Titmuss (1968) who also wanted to avoid 'a poor service for poor people'.

Barber suggested that the first of New Labour achievements was to provide the money and to begin to abolish poverty. On the other hand, he stressed the size of the problem: in international comparisons England was tending to come far too close to the bottom. In order to move away from being an 'under-performing system' Barber advocated a policy approach described as 'high challenge, high support'. He suggested that there had been twenty-five years of history when England spent ten years in low challenge, low support, until the Thatcher government increased the challenge but failed to provide support. Barber proceeded to convert that approach into a set of principles. The first was that 'All students can achieve': 'if we set high standards and expect every student to meet them; and recognise that for some students, in some circumstances, teaching those high standards is more difficult. They will need extra assistance and time.'

The next principle is 'Don't compromise on quality: invest in it'. A third principle states that 'A government that demands quality must provide it too.' Barber wants a culture in which everyone takes responsibility for student outcomes. He approves of the Blair soundbite 'all money is for modernisation'. Barber then provides us with a framework of continuous improvement centred around 'high challenge, high support': ambitious standards; devolved responsibility; good data/clear targets; access to best practice and quality professional development; accountability; intervention in inverse proportion to success (rewards, assistance, consequences). (He distinguishes between successful schools; all schools; under-performing schools; failing schools and failing LEAs or districts.)

More specifically, Barber claims some early successes for three broad strategies: the literacy and numeracy programmes at primary level; the transformation of secondary education; and the modernisation of the teaching profession. This is followed by a detailed description and evaluation of the national literacy and numeracy strategies. He quotes the Canadian educator, Michael Fullen, who said that England had embarked on 'the most ambitious, comprehensive and aligned national strategies anywhere in the world' (Earl *et al.*, 2000).

The claims for improvement in literacy and numeracy are supported by figures showing the steady increase of pupils at level 4 or above in key stage 2 English and Mathematics tests (DfEE, 2000, Statistics). Other evidence was obtained from a survey of primary school headteachers on literacy. At this stage there is a switch away from results to aspirations: 'the transformation of secondary education'. The plans are set out in some detail, especially 'teaching and learning in the middle years (age 11–14)'.

One of the specific projects is *Excellence in Cities* (EiC) (1999). This programme involves another principle: 'equity and diversity' associated with four core beliefs (p. 30):

1. High expectations of every individual.
2. Diversity (EiC is designed to increase diversity of provision in secondary education in the major conurbations – EAZs and City Learning Centres).
3. Networks (each pupil should see himself as a member not just of a specific school community, but of a wider learning community . . .).
4. Extending opportunity.

To turn these beliefs into reality there are seven strands of the policy:

a) The gifted and talented.
b) Removing barriers to learning.
c) Behaviour support.
d) Beacon schools.
e) Specialist schools.
f) New City Learning Centres, and
g) Education Action Zones.

The programme started only in September 1999 but, according to Barber, already there had been substantial reductions in truancy and exclusion and improvements in pupil attitudes.

> It has broken down the isolation of many inner-city schools and encouraged a new sense of shared endeavour. We believe these are vital signs of improvement. Ultimately, the programme should result in a complete re-engineering of secondary education. Instead of fitting students into the system as we did in the twentieth-century, we would build the system around the needs and aspirations of students.
>
> (p. 31)

This is followed by a section on 'the modernisation of the teaching profession' which admits that 'there are major challenges':

- major teacher shortages – science, maths, foreign languages and music;
- particular recruitment and retention problems of schools in challenging circumstances;
- shortage of good candidates for leadership positions, particularly in London and the south east.

That is the position: the new vision of 'a modernised teaching profession' has five aspects:

1   strengthening leadership;
2   linking pay and performance;
3   improving professional development;
4   strengthening the preparation of teachers;
5   providing greater support (major investment in school buildings; the provision of standards, teaching materials, planning guidance, data and best practice advice through the internet; the use of technical expertise for maintaining ICT systems; training and developing over 20,000 additional teaching assistants – especially for literacy and numeracy; and, finally, reducing bureaucratic burdens.

Barber admits that this programme is not without difficulties:

- too few teachers see the big picture of reform;
- avoid negative portrayal of schools and teachers;
- avoid perception of reform as 'top-down';
- the difficulty of LEAs in between central government and the schools;
- funding has been too complex and lacking transparency.

The future, according to Barber:

- The first task is to see things through.
- If it all works, the result will be schools with high autonomy and high performance.
- School reform will globalise.
- The central question for public authorities will cease to be 'who provides?' instead they will ask 'how is the public interest to be secured?':

> For most of the 20th century the drive for educational progress came from the public sector, often in combination with the religious or voluntary sectors. Towards the end of the 20th century, as frustration with existing systems grew, this legacy was challenged by a growing vibrant private sector . . . the challenge for the 21st century is surely to seek out what works. The issue is not whether the public, private or voluntary sector alone will shape the future, but what partnerships and combinations of the three will make the most difference to performance.
>
> (p. 39)

The paper concludes in an interesting but controversial way:

> Public authorities will need to invest more in education than ever before, partly because of technology and pressure to improve teachers' pay, conditions and professional development, but mainly because they will be striving to achieve much higher performance standards for *all*, not just

some, students. Meanwhile, those parents able to will spend more money than ever on their children's education. Some may choose private schools, depending on the quality of public provision locally, but many will spend on resources for the home and on out-of-school learning opportunities of all kinds. The challenge for government will therefore be, not only to provide high quality schools, but also to provide the equivalent of the home and out-of-school learning opportunities for those students whose parents do not have the will or the means to provide them. This will be crucial from an equity as well as from a performance point of view, and opens up an entirely new area of public policy.

(p. 40)

Barber's paper is a persuasive, perhaps brilliant exposition of New Labour policies and, to a lesser extent, achievements of 1997–2001. But it is typical of New Labour documents on education in its ignoring fundamental beliefs and values, concentrating instead on a managerial, technicist approach to the delivery of traditional education. Despite the use of the word 'vision' there seems to be no creative ideas about a better kind of school or curriculum to match the needs of a democratic society in the twenty-first century. It also accepts implicitly, if not explicitly, the continuing existence of independent schooling more or less unchanged. We are simply offered a more effective way of managing an imperfect machine.

Before continuing with my own evaluation of the four-year period, however, I would like to refer to the views of others who are less enthusiastic than Michael Barber about the way that New Labour has approached education in its first term of government.

Some critical comments on education policies and achievements 1997–2001

There are too many books and articles about New Labour education to allow comprehensive treatment of every one of them. I will have to be selective, but I will try to select in a way that does not distort the views of left-of-centre educationists.

General critique of New Labour and education

A number of writers have made much of the fact – completely ignored in Michael Barber's paper – that there were many issues on which too little was different from the Thatcher–Major policies. Ball (2001), for example, points out that:

The three key non-governmental agency figures from the previous Conservative administration have been retained, Woodhead at the Office for

Standards in Education, Tate at the Qualifications and Curriculum Authority and Millett at the Teacher Training Agency. It is hardly a startling conclusion, then, to suggest that despite the flurry of policy activity in and
around education under Labour we need to attend as much to the continuities as to the differences between Labour and the Conservatives.

(Ball, 2001, p. 45)

The continuity has often been perceived as a willingness to persist with Tory
attitudes and policies as well as personnel. The policies included an eagerness
to hand over schools and some LEA responsibilities to the private sector, a
somewhat punitive attitude towards teachers, and a failure to abandon selection.
These are 'negative ideas' but none the less important for that: part of the
history of ideas is the persistence of some attitudes when they were expected
to change or fade away. Ball (2001) points out that some of the continuities
from Conservative to Labour 1997 were global trends rather than New Labour
aberrations, for example, three primary interrelating principles:

- *Choice and competition.* The commodification and commercialisation of
  education.
- *Autonomy and performativity.* The managerialisation and commercialisation
  of education.
- *Centralisation and prescription.* The imposition of centrally determined assessments, schemes of work and classroom methods.

(Ball, p. 46)

For those who were disappointed about Labour's commitment to social justice,
1997–2001, Ball reminded us of Tony Edwards's (1998) perception of Labour
policies on setting, selection and choice, for example, as representing a 'confused or at least weak commitment to social justice'.

The explicit commitment to tackling exclusion does not seem to be
matched by efforts to maximise inclusion. What I mean by that is that
the exclusion effects of educational processes themselves remain un-
addressed. As Whitty (1998: 2) puts it 'the government has adopted a
fairly conventional view of educational knowledge and avoided awkward
sociological questions about its selective nature and social functions'.
O'Brien (1998: 3) points out that Labour's education policies can be understood and analysed as 'a synthesis between market and social democratic
values' or rather a dichotomy 'informed by two separate strands of philosophical thought'.

(quoted by Ball, 2001, p. 47)

So much for the general question of 'continuity' between Tory and New Labour
education. It may now be useful to look at more specific aspects of education and

New Labour policies or initiatives. (Ball reminds us that at the 1998 Labour Party conference 47 education initiatives were mentioned).

Early years and primary education

Promises had been made to increase the number of nursery places, and to keep the size of classes below 30. Money was made available to enable those promises to be kept. That was good, even if some critics complained about the baseline tests that were imposed on 5-year-old children. New Labour was also criticised generally for retaining too much testing from the previous Conservative regime and for increasing the intensity of pressure in primary schools by retaining league tables and the imposition of standards for individual schools. OfSTED, since the departure of Chief Inspector Woodhead, has frequently complained about over-assessment in primary schools and the distorting effect this has had on the curriculum. In particular, the reduced amount of time being spent on the arts and music, resulting in an unbalanced primary curriculum.

Peter Moss (2001), an international expert on early childhood education, wrote a review of Labour performance 1997–2001 with an interesting title *Renewed Hopes and Lost Opportunities: Early Childhood in the Early Years of the Labour Party*. It began encouragingly:

> The first thirty-six months of the Labour Government have seen un-paralleled attention and resources devoted to early childhood services. Educational provision has been made for all four-year-olds and is to be extended to at least two-thirds of three-year-olds by 2002; a National Child Care strategy has been proposed, and is being implemented by early years development and child care partnerships, informed and guided by child care audits and local early years development and child care plans; the *Sure Start* initiative targets children under three and their families in disadvantaged areas, with 250 local programmes envisaged by the end of 2002; a programme of Centres of Early Excellence, intended to highlight 'best practice', has been launched; new sources of funding have been provided.
>
> (p. 73)

But Moss goes on to complain that instead of all that flurry of initiatives, it might have been better to re-think the whole of early years provision (by which he means 0–6 years). He concludes his evaluation as follows:

> The Labour Government has brought about an unparalleled and invigorating change of climate, with a recognition of the importance of early years and a willingness to act and spend money. Yet renewed hope mingles with an uneasy sense that an opportunity to transform early childhood services has been slipping away as the imperatives of other projects force

hurried responses. What has been missing is a process of collective reflection about early childhood, early childhood institutions, pedagogical work and early childhood workers.

(p. 81)

In the same volume, Peter Woods, Bob Jeffrey and Geoff Troman wrote a combined evaluation on *The Impact of New Labour's Educational Policy on Primary Schools* (2001). This paper begins rather critically:

The shift in emphasis in official policy from the liberal and egalitarian view of the 1960s and 1970s to one dominated by economic considerations, focusing on the need for a highly skilled workforce to enable the country to compete successfully in the global economy, brought a more instrumental, technicist approach on the part of government to primary teaching in the 1980s and 1990s. Primary teachers have a broader conception of educational aims embracing the whole child and many have felt a conflict of values in implementing government policy.

(p. 84)

The authors complain particularly about New Labour's *technicist* attitude exemplified by the literacy and numeracy strategies:

The model, as with the National Curriculum in general, is based on 'performance', with fixed goals, task analysis and testing, and the exclusion of any alternative views. This warrants a high level of prescription. The underlying philosophy has been challenged (for example, Cox, 1998). There is little in the official documents about the creative uses of literacy or 'critical awareness', of meaning and understanding.

(pp. 84–5)

In addition to their own research, the authors quote Galton's (1999) study: 'This has to be seen within the context of the 'low-trust society' (Giddens, 1990; Troman and Woods, 2001). Teachers are no longer trusted to implement reform, and must be directed and monitored' (p. 91). Woods *et al.* claim that although some interest was originally shown concerning the problem of creative and cultural education and a national advisory committee was set up, which reported in 1999, 'since then the Report has become marginalised' (p. 92). The problem of a technicist attitude which does not encourage a broader curriculum and creative work remains.

This was not an isolated research finding; there were many others making similar criticisms including, for example, a study by Professors Maurice Galton and John McBeath who showed that the pressures of testing and targets under New Labour had too often resulted in a primary curriculum that was ill balanced: the arts and music were frequently squeezed out, and even science and technology had insufficient time. Teachers also complained that they had little time for individual feedback with pupils; and young teachers found that classroom teaching was less satisfying than they had expected (Galton and McBeath, 2002, *Primary Teaching 1970–2000*, report commissioned by the NUT).

Secondary education

More money has been spent on secondary education, especially on information and communication technology. But, despite *Excellence in Cities* and other initiatives, the problem of inner city schools, including truancy and exclusions as well as poor levels of achievement, has remained. Above all, many Labour-supporting educationists were critical of New Labour's attitude to comprehensive schools, selection and the failure to deal with independent schools in a constructive way. The whole policy for secondary schools was seriously distorted by decisions that really meant continuing with Conservative policies about choice, the market and privatisation.

Professor Clyde Chitty (2002) has described the origins of some of New Labour ideas on secondary education in an interesting way. He made a link between the 'standards not structures' motif in *Excellence in Schools* (1997) and in the Education Act (1998) with an earlier book by Peter Mandelson and Roger Liddle (1996), *The Blair Revolution: Can New Labour Deliver?*

> New Labour must now spell out with greater clarity what its new education policies mean in practice and how its new emphasis on standards not structures can in time transform state education.
>
> (p. 93)

Neither Mandelson nor Liddle could be seen as experts on education; so why should Blunkett take notice of them? Other significant phrases in Mandelson and Liddle also find their way into the White Paper and legislation: for example, 'zero tolerance of failure', Chitty comments that:

> A survey of comprehensive education in Britain undertaken in the academic year 1993–4 [reported in Benn and Chitty (1996)] emphasised the crucial importance of related issues concerning structure, selection and admission criteria, which the White Paper neatly side-stepped.
>
> (Chitty, 2002, p. 96)

Chitty locates the origins of some ideas from *Excellence in Schools*:

> The Major government of 1992–7 bequeathed to New Labour a sharply divided system of secondary state schools in England and Wales. Any attempt by David Blunkett to create a unified comprehensive structure subject to fair and transparent admissions rules could not ignore the existence of 163 grammar schools concentrated in English counties such as

Buckinghamshire, Kent and Lincolnshire and in many of the larger conurbations; 15 City Technology Colleges and 1,155 Grant-Maintained schools
accounting for 19.6% of the students in secondary schools and for 2.8% of
those in primary schools; and a growing number of specialist schools and
colleges that were now able to 'select' students at the age of 11 on the
basis of their 'aptitude' for particular subjects such as technology, languages,
sports or arts . . . the Blair administration has proved singularly reluctant to
tackle the administrative confusion caused largely by Conservative policies.
Indeed, the 1997 White Paper itself was distinctly lukewarm in its defence
of comprehensive schooling, arguing that progress towards a more unified
system in the 1950s and 1960s had served to undermine 'the pursuit of
excellence' . . . This curious defensiveness about the comprehensive reform
was accompanied by both a failure to give a clear lead on the question of
grammar schools and their future and a determination to persist with the
Conservative policy of 'selection by specialisation'.

(Chitty, 2002, pp. 96–7)

Chitty traces the evolution of this New Labour policy from Labour's 1995 policy
document, *Diversity and Excellence: A New Partnership for Schools*, where it was
argued that the Labour Party was 'implacably opposed to a return to selection
by the 11+', but it was also made clear that the grammar schools would not be
dealt with as an issue of national policy (Chitty, 2002, p. 97). The story continues to the Labour Party conference in October 1995 when delegates were
unhappy with the policy document. There was an acrimonious debate during
which David Blunkett placated the audience with his famous 'Read my lips.
No selection, either by examination or interview, under a Labour government.'
This assurance was enough to satisfy the audience and remove the demand for
abolition of all grammar schools. Chitty continues with the story as follows:

It soon became clear, however, that 'no selection' actually meant 'no *further*
selection'; and when David Blunkett began using this new slogan in
speeches and media interviews, he was not guilty of a simple slip of the
tongue: he was, in effect, announcing a *change of education policy*. As Roy
Hattersley has pointed out on a number of occasions, 'no selection' signi-
fied an end to the existing grammar schools; 'no *further* selection' was a
guarantee of their retention. In Hattersley's view, David Blunkett made a
specific pledge to see him through a very difficult education debate knowing
full well that Tony Blair would not allow him to honour it. But, replying
to this charge on the BBC Television *Breakfast with Frost* programme on
30 November 1997, the new Education Secretary protested that when he
had used the words 'no selection' in the 1995 debate, he had actually
intended them to mean 'no *further* selection'. There had, therefore, been
no change of policy.

(Chitty, 2002, pp. 97–8)

In an interview with *The Sunday Telegraph* (12 March, 2000), David Blunkett claimed that it was all a joke.

Clyde Chitty also referred to very important research by Professor Tony Edwards (1998) which reviewed research evidence on specialisation and selection. Edwards organised his review around three claims made in support of a change in policy:

- That parents actually *want* greater curriculum choice;
- That specialisation is quite different from selection;
- That diversity through specialisation will raise educational standards *in* and *beyond* the specialist schools themselves.

Chitty summarises the Edwards' findings as follows:

1 There is no evidence of parental demand for more specialised forms of curriculum.
2 In the British, and particularly the English, context, specialisation as a means of diversifying and modernising the school curriculum confronts a formidable obstacle – the continuing high prestige of the 'traditional academic' curriculum.
3 Specialisation is hard to separate from straightforward selection, and certainly in conditions where schools compete for students.
4 'Selection by interest' also tends to produce socially segregated intakes.
5 The early identification of 'aptitude' for particular subjects, defined as *promise* rather than *achievement*, remained a problem without technically well-grounded and educationally acceptable solutions.
6 Without valid evidence that 'specialist schools' are in fact more effective, the extent to which they are preferentially funded is inequitable.

(Research Information on State Education: RISE, 1998,
quoted by Chitty, 2002, pp. 101–2)

Chitty's criticisms were shared by large numbers of educationists who resented this manipulative change of policy that threatened what they saw as an important principle – comprehensive education without selection.

The secondary curriculum (including 14–19)

In terms of the secondary curriculum the picture is not so bleak: useful modifications were made and best of all, citizenship education was introduced as part of the national curriculum. For the 14–19 age group there must be a mixed report. Labour has been anxious to make better provision for this age group and has devoted resources to the neglected further education sector. They have, however, shown timidity in dealing with examinations and qualifications, and have failed to deal adequately with the academic/vocational divide. Worse still, they came dangerously close to sanctioning inferior courses, under the guise of vocational opportunities, for 14–16 year old boys (and some girls) who disliked the curriculum on offer.

In a book written two years after the election, Ann Hodgson and Ken Spours (1999) wrote a sympathetic evaluation of New Labour and education 14–19, but made a careful distinction between the compulsory and post-compulsory phases:

> New Labour's approach to compulsory education is dominated by the desire to raise educational standards by centralized initiatives and regulatory systems . . . The desire to bring about change quickly has led to a tough accountabilty-driven approach to providers which brooks no opposition and has led to considerable antagonism from the teaching profession . . . In contrast to this assertive, centralized approach to compulsory education, New Labour's approach to post-compulsory education and training is much more cautious, experimental and voluntarist. Although in some areas, such as the New Deal, there is an element of compulsion and regulation, for the most part, New Labour has continued to follow the previous administration's permissive or voluntarist approach.
>
> (p. 2)

Teacher education and professionalism

Labour began badly in 1997 by failing to remove the unpopular Chris Woodhead as Chief Inspector until he began to 'bite the hands' of Blair and Blunkett. This was a missed opportunity because Woodhead symbolised an anti-professional view of teaching and teacher education. Presumably for similar reasons, that is, wanting to appear to be tough on standards and teachers, the Teacher Training Agency (TTA) was not abolished, as promised in 1994, but continued its 'command-and-control' regime which not only failed to produce the number of teachers required but also failed to enhance the professionalism of teachers. The Labour Party's decision to keep its promise about establishing the General Teaching Council helped to redress the balance, together with better provision for teachers' professional development, but teacher shortage and teacher quality remained as massive unsolved problems. Instead of developing a policy of enhancing the professionalism of teachers, including appropriate pay and conditions, we have had a series of quick fixes, presumably from the bright young people at No. 10. For example, there was the fast track scheme, aiming to attract well-qualified graduates into the profession (£5,000 and a laptop) and the new version of 'payment-by-results' – performance related salaries (an extremely expensive, near-total failure). Teaching morale continued to be low throughout the first Blair government; teachers continued to threaten to take action against key stage testing and other unnecessary paperwork.

Professor Peter Gilroy, then chair of the Universities Council for the Education of Teachers, wrote an evaluation of *New Labour and Teacher Education in*

England and Wales: The First Five Hundred Days (1998). He was very critical of the damaging effect that the new arrangements for initial teacher training were having on universities and on the profession, especially the use of performance tables and a generally bureaucratic attitude towards professional education (see also Gilroy, Edwards and Hartley *Responses to Uncertainty*, 2002).

Higher education

Professor Alan Smithers (2001), in a general review of New Labour and education from 1997, singled out higher education as an area of weakness: 'The Blair government made no bones about it. On election its priority was school education. But even so its treatment of higher education which has left both students and universities impoverished amounts to wilful neglect' (p. 421).

This may have been because both Labour and Conservatives were waiting for Ron Dearing to produce his report, *Higher Education in the Learning Society*, which did not appear until July 1997. It was a very large document covering learning, teaching in higher education, quality assurance, and, above all, reforming the financing of the universities. Dearing pointed out that the finance position of universities had reached a crisis point because the higher education unit of resource had been reduced by 25 per cent since 1989. The Dearing proposal was that students would have to make a contribution towards tuition, but that less affluent students could be exempt. The Dearing solution was a loan which would be repaid when their salary was high enough. The Labour government accepted most of the report but changed the Dearing proposal for a much less straightforward scheme of its own which was disliked by both students and university authorities. The Labour Party plan was to abolish maintenance grants and the fees were to be means tested. At first top-up fees were completely forbidden, but later on it was suggested that top-up fees would be allowed only under certain circumstances. Thus financing became related to control over universities' policies on access. This was not only a very muddled proposal but it failed to solve the problem of providing universities with extra money immediately. At the Labour Party Conference in 1998 Blair added to the confusion by announcing a new target of an extra half a million places by 2002. This was associated with his desire to see 50 per cent of the 18–30 age group benefiting from higher education of some kind (by 2010). These targets were very difficult for some universities to achieve, but if they failed they were threatened with fines which would add to their financial difficulties.

The basic problem of paying for higher education was unsolved, but there was another equally important difficulty – equality of access. The idea of an 'access regulator' which was being discussed at this time was supported by both Tony Blair and Gordon Brown. The notion was essentially sound, but neither the Prime Minister nor the Chancellor of the Exchequer seemed to have thought out a clear policy about removing unfair access to universities, especially the privileged position of students from independent schools.

The government was right to attempt to increase the proportion of the age group receiving some kind of higher education, but did not succeed in narrowing the gap between middle-class and working-class 18 year olds in that respect. The general record on higher education was not good. The unit of resource (that is, the average amount of money spent *per student*) declined dramatically. The government was accused of wanting to increase participation without being willing to pay for it: they failed to produce a clear and fair policy on the funding of higher education, partly through an unwillingness to upset middle-class parents.

Lifelong education and the learning society

There was a certain amount of rhetoric from 1997 onwards about the need for a learning society. It was a good concept backed by a number of respectable academic ideas (e.g. Stewart Ranson, *Towards a Learning Society*, 1994) but the reality of many new proposals did not match the easy slogan which could hardly be opposed in principle. On the whole there was a gap between effort and achievement which could only be rectified by better quality ideas. There have been many initiatives – too many – but they have often been based on educational views that are difficult to justify. Research evidence as well as the views of education theorists have too often been ignored in favour of the quick-fix bright ideas of spin doctors and advisers at No. 10. I will look at some examples in the next section on policy inconsistencies and conceptual confusions. There has been an unfortunate tendency to continue the Tory tradition of branding any educational expert as part of the educational establishment as an excuse to disregard any advice given.

Local Education Authorities and privatisation

Before 1997 under Conservative regimes, there was a good deal of hostility towards LEAs, and their powers were drastically reduced. One reason for the Conservative hostility was that some major LEAs were Labour controlled and appeared to be antagonistic towards Conservative policies. This did not mean, however, that New Labour would be automatically on the side of LEAs. As we have seen, in many respects New Labour was highly centralist and did not find it easy to define a clear role for local authorities. It seems that they too were tempted by the idea of abolishing LEAs, but were perhaps concerned at the possibility of many protests against the destruction of local democratic involvement in education. Their solution seems to have been to keep LEAs in existence but to limit their responsibilities to a much greater extent than the Conservatives, partly by encouraging privatisation of various kinds.

On the question of privatisation Colin Crouch (2003) has written a devastating critique of New Labour policies (especially education). I will not attempt to summarise the argument, but will refer to his Fabian paper from time to time. It should be read by all who are interested in this topic. His basic contrast is included in the title, *Commercialisation or Citizenship: Education Policy and the Future of Public Services*. Crouch maintains that in the history of the Labour Party, and especially during the Attlee government, a distinction was made between the kinds of things in a mixed economy that might be left to buying and selling in a market and those public services like health and education which should be kept separate from the profit motive. Commercialisation was contrasted with citizenship rights.

This was a useful distinction which can be refined to indicate that the government does not have to nationalise every firm supplying paper or equipment to its schools, but there are professional services which must be kept out of the marketplace.

Crouch shows, however, that this fundamental distinction has been threatened by the New Labour urge to modernise, which they seem to equate with commercialisation. Private companies were, under the Conservatives, involved in inspecting schools and even running a few schools (the unsuccessful City Technology College venture). But the process has gone much further with New Labour – so much so that the idea of professional non-profit making education is under threat. It would seem that New Labour has not considered the unintended consequences of wholesale commercialisation of education services that has included taking over some functions of LEAs and schools.

The problems include the following:

1 Part of the expertise of private firms is to select carefully their target customers. In education this is not possible because the state has the responsibility to educate everyone. This does not, however, prevent private firms from 'cherry-picking' the most profitable educational schemes on offer.
2 There is much talk about 'the market', which is far from a 'free market'. The result is that a few privileged private firms are allowed to compete in a very limited sense.
3 Another fallacy of the market analogy is to pretend that the customer is the pupil. This is an error. It is the government that pays and chooses the supplier. The pupils or their parents have little or no choice.
4 A variant of the 'cherry-picking' problem is the fact that the quasi-market allows schools to try to attract as many 'good' pupils as possible and reject those who are likely to be more difficult to teach (and to reach targets).
5 A consequence of the above example is that there will be a tendency for some schools, and LEAs to be left with problem cases.

In the case of LEAs, the government must define carefully the functions that it wishes to preserve. LEAs may appear to outside managers as an unnecessary tier in the system, but they have two important functions: first, they provide local democratic accountability; second, they are responsible for professional local monitoring of schools, teachers and policies. Regarding LEAs as a different kind of competitor in the marketplace is not acceptable. It is ironic that since 1997 an important performance indicator for LEAs has emerged – a willingness to co-operate with private firms. Competitive tendering has a place in local education, but care must be taken not to lose the benefit of professional knowledge and experience. For example, when a new school is to be built, the LEA is obliged to do all the preparatory work, at their expense, but then tenders are invited from private firms to take over. If a private firm is successful, they reap all the benefits of the LEA work, and may also be given the land for nothing.

A further disadvantage is that in a competitive market LEAs have to compete with each other rather than co-operate and share knowledge and experience. One of the fallacies of privatisation is that such professional experience can be pre-specified and packaged as a contract. In terms of cost, privatisation has tended to be more expensive (for example, they employ ex-LEA staff but pay them more). One of the weakest features of privatisation is that when an LEA takes over functions of another LEA, or a school takes over another school, they become, in effect, private firms, no longer part of the public system, but simply offering a commodity for a price.

Summary of New Labour's educational achievements and disappointments

The final verdict has to be a mixed one:

1 More money has been devoted to education; but not all of it has been used for the best educational purposes.
2 Standards, as measured by key stage tests, have improved but there are complaints about the narrowing of the curriculum, especially harming the arts and creative work.
3 Citizenship education has been the most important achievement, educationally, of New Labour.
4 There has been some relaxation of the tight central control of teacher education, but the work of TTA and OfSTED is still too intrusive.
5 Some progress has been made on reforming provision for the 14–19 age group, but Labour has been timid, especially in relation to examinations.
6 Higher education has received some more funding but not nearly enough, and this has produced problems and has prevented the policy of extending higher education to a bigger proportion of the age group, especially working-class boys and girls.

More seriously, there have been contradictions, U-turns and broken promises.

U-turns and inconsistencies

Primary education

There had been a promise to abolish key stage testing and league tables. In fact, there were more tests, more league tables, and more standard setting for individual schools.

Secondary education

The promise to incorporate the remaining grammar schools into the comprehensive system and to abolish selection was not kept. Instead, the government established impossible hurdles to be overcome in the balloting of parents before grammar schools could be converted into non-selective schools. Worse still, the amount of selection increased: the government embarked on a policy of specialist schools, beacon schools and more faith schools, all of which encouraged the growth of a 'multi-tier system' of secondary education rather than a policy of good schools in all areas. This was associated with incorrect judgements about the quality of comprehensive schools. New Labour ignored their continuing record of improvement; the use of such language as 'bog-standard' comprehensives was not only insulting but did not correspond with research findings.

The promise in opposition to take action on 'A' levels and narrow the gap between academic and vocational courses was not kept: in office, a much less ambitious policy of tinkering with 'A' levels was adopted. The government seemed to have an obsession about retaining traditional tests and qualifications.

The major contradiction was, however, paying lip-service to 'social justice' and 'inclusion' whilst encouraging market ideas and selection which necessarily involved having losers as well as winners.

Independent schools, are, as Barber has clearly shown, no longer one of Labour's traditional problems: they are now to be treated as a national asset to be exploited. Integration without any loss of privilege for the wealthy. Such a change is only possible by greatly weakening social justice as a fundamental principle.

Higher education

Before the election a promise was made about no top-up fees, but after 1997 there was an immediate discussion of loans instead of grants.

Teacher education

A promise was made to abolish TTA; in fact, it was strengthened and given more extensive powers.

Commercialisation/privatisation

So great has been the programme of commercialisation embarked upon by New Labour that it constitutes a serious departure from what prospective voters were led to expect in the 1997 manifesto and election speeches. It is probably the most serious departure from Labour values and policies in education.

The only excuse for so many changes of policy since 1994 would be if there really existed a coherent 'Third Way' in education which was acceptable to the Party and the country. There are many problems about the 'Third Way'. First, does it exist or is it disguised Toryism or Thatcherism as Clyde Chitty (2002) suggested? If there is a 'Third Way' what exactly does it mean, especially as applied to education? I shall look at these questions in detail at the beginning of Chapter 12, as a way of examining possible future policies in education.

Conclusion

It is important for any political party to take account of social, economic and technological change. It is also essential for a party to hold on to its fundamental values and principles. There may be a problem of deciding whether changes in policy represents abandoning certain values or merely developing new means of achieving them. For the Labour Party high priority has always been accorded to social justice or fairness or equal worth. It would be difficult for any Labour politician to propose abandoning that fundamental value. But a government might point towards it as a fundamental value but at the same time introduce policies that steered away from it.

I suggest that this is what has happened to New Labour and education since 1994. Blair and some of his colleagues still pay lip-service to 'equal worth' but in practice they have substantially moved away from the ideal of a common educational experience for all, with a common curriculum in non-selective schools. What they seem to want instead of a comprehensive system is a hierarchy of schools descending in cost and often quality from independent schools to grammar schools to beacon schools, 'advanced' specialist schools to less prestigious specialist schools to the kind of secondary school they would never send their own children to.

These basic value changes are 'compensated' for by attempting to raise 'standards' in all schools by a culture of targets, testing and league tables. Such a system is being increasingly commercialised and privatised to fit in with New Labour's vision of modernisation in education.

Inequality of access to worthwhile education is accepted cynically and disguised by talk of meritocracy (a completely non-socialist concept as Michael Young (1958) demonstrated).

These policies represent such a betrayal of fundamental values that the New Labour educational programme 1997–2001 should not be allowed to continue without radical changes. Chapter 12 will examine some alternative policies which would retain the fundamental values of the Party.

12 The future of Labour education 2001–10 and beyond

Targets or worthwhile learning?

Labour policy has been a bastard Thatcherism: league-tables, bloated CEOs, privatisation, 'choice' in the public sector . . . These policies have now landed the Party in the mire, where it is sinking fast: not just because as policies they are unpopular, but because the absence of the Conservative Party as a serious competitor has relieved Labour of the need to give its policies ideological and political coherence, and because the Labour Party, even New Labour, has a collective memory which cannot be expunged. Bastard Thatcherism, therefore, has been modified in ways which render it more palatable to MPs but even more incoherent. Nevertheless, in this combination of bastard Thatcherism and collective memory, it is bastard Thatcherism which the present leadership of the Party obviously favours.

(McKibbin, 2003)

Nevertheless, New Labour persisted in its ideological presentation of Britain as a meritocracy where even the socially excluded could rise into the middle class. Blair commented early in 1999 in a speech to the IPPR that his government had a ten-year programme to tackle poverty and social exclusion: 'At the end of it, I believe we will have an expanded middle class and ladders of opportunity for those of all backgrounds. No more ceilings that prevent people from achieving the success they merit.'

(Tomlinson, 2001, p. 131)

Introduction

The purpose of this chapter is to discuss the future of Labour Party education policies. I will begin by an examination of the Labour Party manifesto for the general election 2001. This will be followed by a discussion of the 'Third Way' and its application to education. I will then look towards the future of education and the Labour Party, beginning with a critical evaluation of how New Labour has tackled or proposed to tackle four educational issues: (1) equality and education; (2) assessment and selection; (3) the comprehensive ideal and independent schools; and (4) citizenship education and changing the culture of schools. Finally, I will look forward to other possible future Labour policies in education.

As a result of John Smith's death and Tony Blair's election to the leadership of the Labour Party in 1994, those who represented a more enlightened view of education lost out to political and educational advisers such as Michael Barber and Andrew Adonis whose educational ideas were mainly technicist, managerial and of doubtful acceptability from a socialist point of view. The Blair notion of modernisation and the 'Third Way' was antagonistic to the comprehensive ideal, accepting instead selection for secondary schools, setting and streaming and an emphasis on targets, testing and league tables, as well as consumerist choice. Worst of all, the government embraced commercialisation and privatisation with increasing enthusiasm.

There were some positive achievements in 1997–2001: for example, more nursery places, more money for education, and some curriculum improvements – especially citizenship education. But Blair and his education team had swallowed too much of the Conservative propaganda on education to make their programme acceptable to socialists. Ann Taylor's carefully planned programme in her Commission on Education (originally set up by John Smith), which had been widely discussed and approved within the Party, was pushed aside. The Party was still seriously divided on education, but for the moment quiescent.

Events and ideas leading up to the election 2001, including the election manifesto

Blair's pre-election speeches

In February 2001 Blair made a policy speech during a visit to a north London school. He took the opportunity to outline his agenda for the future after the May election that he was confident of winning. The speech was concerned with policies in general, but taking place as it did in a school, much of the text dealt with education. One promise was the 'modernisation' of the comprehensive system. Specialist schools would be doubled over a 5-year period reaching a total of 1,500 by 2006, when they would form 40 per cent of all secondary schools. New specialist schools for engineering, science and business would be included. Blair also said that he wanted more partnership between public and private sectors in the provision of services – including education. This was seen as a decision not to disturb the existence of independent schools as a separate sector.

Only four days later Blair made another speech, specifically on education, when addressing headteachers at No. 10. This was on the same day as the publication of the Green Paper, *Schools: Building on Success*, and covered much of the same ground – see below.

Schools: Building on Success *(February 2001)*

The Green Paper began with a list of the government's claims for success: the Sure Start pre-school programme; literacy and numeracy strategies; smaller infant class size; *Excellence in Cities*; Education Action Zones; specialist schools; the expansion of ICT; the General Teaching Council; the National College for School Leadership; increased pay for teachers who passed the threshold test; Advanced Skills Teachers; many more teaching assistants and mentors.

The future would concentrate on secondary education. The Green Paper proceeded with an outline of four key points: first, 'diversity must become the norm, not the exception'. Private and voluntary sectors would be encouraged to run schools on a contract basis. Second, to concentrate on early secondary years, especially those pupils joining without adequate basic skills. For them the literacy and numeracy strategies would be extended to the 11–14 age range. Third, the expansion of vocational education: new vocational GCSEs, and greater curriculum 'flexibility'. And 'more challenging academic pathways, including acceleration to GCSE and a broader curriculum for the more able'. Fourth, successful schools would be given greater autonomy, red tape would be cut for those schools demonstrating success. In addition, there was a conciliatory statement about the important role of Local Education Authorities, and the need to work with and reward teachers.

Ambitions for Britain: Labour's manifesto 2001

The manifesto was also intended to celebrate the past four years as well as to make promises about the next term and beyond. The Prime Minister's opening remarks mentioned 'ten goals for 2010' that included two on education: 'Expanded higher education as we raise standards in secondary schools' and 'Opportunities for all children' (p. 3). Then pages 6 and 7 are headed 'Investment and reform' and include sections specifically on education.

We will now:

- Ensure every secondary school develops a distinctive mission including specialist schools.
- Diversify state schools with new City Academies and more church schools.
- Direct more money to headteachers, more freedom for successful schools.
- Reform provision for 11–14 year olds to ensure higher standards in English, maths, science and information technology.
- Introduce new vocational options from 14 onwards with expanded apprenticeship opportunities.
- Ensure primary schools offer more chance to learn languages, music and sport, as well as higher standards in the basics.
- Provide a good quality nursery place for every three-year-old.

Under a separate heading 'Renewing Public Services: More Frontline Staff', another promise was made.

We will now deliver:

- 10,000 more teachers. Invest in further rapid promotion and rewards for classroom excellence, more classroom assistants and help with housing costs in high-cost areas.

Finally, the manifesto listed 25 steps to 'a better Britain' which included four on education:

- basic skills for 750,000 people
- every secondary school with a distinct ethos, mission or centre of excellence
- recruit an extra 10,000 teachers
- more power to frontline staff.

This manifesto was seen by many educationists as a continuation of the technicist, managerialist kind of modernisation rather than a new vision of education and society.

The 'Third Way' or bastard Thatcherism?

The Election in 2001 confirmed and strengthened several changes of policy since 1994 which, as I mentioned in Chapter 11, could only be regarded as legitimate if they constituted a coherent 'Third Way' education programme, consistent with Labour values. Some readers may feel that I dismissed the 'Third Way' all too quickly in Chapter 11. It is a complex issue, so I will spend some time in this chapter examining the case against the 'Third Way' more carefully.

Some rejected the 'Third Way' concept as meaningless. Others questioned its application to education as anything more than disguised Thatcherism: for example, Clyde Chitty (2002) condemns the 'continuities' between the Thatcher and Major governments and the policies after 1997. In some respects, Chitty complains, Blair has gone further in the direction of selection and privatisation than either Thatcher or Major. Can this be justified in terms of a genuine 'Third Way'?

What is the 'Third Way'?

One answer was provided by Blair himself in a Fabian pamphlet published in 1998. In that pamphlet there are some new ideas and arguments that should be carefully examined rather than dismissed out of hand. For example, Giddens (2002) has pointed out that the 'Third Way' is not simply a British phenomenon but has been accepted, in some form, by a variety of European countries, including Sweden, Germany and, more reluctantly, France.

I would now like to try to summarise the 'Third Way', as I understand it. I say 'as I understand it' because in my view Blair's pamphlet is not entirely free from ambiguities and inconsistencies (for example, on p. 3 Blair says that values are not absolute, but a few pages further on he also says that they are 'unshakeable'). What I want to do is to present his argument as fairly as I can in a precis, and then to attempt to apply the 'Third Way' to education.

Blair (1998): The 'Third Way'

Blair begins by reaffirming his belief in fundamental social values: democracy, liberty, social justice, mutual obligation and internationalism. He asserts that the 'Third Way' is not a matter of splitting the difference between right and left, neo-liberal capitalism and traditional social democracy. It is a creative partnership between public and private enterprise, based on the assumption of no necessary conflict between the two. It rests on four core values:

- equal worth for all members;
- opportunity for all;
- responsibility;
- community.

All four values are essential for a good, strong society. He stresses that 'What matters is what works' should not be seen as value-free pragmatism but as an application of the four values to real life situations and choices in the modern world. He claims that in the past the Labour Party tended to over-play rights of citizens and to ignore corresponding responsibilities. This distorted society, especially the Welfare State. In the 'Third Way', partnership with private enterprise will be involved, where appropriate, regulated where necessary. The market envisaged is not a free market.

Blair's exposition does not, however, solve the problem. There are several unresolved difficulties – especially some concerning education. Giddens (2002), who was writing in support of Blair's 'Third Way', in a much longer analysis of the thesis, includes a number of implied criticisms that apply to education (in addition to general complaints about too much spin): Giddens recommends that New Labour needs to develop a stronger model of 'the good society' and an ideology that would guide future policies. This was certainly true about education. Giddens also mentioned specific weak policies such as post-school education.

Raymond Plant (2001) also made a telling point about ends and means. Blair likes to give the impression that he is still committed to basic Labour values (the ends) but wants to modernise by changing the means. Plant suggests that it is not quite that easy. For example, the problem of means and ends in the case of comprehensive education. It is quite possible that some educational ideas like the comprehensive school may be seen as a means by Blair but as an end in its own right by Labour educationists who not only have a stronger view of social justice than some Blairites but also have a clear view of the comprehensive ideal.

Blair has stated that sometimes his four values might come into conflict with each other, but he does not say by which principles he would resolve such conflicts. How strong is his commitment to social justice in education or 'equal worth' in his terminology? Most politicians claim to believe in social justice, but what does it mean in practice? How strong is their belief when it conflicts with other values such as 'freedom of choice'? (Crosland found that a difficult question to answer; Blair does not seem to have yet asked the question.)

We must, however, first ask whether Blair's four core values are adequate, especially in terms of educational policy. To some extent he is in tune with well accepted versions of educational philosophy. The way Blair uses 'equal worth' is very like the concept of respect for persons discussed by Richard Peters in *Ethics and Education* (1966). 'Opportunity for all' is equally acceptable. And I can think of few educationists who would object to emphasising 'responsibilities' as well as rights: this has been part of educational discourse for a long time.

It is easy to accept a list of values in isolation; the difficulty arises when one value comes into conflict with another, and a decision has to be made about which takes priority. Blair gives no guidance about principles for establishing such priorities. In addition, it will be important to have clearer definitions of the four core values with some examples. This may help in the process of establishing priorities. But it is more likely that every case of one value being preferred over another will have to be argued out individually. Without this, policies may be established simply by personal taste, rather than by any process that would stand up to careful public scrutiny. Even if there were complete agreement about the meaning of both 'equal worth' and 'opportunities for all', there would still be a problem in English society (much more so than in many other countries): that is, the tradition of upper-class parents buying educational privileges for their children. This practice has often been justified, implicitly or explicitly, in terms of liberty – the right to spend money for the benefit of one's own children. From current evidence it would seem that Blair wishes to resolve the conflict by favouring freedom rather than social justice.

There are so many examples of conflicting value situations that it may be more useful to establish educational policies individually by arguing the strength of value components compared with other values in each case. In other words, a list of four values is not enough; and when it comes to making decisions about a contentious issue such as comprehensive education, it becomes necessary to specify the strength of any values involved in the decision making. Throughout the history of the Labour Party, social justice has been regarded as a fundamental value, but individuals and groups have attached greater or lesser strength to that value compared with other priorities such as economic efficiency in the case of Sidney Webb or freedom of choice in the case of Tony Crosland.

Despite Blair's first core value being 'equal worth' it would seem from post-1997 policies that social justice, as it is normally understood, is *not* the top priority.

Seeing social justice as a relatively weak value has nothing to do with 'modernisation': that view of secondary education (that is, one involving selection and segregation), was, as we saw in Chapters 1 and 2, a feature of Sidney Webb and other early Fabians. Their view of social justice stretched as far as 'education for all' but still accepted the idea of much better quality education for a few who would travel up the ladder of opportunity into the world of a higher social class. It would seem from Blair's use of such terms as 'meritocracy' and 'ladder of opportunity' that he has departed from the traditional Labour value of social justice expressed in the metaphor of 'the broad highway'. He has reverted to a pre-comprehensive model of secondary education involving not only differentiation (which is desirable within the comprehensive scheme) but also to methods of selection which are contrary to the principle of 'equal worth'. I shall return to this discussion later in the chapter.

The 'Third Way' or 'Webb's Way'?

I began this chapter by being doubtful about the wholesale application of some aspects of the 'Third Way' to education. Blair's 'Third Way' in education shares a number of features with Sidney Webb's way: too much bureaucratic planning and control (targets and testing in primary and secondary schools); a high degree of central control of teacher education; and expansion of higher education as a greater priority than other forms of 'lifelong education'. And although this is nowhere stated explicitly, New Labour's liking for selection and specialist schools must rely on a view of aptitude and intelligence far closer to Webb and the eugenicists of the early twentieth century than would be acceptable by psychologists and educationists today. Far from being a modernised view of secondary education, some of the New Labour plans outlined in 2001 (summarised above) are extremely old-fashioned and unscientific. Blair's acceptance of meritocracy and the 'ladder of opportunity' are particularly objectionable.

In its present form, the 'Third Way' in education will not do as a set of policies, not least because it conflicts with fundamental Labour values; and it is not acceptable pragmatically because it does not work. There is no evidence to show that privatising schools and educational services is more efficient.

The future of Labour education

Throughout this book I have suggested that Labour education policies should be related to a vision of a better society. Failure to do this may account for many of the disappointments of Labour administrations, including 1997 onwards. It might be suggested that Blair provided something like a new vision when he abolished the traditional clause 4 of the Labour Party constitution. The change included a commitment to socialism, which had not been part of the 1918 clause 4, and went on to advocate 'a community in which power, wealth and opportunity were in the hands of the many not the few'. This is hardly a comprehensive vision of a better society and is somewhat vague, but even as it stands, it suggests more than Blair's educational policies as described in Chapter 11 and summarised earlier in this chapter. Future Labour education policies must aim at something much more ambitious than what has been achieved so far. This will not be possible until 'bastard Thatcherism' is replaced by policies that are compatible with truly democratic values. Before outlining how that might be achieved, I would like to discuss four specific problems of British education which have not yet been solved by the Labour Party.

New Labour: modernisation and education – four issues and problems

At this stage it may be useful to look at a number of key controversial educational issues involved in New Labour educational initiatives. A key concept for 'Third Way' education is modernisation: for New Labour how could it be otherwise? Perhaps modernisation takes priority even over the four core values? Blair has claimed that modernisation is not to be achieved at the cost of losing fundamental Labour principles. I would like to re-visit New Labour education policies in order to test whether modernisation of the Blair kind has been consistent with Labour values, and also the extent to which changes will be necessary in the future.

There are several problem areas that need to be discussed in the context of the educational modernisation programme since 1997. I will discuss them in the following order:

1   equality and education;
2   assessment and selection;
3   the comprehensive ideal (and the problem of independent schools);
4   citizenship education and changing school culture.

1 Equality and education

How do the core values of equal worth and opportunities for all fit in with Blair's educational policies? Social justice and equality of opportunity are well established Labour values, but it has not always been clear how they work in practice. For R.H. Tawney equality was a basic principle for socialism, and he sometimes despaired of it ever being achieved – especially in education. Later in the twentieth century, Tony Crosland also struggled to find a solution to the education and equality paradox. He failed. What about Tony Blair?

It is clear that in education equality of opportunity is not enough. On the other hand, equality of outcome in education is impossible: it would be immoral to hold back the most able to the level of the slowest learner, and some students will want to pursue a subject in greater depth than the average – is this to be forbidden? Clearly no. It is differentiation of a desirable kind. That is not the real problem. In education as far as outcomes are concerned the sky must be the limit. The problem is not at the outcome end but at the beginning. Some children start with parents with more cultural capital, as well as money, and will probably be given better qualified teachers: in England for a long time this was the educational norm. But in a democratic society we need some kind of positive discrimination. It is difficult to decide how much and what kind.

The Education Priority Areas project arising out of the Plowden Report was based on the idea of positive discrimination – that is, identifying 'deprived areas' and spending more money on their primary schools. To treat unequals equally cannot be accepted as fair treatment.

The trouble in England is that the whole tradition in education is against positive discrimination. The children of the rich are given better schools (either in fee paying schools or in well equipped schools in leafy suburbs) which have little difficulty in attracting good teachers. To some extent the balance could have been redressed on the Educational Priority Areas principle (which was unfortunately terminated by Thatcher). There is no evidence that any of the new policies, for example, Education Action Zones, is a successful application of the idea of positive discrimination. They have, unfortunately, been distracted by conflicting ideas of commercialisation and privatisation.

At the same time we must also accept the need for positive discrimination at other points in the educational process, for example, university entrance. In the year 2000 and later, Bristol and other universities were quite right to say that a boy from Eton with four A grades at advanced level is probably not as good *potentially* as a student with exactly the same grades from a comprehensive school in a deprived area. To apply positive discrimination in this way is both fair and efficient (research has shown that the high scoring boy or girl from a comprehensive is likely to be better as a long-term bet academically than one from an independent school whose success probably owes more to smaller classes and better resources, rather than superior brain power.

Equality of opportunity may not be enough (as Crosland observed) but equality of achievement is neither possible nor desirable. It is not possible because individuals do have different personalities, partly innate, and in any kind of achievement – sporting, academic, artistic – some have 'natural' talents which should be encouraged rather than limited. To stifle interests and potential is anti-educational (even if widely practised). It is also undesirable to deny any child the good luck of having parents who support and assist the educational process rather than impede it. But one function of state education at all levels should be to try to bring out the potential of those who are not so fortunate as, for example, the son or daughter of a Prime Minister.

Unfortunately, most education systems manage to do the opposite: pursuing the policy of 'unto those that have, more shall be given'. So the Prime Minister's son was not sent to the nearest school but to one chosen partly for its academic record. The teachers understandably made sure that he received a 'fair' share of individual attention, and when 'A' level time approached, he was sent for private tuition just to make sure. This can be put down to good fortune – in other respects he may have had some disadvantages. Such variations of good fortune are inevitable but the school task should be to apply discrimination on the side of the less fortunate. This is extremely difficult to enforce, but it should be accepted as a part of the school's mission. Perfect justice may be impossible but we should aim at achieving as much as we can. For many schools this will require a dramatic change of ethos. It will also require a revision of some organisational practices, especially those involving selection. As well as having appropriate forms of positive discrimination, we should be careful to avoid introducing hurdles which are, in effect, ways of benefiting those who are already privileged. The Blair plan for retaining selection for grammar schools in some areas and for increasing the number of specialist schools does not meet the requirement of social justice as a value.

That may be where assessment comes into the plan. And it is here that New Labour or 'Third Way' policies need re-thinking.

2 Assessment and selection

It is useful to make a distinction between two kinds of assessment: professional and bureaucratic. Professional assessment is used by teachers to improve the performance of their pupils; bureaucratic assessment is demanded by an authority for purposes of control and accountability. Both are legitimate if used wisely; but it is generally agreed by informed observers, including OfSTED, that bureaucratic assessment has been over-used in recent years, especially since the Education Reform Act (1988), when the national curriculum and the proposed assessment of all ten subjects would have made the English system the most centrally controlled in the world. In 1993, however, teachers boycotted the key stage tests and the Conservative government sought the assistance of Ron Dearing in simplifying the national curriculum itself as well as the testing process. The result was an improvement, but since 1997, the demands of targets and testing have been excessive. So much so that school assessment was quoted by Professor O'Neill (2002), in her Reith Lectures as a good example of over-accountability replacing trust in society to the detriment of professionals and their clients.

This distortion of assessment need not have happened. After 1988, the Task Group for Attainment and Testing (TGAT), chaired by Professor Paul Black produced an enlightened model of national curriculum assessment, but it was misused by the Conservative politicians and became a bureaucratic nightmare for teachers.

There were two main reasons for this error: first, the national curriculum itself was too detailed and over specific; second, the Conservative government wanted to use national curriculum assessment as a means of providing data to help parents choose schools in a quasi-market situation. That is, the assessment data was used to produce league tables putting schools in a supposed rank order, on the assumption that parents would choose only 'good' schools and that eventually poor schools would be driven out of the market.

This was a missed opportunity: the TGAT model could have been accepted to enable teachers to use assessment professionally and also provide useful bureaucratic data. But the combination of an over-prescriptive national curriculum and the quasi-market distorted the relation between curriculum and assessment, and prevented teachers using the assessment data professionally, for the benefit of the pupils. It may not be too late to put this right. The original intention of TGAT was that assessment should be used to monitor pupils' achievement and to provide useful feedback to pupils about their progress. Paul Black and his colleagues had specifically distinguished between using average scores for an age group as norms and their use as a pass/fail borderline. Pupils would be graded into 'levels' but a level covered, on average, a two-year period of development. Politicians, however, insisted on the concepts of pass and fail, that were needed for league tables, in their opinion, and what had been intended to be useful guidelines indicating individual pupil's progress was transformed into a means of establishing targets for schools and for the nation as a whole. Professional assessment had been sacrificed in order to produce not only bureaucratic, managerial data, but also to provide parents with 'evidence' on which to base their choice of schools. After 1997, the Labour government should have remedied this practice, but they have aggravated the problem.

SELECTION

One of the tasks of a schooling system is to educate and train future leaders. In an expanding capitalist economy it is necessary to do more than merely replace existing workers because expansion makes various institutions hungry for more and more of those with the required skills, capabilities and qualifications.

Servicing the labour market is an important function of the education system in a modern industrial society. But it is not the only one and it is not the most important. Educating the young so that they become well-rounded individuals who can live in, and contribute to, a good society is more important. The idea of educating individuals for work, to be citizens and to become (in Bruner's term) 'more human' is a simplified model but it can serve usefully to contrast the popular view that schools exist mainly to prepare the young for work. This three-dimensional model can be a socialist model, provided that we define the individual, citizenship and the good society in appropriate ways.

What has this to do with selection? In an education system dominated by the labour market, there will be a tendency for the system to select early in order to begin the process of 'allocation', that is, channelling young people towards certain qualifications and jobs. That kind of selection may be inevitable but if it begins too early it is not only unfair but inefficient.

If selection of any kind takes place early, the danger is that of mistaking achievement for real potential, giving better chances to those selected and allowing ultimate success to be a self-fulfilling prophecy. This is both unfair and inefficient: it is unfair because early selection will tend to discriminate against those from the lower social classes, and some kinds of minority groups;

it is inefficient because early selection does not necessarily choose those who are potentially the best.

Socialists tend to be more impressed by the 'fairness' argument, and that is one reason why they oppose 11+ testing for secondary schools or testing at any age which makes irreversible decisions in education, that is, eliminating later choices. Non-socialists (and some in the Labour Party, for example, Sidney Webb) have been more concerned about economic efficiency – that is, selecting the best candidates for certain kinds of jobs which will improve our international competitiveness. But the research does not support that point of view.

Eventually some individuals will end up as high earners in high status jobs and others will earn less in jobs requiring less ability. That is inevitable. But in a good society, schools will make that process as fair as possible; they will also do as much as they can to preserve the principle of 'equal worth' for all pupils and all adults. A good society will also make sure that the gap between the highest earners and the lowest is not too great.

Since 1997 not only has the gap between rich and poor widened (with Tony Blair refusing to apologise for this) but also the New Labour plans for secondary schools will undoubtedly result in children being selected for places in a hierarchy of schools of very different quality. This means that Blair is failing to live up to his own stated value of 'equal worth'.

3   The comprehensive ideal (and the problem of independent schools)

Two aspects of the comprehensive ideal have been partly explored above in the sections on equality, and assessment and selection. The two sections also explain why Raymond Plant (2001) was correct in suggesting why for many Labour Party educationists the comprehensive school was more than a means to an end, but should be considered to be an end in itself (see discussion on the 'Third Way' earlier in this chapter). A socialist education policy must prefer a strong version of social justice and non-selective secondary schools.

Blair and his colleagues, however, have moved away from the comprehensive ideal and reverted to education based on 'meritocracy' and the out-of-date model of the 'ladder of opportunity' favoured by Sidney Webb in 1902 as part of his 'capacity-catching' machine. I have used the word 'ideal' in the title of this section because it is about more than the problems of comprehensive schools or what to do about the Independent Schools and the remaining grammar schools.

At this point it may be helpful to put the English debate into an historical and international context. (Interestingly the same problems hardly exist in Wales and Scotland where comprehensive education has been accepted as Labour policy.)

By the second half of the nineteenth century the 'common school' was spreading rapidly throughout the USA; by the 1920s the comprehensive high school was established in all states of the USA. At the same time in England the situation was quite different. Why? The answer is that the US was building state systems of education from scratch, whereas in England there was a long tradition of 'secondary' schools (that is, public schools plus grammar schools) for small elite or potentially elite groups. In England discussions about secondary education inevitably looked backwards rather than forward.

In 1926, prompted by R.H. Tawney and others within the Labour movement, the Hadow Committee produced a report recommending secondary education for all, but they were unclear about how the system should be organised. In 1938, the Spens Report, on the basis of the elite tradition of education plus some very shaky psychological evidence, recommended what became known as the 'tripartite' system of grammar, technical and modern secondary schools for children with supposedly different kinds of minds.

This completely unscientific view was reinforced in 1943 by the Norwood Committee (which was, as we saw in Chapter 3, much criticised by the Labour Party and others). In 1944 the Education Act remained neutral about comprehensive schools; and in 1945 the Labour government missed the opportunity of giving a decisive lead when it implemented the 1944 policy of 'secondary education for all'. For a while the Party was distracted from the goal of comprehensive secondary education by the false hope of parity of esteem for all three kinds of school. When it became clear that parity was impossible for social reasons, then the comprehensive solution became official Labour policy.

The debate continued throughout the 1950s and 1960s, but by the late 1960s it seemed that the battle had been won. From 1970 to 1974 Margaret Thatcher as Education Secretary, agreed to more and more LEA comprehensive plans.

A reaction was, however, building up inside the Conservative Party, and spreading gradually to the media. James Callaghan, as Prime Minister 1976–79, has been blamed for taking heed of this reactionary propaganda and 'stealing the Tories' clothes', criticising education generally and questioning the success of comprehensive schools. Despite the fact that the evidence showing the general success of comprehensive schools was and is strong, the Conservative attack continued during the Thatcher and Major years. More surprisingly, it has continued into the New Labour regime since 1997.

By the mid-1970s comprehensive secondary education was generally, but not totally, accepted in the Conservative Party as well as in the Labour Party. What has happened since then?

There are at least three answers to that question. First, the Black Papers expressed the views within the right wing of the Conservative Party that had been lying dormant but never completely extinguished, namely, a belief that true secondary education should be the preserve of the few rather than the majority. Second, during the Thatcher–Major years, every opportunity was taken by the right wing to criticise schools and teachers generally, and to compare comprehensive schools with the higher standards of education in pre-comprehensive days. Third, the idea of choice was used by those favouring the retention of grammar schools. The fact that choice was largely illusory and that the most that parents could expect was the right to express a preference for a school was disguised in the rhetoric of market solutions. Once choice had been introduced, however, it was probably irreversible: no government could in future propose that 'choice' would be abolished. This was not a good reason for continuing the deception and pretending to offer more choice than could possibly be delivered. The sensible route for the Labour Party in 1997 was what had been promised by Ann Taylor following her Commission on Education – abolishing league tables and playing down choice without eliminating it completely. This could have been accompanied by a campaign to restore public confidence in our schools and teachers. Research shows that the continued criticisms of the comprehensive plan (as opposed to some individual schools) cannot be justified. Standards are high and still rising. The New Labour attack on comprehensive schools is strangely ideological – the ideology of the 'Third Way' which appears to believe that private is better than public, and that selection is more important than a common culture.

An important feature of the comprehensive idea was the notion of devising a common curriculum suitable for all pupils in a modern democratic society. We saw in earlier chapters that long before Kenneth Baker embarked upon his national curriculum in 1988 there were several interesting attempts to devise a curriculum suitable for secondary education for all in comprehensive schools. One serious attempt was the 'entitlement curriculum' devised and piloted by Her Majesty's Inspectorate (HMI). The entitlement curriculum was based on the idea that if education is compulsory, then pupils have a right to expect a worthwhile education programme and that the essential aspects of a common curriculum should be nationally agreed.

The HMI entitlement curriculum (DES, 1975) was careful to avoid taking over the whole curriculum of any school because there should always be space left for individual and local needs and preferences. Unfortunately, the Baker national curriculum was so detailed and specific that there would have been little time left over after the requirements of the ten compulsory subjects (plus religious education) had been met.

It would be a pity if the mistakes of 1988 were allowed to discredit the whole idea of a common curriculum for comprehensive schools. The basic idea is sound and necessary. The common curriculum idea rests not only on the entitlement argument but also on the idea of common culture. Part of the advantage of a comprehensive school is that young people irrespective of class, religious or ethnic group, have educational experiences in common. The common curriculum is therefore much wider than the acquisition of academic knowledge.

The essential point is that the comprehensive school is not simply concerned with pupils attending the same school, but in sharing important aspects of human development in the process of growing up. Segregation by type of school is unhealthy in a democratic society, whether it is social selection by means of fee-paying in independent schools or intellectual selection and segregation in different types of secondary school. This is an essential part of the

Labour Party policy of a 'common educational highway' that is so different from Webb's 'ladder of opportunity' or Blair's 'specialist schools'.

As we have seen, Blair's views on education are meritocratic rather than socialist. Either he or his colleagues have not read Michael Young's *The Rise of the Meritocracy* (1958), or they have failed to understand its ironic conclusion. Tony Blair, David Blunkett and, more recently, Estelle Morris, have all used the word 'meritocracy' as though it were an accepted feature of Labour educational philosophy. This is totally incorrect. At the height of the debate about comprehensive schools and grammar schools Michael Young (1958) wrote his book as a fascinating account – a fable – of what would happen in a society that ran its educational system on the principle of IQ plus effort equals merit, selecting those for a different kind of education by means of intelligence tests and evidence of hard work. Far from this being a solution to the educational problem of allocating students into differential career possibilities, the result was clearly a nightmare: a society in which the whole of social life was dominated by one aspect of human performance. The main reason for Young's rejection of 'meritocracy' was that it elevated one aspect of human life and development into a supreme arbiter. This not only resulted in all kinds of unfairness, but also impoverished human life, ignoring artistic and creative abilities. Since 1958 Young's position on meritocracy has been greatly strengthened by recent developments on the nature of intelligence such as Howard Gardner (1984) *Frames of Mind* which showed that the intellectual aspects of development are by no means the most important for success in life. Another line of research (Goleman, 1996), argued that emotional intelligence is even more important. The main point is, however, that to replace social selection by intellectual selection would only be a partial step towards a better society. The socialist vision of a good society involves treating all citizens and future citizens with equal respect, socially, legally and educationally. Blair quotes 'equal worth' as one of his major values, but meritocracy is not compatible with that value, as Michael Young so clearly showed.

INDEPENDENT SCHOOLS

The problem of independent schools in England is quite different from the relationship between the state and education elsewhere in the world. It is an important problem for a number of reasons: first, although independent fee-paying schools only account for about 7 per cent of the age groups, they have disproportionate influence both on education policy, higher education, and access to the professions and other 'top jobs'. They are schools for the already privileged which are concerned to maintain and magnify those privileges. For example, the 7 per cent of 13-year-old boys (and girls) from independent schools manage to scoop almost 50 per cent of places at Oxford and Cambridge.

The Labour Party has always found this kind of social privilege objectionable in a democratic society. R.H. Tawney added a related argument that in England, state education was run by people who did not use its schools for their own children. He referred to this situation as a 'tragedy'.

A number of attempts have been made to find a solution to this English problem. The best opportunity was in World War II when rationing, social solidarity and genuine moves towards equality might have made many of what were then called 'Public Schools' amenable to some kind of democratic reform. As we saw in Chapter 3, however, the opportunity was missed – deliberately. Rab Butler excluded discussion of public schools from the 1944 Education Act by 'shunting the issue into a siding'. The Fleming Committee produced a rather half-hearted report recommending an impracticable form of integration involving LEAs buying places for less privileged pupils – at a time when every penny would be required for bringing the maintained schools up to a better standard.

Very little use was made of the Fleming proposals and the public schools gradually regained their pre-war position of dominance and privilege. Tony Crosland saw the injustice of the situation in *The Future of Socialism* but did not propose a solution of any kind; instead he set up the Public Schools Commission which produced its First Report in 1968. The committee was chaired by Sir John Newsom. The terms of reference focused on the word 'integration', and the Commission, unfortunately, failed to reach a unanimous decision. The majority report rejected the idea of 'outright integration'. The report was excellent in its compilation of statistics and other information, but it did not come up with a solution that was acceptable in 1968.

The Second Report of the Commission, chaired by Professor David Donnison, reported on direct grant schools in 1970, and encouraged the Education Secretary, Shirley Williams, to give the prestigious day schools the alternative of going completely independent or joining a comprehensive plan. Most chose the independent route; probably integration was never a serious consideration.

The problem did not go away and continued to be a subject for discussion in Labour left-wing circles. It should, however, be part of any future Labour Party secondary education reform.

There are several issues and principles involved. First, independent schools certainly offend against the principles of social justice, or fairness or 'equal worth'. However, they cannot simply be abolished: that would offend too starkly against the principle of individual liberty. Although it is quite possible to mount a good argument that freedom is always relative and that for the sake of the common good, England would be a more democratic place without independent schools, simply to try to abolish them, would be a political non-starter and we must find a compromise of some kind.

The compromise should tackle two related problems. The first problem is that it is undesirable in a democratic society for an affluent social elite to have their children educated in a way that segregates them from the rest of the community. Somehow, independent schools should be encouraged to admit a large proportion of pupils from non-elite backgrounds. The second problem is that public school pupils tend to be admitted to prestigious universities in much greater numbers than is fair. This may be an easier problem to solve.

University admissions tutors can be helped to make reasonably accurate assessments of how far students' 'superiority' should be attributed to their school rather than their ability. This would have a double advantage: first, making independent schools less attractive to ambitious parents (and a doubtful investment). Second, it would reduce the domination of top universities by the public school ethos as well as by its products. This reform of university admissions should go even further. All universities should be invited to reconsider their mission in terms of the kind of students they want to accept. Limiting admission to any department to, say, four A's at 'A' level is a relatively new idea, and is not necessarily a good one. Some universities now even claim that they would like to restrict admissions even further – to the top 4 or 5 per cent of sixth formers. Why? They have developed this policy as a result of supply and demand for places but it is very naive to believe that there is any way that an examination can infallibly make such discriminations. And by what right, apart from the market, do they demand to be so selective? It might well be better for a university to be more relaxed and take the top 10 or 20 per cent of students. This would not, of course, prevent some departments making specific requirements: it is reasonable, for example, for someone wishing to read physics to have reached a high standard in mathematics. But that is very different from current practices in Oxford, Cambridge or elsewhere. A review of admissions policies is over-due.

There is a third set of issues concerned with independent schools being boarding schools and efficient at substituting for absentee parents. It has even been claimed by the Independent Schools Council (ISC) that it would be cheaper to send children who are officially in the care of local authorities to boarding schools (with fees of about £18,000 p.a.) than to send them to children's homes where 75 per cent fail to achieve any qualifications at school. It cannot, however, be left to the independent schools to pick only very bright children in care and to leave the difficult cases to local authorities.

The solution to the independent schools problem is a mixture of regulation and kindly integration. I was once told by an ISC 'insider' that of all independent preparatory and senior schools, about 40 per cent were 'really not very good'. Before sending children in care to independent schools, they would have to be tested for quality. Requirements would include regular OfSTED inspections.

In fact, all independent schools should be regularly visited by OfSTED. It would also be important to take the opportunity of looking at their charitable status, and scrutinising their charters. (Many, including some of the best known independent schools, were originally founded for the benefit of 'poor' scholars.) This combination of careful (but not excessive) regulation and useful integration could not only solve a long-standing problem but also indicate a truly beneficial public/private partnership. This would not be a total solution but would be a useful start, combined with other kinds of 'integration', but it would have to be stipulated that independent schools would not be allowed to accept only bright pupils: other criteria, including need, would be important. Gradually real integration would take place, but this should be on the basis of equality between private and public, unlike the Blair attempts to promote co-operation between the two sectors which gives the impression of independent schools volunteering to help out their weaker brethren. Independent schools, as well as universities, should be encouraged to adopt policies of 'inclusion', rather than to rest on their reputation for being exclusive institutions.

4 *Citizenship education and changing the culture of the school*

In Chapter 11, I drew attention to citizenship education as the outstanding idea, or set of ideas, generated in education during the period 1997–2001. Citizenship education is important for its intrinsic value, as well as its potential to exert a benevolent influence on the culture of schools and schooling. It is important in terms of curriculum, pedagogy and organisation and structure of schools. This last point has been neglected by New Labour. Official statistics tell us that 50,000 pupils on an average day are truanting. This, together with large numbers who are excluded from school indicate a problem of some kind. It is a paradox that in a democratic society that values education enough to make it compulsory, many young people apparently have no desire to benefit from what is offered them.

Additional evidence about the problem was provided by Michael Barber when he was Professor of Education at the University of Keele. He was involved in a study showing that many secondary school pupils were bored and disaffected with their schools to such an extent that their time at school was largely wasted. Part of the problem is that many schools are insufficiently demanding, but others manage to alienate their students by the authoritarian atmosphere of the school and very poor teacher–pupil relations. There are many studies showing that there are still too many schools that are inappropriate for the twenty-first century. This remains true despite those who have been involved in the 'improving schools' movement.

The basic problem is that in many respects the school is a nineteenth-century institution. The nineteenth-century school was one of several public institutions invented to solve social problems, especially in the rapidly developing urban areas. The institutions included prisons, workhouses and schools, all of which resembled factories in their organisation. Schools in particular have not always kept pace with the kinds of social change which should have transformed their organisation and ethos. Some are still authoritarian, unhappy places for young people. So much so that too many leave school as soon as they legally can (if not sooner); many who leave to work on monotonous routine tasks in dull factories still say they prefer going to work to staying at school.

What has this to do with citizenship education? The model of citizenship education which was proposed and accepted in 2000 was enlightened in several ways. First, citizenship education was defined so that it included not just knowledge about politics and citizenship but also active participation in democratic procedures inside the school as well as in the world outside. This will necessitate, for some schools, radical changes in their ethos and organisation. Second, citizenship education will, in this way, have a knock-on effect on many other aspects of educational procedures. If it does not, it will be a failure. It will be essential for Labour governments to understand the importance of this particular issue. Citizenship education must not become just another subject, but must be seen as central to the necessary transformation of schools into more moral and liberal teaching-learning environments. This kind of modernisation, however, is quite different from the technicist, managerialist approach adopted by New Labour 1997–2001.

The above four examples have illustrated some of the key ideas of democratic education and the problems that still face New Labour. There are others. At the level of principles and ideas, New Labour needs to focus much more on such important concepts as inclusion, culture and curriculum planning in the widest sense (that is, covering pedagogy as well as content and assessment). At the level of detailed policies there are several changes of direction needed that will be discussed in the next section.

An alternative education policy: a fourth way for the Labour Party?

I have referred several times to the need for the Labour Party to have a clearer vision of the future of education. This necessarily depends on a vision of a better society. Many others from R.H. Tawney to Tony Giddens have made this point. Some of the criticisms of New Labour and the 'Third Way' have been concerned with the fact that the fundamental ills of modern capitalist society have not been addressed. For example, 'tough on crime and tough on the causes of crime' makes a good soundbite but we have not seen New Labour politicians prepared to examine the underlying problems of modern society. New Labour has seemed to accept the greed and selfishness, intensified during the Thatcher years, rather than try to mitigate their influence. They have, for example, shied away from a policy of taxing the rich in order to redistribute wealth in an increasingly unequal society. Peter Mandelson is on record as saying that there was nothing wrong with being 'filthy rich', and Tony Blair appears to enjoy the company of the very rich. Part of the vision of a better society would be greater equality in that respect, as well as greater equality in education, as discussed above. A democratic Britain would enjoy much greater social justice in all aspects of life and there would be less emphasis on ever-increasing consumer goods and economic expansion. More attention would be paid to general quality of life, including concern for the environment. Lack of that kind of vision has encouraged New Labour to embark upon a policy for secondary education which will increase inequality rather than diminish it. They have failed to learn the fundamental lesson that if you encourage choice and differentiation there must be losers as well as winners in a competitive race to find the best schools. This cannot be concealed by pretending that the variety of schools proposed are different but equal. New Labour must also switch the emphasis of modernisation away from aspects of technical 'efficiency' to methods of making schools better, more humane, places of teaching and learning where the stress will be on teacher professionalism and a school ethos focusing on the quality of human development rather than measuring limited aspects of academic achievement.

These are some general principles for New Labour to follow. It may also be useful to spell out a few more examples, in addition to the four discussed above.

It is important that Labour learns from recent mistakes. They should move forward in ways consistent with fundamental values. There are several examples in this category: league tables were in tune with Tory policies emphasising competition and choice but not with Labour values of co-operation and community. On the other hand, parents are entitled to information about their schools according to the principle of open government. But any information should be carefully explained: raw data can be misleading. Above all, statistical information about schools should be used mainly for professional purposes and school improvement. Targets and testing are in a similar position to the league tables mistake. They need not be abolished completely but should be used with greater discrimination. Their misuse has overburdened teachers and resulted in an unacceptable 'culture of targets'.

In some ways New Labour's modernisation of education has been curiously old-fashioned. Teachers and headteachers were, for example, irritated by being instructed to introduce streaming, setting or fast-tracking as a means of differentiation. There are schools that cope with differentiation very successfully in unstreamed classes; there are others which practise streaming without success. What is needed is something much more sophisticated than crude methods such as streaming or setting which only provide very rough groups of ability. In schools in Western Australia, for example, each pupil has an individualised timetable allowing perhaps a pupil to be two years ahead of his age group in mathematics, one year ahead in science but average for most other subjects. With computerised timetabling this is no longer a difficult task and allows much great flexibility than streaming or setting without the disadvantage of labelling any pupil below average or backward. To instruct schools to stream or set is to attempt to deal with very complex questions of differentiation in a very simplistic way.

Commercialisation and privatisation by Conservatives has been 'tested to destruction' by New Labour. Most schemes described in Chapter 11 have failed and should be abolished. Only a few might be retained and kept under careful scrutiny: Education Action Zones might be in that category.

In Chapter 11, Peter Moss and others recommended much more planning of the education service as a whole. Although it is necessary to sub-divide education into phases such as early childhood, primary education, etc., we should always have in mind the concept of continuity or lifelong learning. For example, the present national curriculum is in a mess, partly because it was badly designed in 1988, and partly because the various modifications and 'improvements' have whittled away the principle of a common entitlement curriculum outlined earlier in this chapter. The Labour Party now has an opportunity to re-plan a 5–16 curriculum along democratic lines, incorporating the well-planned programme for citizenship education. The new curriculum should be closely related to a rational policy of assessment. Assessing the new national curriculum would need careful planning, incorporating the best aspects of the TGAT model but being careful to achieve a better balance between professional assessment and bureaucratic data collection which must be kept to a minimum, but not completely abandoned because some record-keeping is an essential feature of modern teaching and learning.

GCSE, GCE or a British baccalaureat? New Labour has been over-cautious in moving away from the 'A' level 'gold standard'. The IPPR proposals for a baccalaureat-style qualification was good when proposed, but could now be improved upon. Essential features of the reform would be, first, to blur the distinction between 'academic' and 'vocational'; second, to make sure that no qualification is a 'dead-end' (the principle of lifelong learning); and, third, encouraging as many young people as possible to continue with some form of worthwhile education and training beyond compulsory schooling. In that respect England is behind most Western European and North American countries, probably for reasons discussed above.

In higher education, the Labour Party is on the right lines in wanting a higher participation rate, especially for working-class students but there must be a clearer policy on university admissions systems, including an element of positive discrimination. The whole question of tuition fees, maintenance grants and student loans needs radical examination. Universities also need to develop much better links with their local communities.

Both Parties when in government have criticised and undermined the work of Local Education Authorities. Their functions need to be clarified and where appropriate strengthened. It should be remembered that LEAs have an important role in local democratic control of education. This has not always worked well in the past, but local democracy should be improved rather than weakened.

The education of teachers and teacher professionalism is of crucial importance in a modern education system. New Labour has paid lip-service to the professional development of teachers (and embarked upon some projects on Continuous Professional Development). But at the same time New Labour actions have served to de-professionalise teachers: for example, by emphasising the literacy and numeracy hours; it should be made clear that they are completely optional for schools and teachers. Another example is the imposition of crude versions of performance-related pay, ignoring the importance of professional team work. Another is the fact that the Teacher Training Agency is so powerful and sometimes too intrusive: it should either be abolished or become subordinate to the General Teaching Council. The behaviour of OfSTED to teachers, schools and university departments of education has improved enormously since the departure of Chief Inspector Woodhead, but such improvements should not be left to chance. Inspection is a useful service but professionalism should be respected. It is no exaggeration to assert that the key to school improvement is almost entirely dependent on the goodwill and professionalism of teachers.

I have not attempted to prescribe a completely modernised educational plan, I have merely set out a few principles that are in harmony with Labour Party values backed up by some specific examples. Any general plan must also bear in mind the need for schools to be given space to indulge in their own school-based curriculum planning and organisation. I have also not devoted much time to the information and computer technology aspects of modernisation – for two reasons. First, what is now available to schools changes so rapidly that any specific recommendations will be out of date by the time this book is published. Second, ICT is a very important feature of modernisation but it is not the most important: far more crucial are the questions of school organisation and the values underlying recommended changes which I have discussed extensively.

Conclusion

One of the gaps in Labour Party policies since 1900 has been the failure to appreciate the importance of education. At best in the early years education was treated as another social service making heavy demands on public spending. The job of the Prime Minister and Chancellor of the Exchequer was often to restrain the ambitions of the Minister of Education.

This changed with Callaghan who was genuinely interested in education but took the Labour Party in the wrong direction by imitating the Conservative complaints about schools and teachers. Blair has made a similar mistake, but on a more massive scale. He seems to have accepted the Conservative policies of Thatcherism, rather than developing a Labour policy which would put education at the centre of the Labour vision of a good society.

Postscript October 2003

One of the motives for writing this book was to examine the continuities and discontinuities of Labour Party ideologies and education policies from 1900 to 2001. My reading of key texts about Labour history confirmed my suspicion that the Labour Party was not only a broad church but also continued for over one hundred years with ideologies that were always in tension and often in open conflict. One of the best stories about Labour Party politicians was the account that one Labour Cabinet Minister said of Herbert Morrison that he was his own worst enemy: 'Not while I am alive he aint' said Ernie Bevin. The beauty of the story is that it could be, and often has been, ascribed to quite different members of the Party.

There has been a tendency to personalise opposing differences within the Party. In education, a key difference concerned the main purposes of education: some early Fabians, like Sidney Webb, stressed the economic advantages of improving education and advocated selection for secondary schools; others saw the Labour Party as a means of improving society morally and socially and saw the purpose of education in more general terms, and related education to equality of opportunity and social justice. That difference has survived into the twenty-first century, even if some of the politicians advocating the economic advantages claim to be motivated by moral arguments. New Labour generally has taken the economic line in justifying education as a top priority.

Another strand in this account of the Labour Party has been the neglect of education by Labour leaders; when they do develop an interest in education they have, unfortunately, got it wrong. That was particularly the case with Callaghan and is increasingly so of Blair. It is important, however, not to personalise these trends too much. Today there is a tendency to demonise Tony Blair for New Labour policies, including education, when they are clearly the ideas of a group within the Party, not a single individual.

Another curiosity of education policy since 1900 has been the fact that independent schools have been seen as a barrier to greater equality and social harmony, yet rarely has any Labour leader attempted to formulate a policy to solve the problem. This is interesting not only as a major issue in its own right, but also as an indication of a feature of the Party that many writers have commented upon, namely, the deferential attitude towards the upper classes, the nobility and the monarchy, and any institutions associated with those groups. This has resulted in New Labour attempting the impossible task of squaring the circle by making use of independent schools in the move towards a fairer system of secondary education.

One of the recurring weaknesses of the Labour Party has been the tendency at times of crisis to forget Labour values and traditions, reverting to Conservative policies. This happened to Ramsay MacDonald in 1930, to Attlee on various occasions, especially in foreign policy, to Callaghan, and to Blair. A low point in morale for Labour came in the summer of 2003 when Blair embarked upon war in Iraq, allied to a very reactionary US President and policy. The decision was justified by using dubious evidence and Blair was accused of misleading the Party and the nation. This departure from an internationalist, peaceful policy of support for the United Nations came dangerously close to splitting the Party, and also revived opposition to some New Labour policies, including education.

This tendency to regress to reactionary policies is related to the point made several times in this book and elsewhere – the lack of a vision of a better society. Too often Labour has been satisfied with carrying through policies inherited from previous Conservative regimes. This was true of many aspects of New Labour since 1997, especially education policies. This was disguised by New Labour's determination to 'modernise'; unfortunately, 'modernisation' was too often equated with a more ruthlessly efficient version of Thatcherism. To some extent the war in Iraq reopened the debate about New Labour policies, especially education.

Finally, it is important not to be too negative about the Labour Party and education. Despite the many criticisms made throughout this book, it remains the case that Labour has been responsible for a number of real improvements in the education service. There have been mistakes and missed opportunities but there have also been important steps forward and new ideas in education; in 1998 the programme for citizenship education clearly comes into this category.

Bibliography

Aldrich, R. (ed.) (1996) *In History and in Education*. London: Woburn Press.

Attlee, C.R. (1949) *The Labour Party in Perspective*. London: Gollancz.

Attlee, C.R. (1954) *As It Happened*. London: Heinemann.

Ball, S. (2001) 'Labour learning and the economy: a "policy sociology" perspective', in Fielding (ed.).

Banks, O. (1955) *Parity and Prestige in English Secondary Education*. London: Routledge & Kegan Paul.

Barber, M. (1997) *The Learning Game*. London: Sage.

Barber, M. (2001) 'High expectations and standards for all, no matter what: creating a world class education service in England', in Fielding (ed.).

Barker, R. (1972) *Education and Politics 1900–1951*. Oxford: Clarendon Press.

Barnard, H.C. (1961) *A History of English Education*. London: University of London Press.

Beckett, F. (1988) *Clem Attlee*. London: Richard Cohen.

Benn, C. (1992) *Keir Hardie*. London: Hutchinson.

Benn, C. and Simon, B. (1970) *Half Way There*. Report on the British Comprehensive School Reform. London: McGraw-Hill.

Benn, C. and Chitty, C. (1996) *Thirty Years On: Is Comprehensive Education Alive and Well or Struggling to Survive?* Harmondsworth, UK: Penguin.

Benn, T. (1995) *The Benn Diaries*. London: Hutchinson.

Bernbaum, G. (1967) *Social Change and the Schools 1918–1944*. London: Routledge & Kegan Paul.

Beveridge Report (1942) *Social Security and Allied Services*. London: HMSO.

Board of Education (1941) *Education after the War* (Green Book). London: HMSO.

Blair, T. (1994) *Socialism*. London: Fabian Pamphlet.

Blair, T. (1994) *The Third Way: New Politics for the New Century*. London: Fabian Society.

Blair, T. (1998) *The Third Way: New Politics for the New Century*. Fabian Pamphlet No. 588.

Blair, T. and Straw, J. (1991) *Today's Education and Training: Tomorrow's Skills*. London: Labour Party.

Blunkett, D. and Crick, B. (1988) *The Labour Party's Aims and Values: An Unofficial Statement*. Spokesman Pamphlet, No. 87.

Board of Education (1943) *Educational Reconstruction*. London: HMSO.

Board of Education (1945) *The Nation's Schools*. London: HMSO.

Briggs, A. and Saville, J. (eds) (1960) *Essays in Labour History*. Basingstoke, UK: Macmillan.

Brookshire, J.H. (1995) *Clement Attlee*. Manchester: Manchester University Press.

Brown, K.D. (ed) (1985) *The First Labour Party 1906–14*. Beckenham, UK: Croom Helm.

Bryce Report (1895) *Secondary Education in England*. London: HMSO.

Bullock, A. (1967) *The Life and Times of Ernest Bevin*. Vol. 2. London: Heinemann.

Butler, R.A. (1973) *The Art of the Possible*. Harmondsworth, UK: Penguin.

Calder, A. (1969) *The People's War*. London: Pimlico.

Cassells, J. (1990) *Britain's Real Skill Shortage*. Policies Studies Institute.

Central Advisory Council for Education (CACE) (1954) *Early Leaving* (The Gurney-Dixon Report). London: HMSO.

Central Advisory Council for Education (CACE) (1959) *15 to 18* (The Crowther Report). London: HMSO.

Central Advisory Council for Education (CACE) (1963) *Half Our Future*. (The Newsom Report). London: HMSO.

Central Advisory Council for Education (CACE) (1966) *Children and Their Primary Schools*. (The Plowden Report). London: HMSO.

Chitty, C. (1989) *Towards a New Education System*. London: Falmer Press.

Chitty, C. (2001) *The Unfinished Revolution: Challenging the Myth of Fixed Innate Ability*. London: Goldsmiths College.

Chitty, C. (2002) *Understanding Schools and Schooling*. London: RoutledgeFalmer.

Chitty, C. and Dunford, J. (1999) *State Schools: New Labour and the Conservative Legacy*. London: Woburn Press.

Cole, G.D.H. (1937) *A Short History of the British Working Class Movement, 1789–1937*. London: Allen & Unwin, Vol. 3, pp. 22–6.

Coleman, J.S., Campbell, E., Hobson, C., McPartland, J., Mood, A., Weinfeld, F. and York, R. (1966) *Equality of Educational Opportunity*. Washington: National Center for Educational Studies.

Conservative Party (1928) *The New Prospect in Education*. London: Conservative Party.

Cosgrave, P. (1992) *The Strange Death of Socialist Britain*. London: Constable.

Council for Curriculum Reform (1945) *The Content of Education*. London: University of London Press.

Cox, C.B. (ed.) (1998) *Literacy is Not Enough: Essays on the Importance of Reading*. Manchester: Manchester University Press and Book Trust.

Cox, C.B. and Dyson, A.E. (eds) (1969) *Fight for Education*. A Black Paper. Critical Quarterly Society.

Cox, C.B. and Dyson, A.E. (eds) (1969) *Crisis in Education*. Black Paper 2. Critical Quarterly Society.

Cox, C.B. and Dyson, A.E. (eds) (1970) *Goodbye Mr. Short*. Black Paper 3. Critical Quarterly Society.

Crick, B. (1969) *The Teaching of Politics*. Harmondsworth, UK: Penguin.

Crick, B. and Porter, A. (1978) *Political Education and Political Literacy*. Hansard Society.

Crick Report (1998) *Education for Citizenship and the Teaching of Democracy in Schools*. London: DfEE.

Crosland, C.A.R. (1956) *The Future of Socialism*. London: Jonathan Cape.

Crosland, C.A.R. (1962) *The Conservative Enemy*. London: Jonathan Cape.

Crosland, S. (1982) *Tony Crosland*. London: Jonathan Cape.

Crouch, C. (2003) *Commercialisation or Citizenship*. London: Fabian Ideas.

Davies, A.J. (1996) *To Build a New Jerusalem*. Tunbridge Wells: Abacus.

Dean, D.W. (1986) 'Planning for a post-war generation: Ellen Wilkinson and George Tomlinson at the Ministry of Education, 1945–51'. *History of Education*. Vol. 15, No. 2, pp. 95–117.

Dearing Report (1997) *Higher Education in the Learning Society*. London: DfEE.

Dearing Report (1999) *Further and Higher Education*. London: DfEE.

Dent, H.C. (1944) *Education in Transition*. London: Kegan, Paul, Trench, Trubner.

Dent, H.C. (1944a) *The Education Act 1944*. London: Unibooks, University of London Press.

Dent, H.C. (1948) *Education in Transition*. Kegan Paul, Trench, Trubner and Co. Ltd.

Dent, H.C. (1970) *1870–1970 Century of Growth in English Education*. London: Longmans.

DES (1966) *Report of the Study Group on the Government of Colleges*. The Weaver Report. London: HMSO.

DES (1972) *Education: A Framework for Expansion*. London: HMSO.

DES (1972) *Teacher Education and Training*. The James Report. London: HMSO.

DES (1975) *Curriculum 11–16*. London: HMI Report.

DES (1975) *A Language for Life*. The Bullock Report. London: HMSO.

DES (1977) *Education in Schools*. Green Paper. London: HMSO.

DES (1978) *Special Educational Needs*. The Warnock Report. London: HMSO.

DES (1978) *A Common Examination at 16+*. The Waddell Report. London: HMSO.

DES (1991a) *Education and Training for the 21st Century*. White Paper. London: HMSO.

DES (1991b) *Higher Education: A New Framework*. London: HMSO.

DES (1992) *Choice and Diversity*. White Paper. London: HMSO.

DFEE (1997) *Excellence in Schools*. White Paper. London: HMSO.

DFEE (1998) *Excellence for All*. Green Paper. London: HMSO.

DfEE (1998) *Teachers Meeting the Challenge of Change*. Green Paper. London: HMSO.

DFEE (1998) Circular 4/98. London: HMSO.

DfEE (1999) *Excellence in Cities*. London: HMSO.

DfEE (1999) *The Review of the National Curriculum: The Secretary of State's Proposals*. London: HMSO.

DfEE (2000) *Statistics*. London: HMSO.

DfEE (2001) *Building on Success: Raising Standards, Promoting Diversity, Achieving Results*. Green Paper. London: HMSO.

Donnison, D. (1970) *Public Schools Commission 2nd Report (Direct Grant Schools)*. London: HMSO.

Donoughue, B. (1987) *Prime Minister: The Conduct of Policy under Harold Wilson and James Callaghan*. London: Jonathan Cape.

Donoughue, B. and Jones, G.W. (2001) *Herbert Morrison – Portrait of a Politician*. London: Phoenix Press.

Earl L. *et al.* (2000) *Working and Learning*. London: DfEE.

Edwards, T., Fitz, J. and Whitty, G. (1989) *The State and Private Education: An Evaluation of the Assisted Places Scheme*. London: Falmer.

Edwards, T. (1998) *Specialisation without Selection*. Briefing No. 1. London: RISE.

Edwards, T. and Tomlinson, S. (2002) *Selection Isn't Working*. A Catalyst Working Paper.

Evetts, J. (1973) *The Sociology of Educational Ideas*. London: Routledge & Kegan Paul.

Fielding, M. (ed) (2001) *Taking Education Really Seriously: Four Years' Hard Labour*. London: RoutledgeFalmer.

Finegold, D., Keep, E., Miliband, D., Raffe, D., Spours, K. and Young, M. (1990) *A British Baccalaureat*. Education and Training Paper No. 1. Institute for Public Policy Research.

Fleming Report (1944) *Public Schools*. London: HMSO.

Foote, G. (1997) *The Labour Party's Political Thought*. Basingstoke, UK: Macmillan.

Ford, J. (1969) *Social Class and the Comprehensive School*. London: Routledge & Kegan Paul.

Freire, P. (1970) *Pedagogy of the Oppressed*. Harmondsworth, UK: Penguin.

Galton, M. and McBeath, J. (2002) *Primary Teaching 1970–2000*. Report Commission by the NUT.

Gardner, H. (1984) *Frames of Mind*. London: Fontana.

Gardner, H. (1991) *The Unschooled Mind*. London: Fontana.

Giddens, A. (2002) *Where Now for New Labour?* London: Fabian Society/Blackwell.

Gilroy, P. (1998) 'New Labour and teacher education in England and Wales: the first five hundred days'. *Journal of Teacher Education*, Vol. 24, No. 3, pp. 221–30.

Gilroy, P., Edwards, A. and Hartley, D. (eds) (2002) *Responses to Uncertainty*.

Glenerster, H. (1970) *Planning for Education in 1980*. London: Fabian, Research Series 282.

Goleman, D. (1996) *Emotional Intelligence*. London: Bloomsbury.

Goodman, P. (1962) *Compulsory Miseducation*. Harmondsworth, UK: Penguin.

Goodwin, H. (1981) 'The Response of Labour to the 1926 Hadow Report', in *History of Education Society. Occasional Paper 6*.

Gordon, P., Aldrich, R. and Dean, D. (eds) (1991) *Education and Policy in England in the Twentieth Century*. London: Woburn Press.

Gosden, P.H.J.H. (1996) 'An essay in missing out: technical eduation in the shadow of the Second World War', in Aldrich (ed.).

Griggs, C. (1985a) 'Labour and Education', in Brown, K.D. (ed.).

Griggs, C. (1985b) *Private Education in Britain*. London: Falmer.

Griggs, C. (2002) *The TUC and Education Reform*. London: Woburn Press.

Gundara, J. (2000) 'Social diversity, inclusiveness and citizenship education', in Lawton *et al.* (eds).

Hadow Report (1926) *The Education of the Adolescent*. London.

Hadow Report (1931) *Report of the Consultative Committee on the Primary School*. London.

Hadow Report (1933) *Report of the Consultative Committee on Infant and Nursery Schools*. London.

Halsey, A.H. (1996) *No Discouragement: An Autobiography*. Basingstoke, UK: Macmillan.

Halsey, A.H. and Gardner, L. (1953) 'Selection for Secondary Education and Achievement in Four Grammar Schools'. *British Journal of Sociology*, No. 4.

Hamilton, D. (1994) 'Clockwork Universes and Oranges'. Annual Conference of the British Educational Research Association. Oxford.

Hamilton, M.A. (1944) *Remembering My Good Friends*. London.

Harris, K. (1982) *Attlee*. London: Weidenfeld.

Haslewood, N. (1981) 'Tawney, the Labour Party and educational policy in the 1920s: a reappraisal', in *History of Education Society. Occasional Publication 6 Labour and Education: Some Early Twentieth Century Studies*. London.

Higginson, G. (1988) *Advancing 'A' Levels*. London: DES.

Hobsbawm, E. (2002) *Interesting Times: A Twentieth-century Life*. Harmondsworth, UK: Allen Lane.

Hodgson, A. and Spours, K. (1999) *New Labour's Educational Agenda*. London: Kogan Page.

Holmes, E. (1911) *What Is and What Might Be*. London: Constable.

Hughes, H.D. (1955) *A Socialist Education Policy*. London: Fabian Society.

Hyndman, H.M. (1881) *England for All*. London: E.W. Allen.

Illich, I. (1971) *De-Schooling Society*. London: Harper Row.

Independent (1991) 'Timid Tory plan for training'. Leading article in *Independent*, 21.5.

Inner London Education Authority (1975) Report on the William Tyndale Schools. The Auld Report. London: HMSO.

IPPR (1993) *Education: A Different Vision*. London: IPPR.

James, E. (1951) *Education and Leadership*. Harmondsworth, UK: Penguin.

Jay, P. (1953) *Better Schools Now*. Turnstile Press.

Jefferys, K. (1987) *Labour and the Wartime Coalition. Chuter Ede Diaries*. Historians' Press.

Jefferys, K. (ed.) (1999) *Leading Labour: From Keir Hardie to Tony Blair*. London: I.B. Tauris.

Jones, K. (1989) *Right Turn*. London: Hutchinson Radius.

Judges, A.V. (1961) 'The educational influence of the Webbs'. *Journal of Educational Studies*. Vol. 10, No. 1 November, pp. 33–48.

Kavanagh, D. (2001) 'New Labour, new millennium, new premiership', in A. Seldon (ed.).

Kinnock, N. (1985a) 'Choice, relevance and standards'. Speech to British Educational Management and Administration Society. *Education*, 20 September.

Kinnock, N. (1985b) *The Future of Socialism*. London: Fabian Society, No. 509.

Knight, C. (1990) *The Making of Tory Education Policy in Post-War Britain 1950–1986*. London: Falmer.

Kogan, M. (ed) (1971) *The Politics of Education*. Conversations with Boyle and Crosland. Harmondsworth, UK: Penguin.

Kogan, M. (1978) *The Politics of Educational Change*. London: Fontana.

Labour Party (1928) *From Nursery School to University*. London: Labour Party.

Labour Party (1945) *Let Us Face the Future*. Election Manifesto. London: Labour Party.

Labour Party (1951) *A Policy for Secondary Education*. London: Labour Party.

Labour Party (1980) *Private Schools: A Discussion Document*. London: Labour Party.

Labour Party (1992) *General Election Manifesto*. London: Labour Party.

Labour Party (1993) *Opening Doors to a Learning Society*. Commission on Education Report, chaired by Ann Taylor.

Labour Party (1997) *Election Manifesto*. London: Labour Party.

Labour Party (2001) *Election Manifesto: Ambitions for Britain*. London: Labour Party.

Lawson, J. and Silver, H. (1973) *A Social History of Education in England*. London: Methuen.

Lawton, D. (1992) *Education and Politics in the 1990s*. London: Falmer.

Lawton, D. (1994) *The Tory Mind on Education 1979–1994*. London: Falmer.

Lawton, D. and Chitty, C. (eds) (1988) *The National Curriculum*. Bedford Way Paper No. 33, Institute of Education, University of London.

Lawton, D., Cairns, J. and Gardner, R. (eds) (2000) *Education for Citzenship*. Continuum.

Lowe, R. (1988) *Education in the Post-War Years: A Social History*. London: Routledge.

Major, J. (1999) *The Autobiography*. London: HarperCollins.

Mandelson, P. and Liddle, R. (1996) *The Blair Revolution: Can New Labour Deliver?* London: Faber & Faber.

Manzer, R.A. (1970) *Teachers and Politics*. Manchester: Manchester University Press.

Manton, K. (2001) *Socialism and Education in Britain 1883–1902*. London: Woburn Press.

Marsden, D. (1971) *Politicians, Equality and Comprehensives*. London: Fabian Tract 411.

McBriar, A.M. (1962) *Fabian Socialism and English Politics: 1884–1918*. Cambridge: Cambridge University Press.

McCulloch, G. (1998) *Failing the Ordinary Child*. Buckingham, UK: Open University Press.

McKibbin, R. (2003) 'How to put the politics back into Labour'. London: Review of Books.

Miliband, D. (1991) *Markets, Politics and Education*. London: IPPR.

Morgan, A. (1987) *J. Ramsay MacDonald*. Manchester: Manchester University Press.

Morgan, K. (1987) *Labour People*. Oxford: Oxford University Press.

Morgan, K. (1997) *Callaghan: A Life*. Oxford: Oxford University Press.

Morris, A.J.A. (1977) *C.P.Trevelyan: A Portrait of a Radical*. Blackstaff Press.

Morris, M. and Griggs, C. (1988) *Education: The Wasted Years? 1973–1986*. London: Falmer.

Morris, W. (1897) *News from Nowhere*. London: Longmans, Green.

Moss, P. (2001) 'Renewed hopes and lost opportunities: early childhood in the early years of the Labour government', in Fielding (ed.).

National Association of Labour Teachers (NALT) (1930) *Education: A Policy*. NALT.

National Commission on Education (1993) *Learning to Succeed*. London: Heinemann.

Newsom Report (1963) *Half Our Future*. London: HMSO.

Newsom Report (1968) *The Public Schools Commission First Report*. London: HMSO.

Norwood Report (1943) *Secondary School Curricula and Examinations*. London: SSEC.

O'Hear, P. and White, J. (1991) *A National Curriculum for All*. London: IPPR.

O'Neill, O. (2002) *The Issue of Trust*. First Reith Lecture. London: BBC.

Office for Standards in Education (OfSTED) *Curriculum 2000: Implementation* (2003) OfSTED.

Owen, R. (1813) *A New View of Society*. Harmondsworth, UK: Penguin.

Parkinson, M. (1970) *The Labour Party and the Organization of Secondary Education 1918–65*. London: Routledge & Kegan Paul.

Pedley, R. (1955) *Comprehensive Schools Today*. London: Methuen.

Pedley, R. (1963) *The Comprehensive School*. Harmondsworth, UK: Penguin.

Pedley, R. (1977) *Towards the Comprehensive University*. Basingstoke, UK: Macmillan.

Pelling, H. (1965) *Origins of the Labour Party*. Oxford: Oxford University Press.

Petch, J.A. (1953) *Fifty Years of Examining*. London: George G. Harrap.

Peters, R. (1966) *Ethics and Education*. London: George Allen & Unwin.

Pimlottt, B. (1985) *Hugh Dalton*. London: Jonathan Cape.

Pimlott, B. (ed) (1984) *Fabian Essays in Socialist Thought*. London: Heinemann.

Pimlott, B. (1992) *Harold Wilson*. London: HarperCollins.

Plant, R. (1984) *Equality, Markets and the State*. London: Fabian Society, Tract No. 494.

Plant, R. (2001) 'Blair and Ideology', in Seldon (ed.).

Power, S. and Whitty, G. (1999) 'New Labour's education policy: first, second or third way?' *Journal of Education Policy*. Vol. 14, No. 5.

Pugh, P. (1984) *Educate, Agitate, Organize*. London: Methuen.

Ranson, S. (1994) *Towards a Learning Society*. London: Cassell.

Rawls, J. (1972) *A Theory of Justice*. Oxford: Clarendon Press.

Research Information on State Education (RISE) (1998) *Specialisation Without Selection?* London: RISE.

Robbins Report (1963) *Higher Education*. London: HMSO.

Rubinstein, D. and Simon, B. (1969) *The Evolution of the Comprehensive School 1926–1972*. London: Routledge & Kegan Paul.

Ruskin, J. (1860) *Unto This Last*. London.

Ruskin, J. (1871) *Fors Clavigera: Letters to the Workmen and Labourers of Great Britain.* Smith, Elder and Co.

Saville, J. (1988) *The Labour Movement in Britain.* London: Faber & Faber.

Seldon, A. (ed) (2001) *The Blair Effect: The Blair Government 1997–2001.* Little, Brown and Company.

Simon, B. (1960) *History of Education 1780–1870.* London: Lawrence & Wishart.

Simon, B. (1965) *Education and the Labour Movement 1870–1920.* London: Lawrence & Wishart.

Simon, B. (1974) *The Politics of Educational Reform 1920–1940.* London: Lawrence & Wishart.

Simon, B. (1985) *Does Education Matter?* London: Lawrence & Wishart.

Simon, B. (1988) *Bending the Rules.* London: Lawrence & Wishart.

Simon, B. (1991) *Education and the Social Order 1940–1990.* London: Lawrence & Wishart.

Simon, B. (ed.) (1972) *The Radical Tradition in Education in Britain.* London: Lawrence & Wishart.

Smithers, A. (2001) 'Education Policy', in Seldon (ed.).

Spens Report (1938) *Report of the Consultative Committee of the Board of Education on Secondary Education with Special Reference to Grammar Schools and Technical High Schools.* London: HMSO.

Stenhouse, L. (1975) *An Introduction to Curriculum Research and Development.* Milton Keynes, UK: Open University.

Stevenson, J. (1984) 'From philanthropy to Fabianism', in Pimlott (ed.).

Stewart, W.A.C. (1968) *The Educational Innovators.* Basingstoke, UK: Macmillan.

Tawney, R.H. (1922) *Secondary Education for All.* London.

Tawney, R.H. (1931) *Equality.* Republished by Unwin Books (1964).

Tawney, R.H.(1934) *Juvenile Employment and Education.* Barnard House Papers, No. 14.

Tawney, R.H. (1943) *The Radical Tradition.* Republished Pelican Books (1966).

Tawney, R.H. (1953) *The Attack.* London: Allen & Unwin.

Tawney, R.H. (1961) *The Acquisitive Society.* London: Fontana.

Taylor, A.J.P. (1965) *English History 1914–1945.* Oxford: Clarendon Press.

Thomson, G. (1929) *A Modern Philosophy of Education.* London: Allen & Unwin.

Titmuss, R.M. (1968) *Commitment to Welfare.* London: Allen & Unwin.

Tomlinson, S. (2001) *Education in a Post-Welfare Society.* Buckingham, UK: Open University Press.

Tomlinson, S. (ed.) (1994) *Educational Reform and its Consequences.* London: IPPR.

Troman, G., and Woods, P. (2001) *The Social Construction of Teacher Stress.* London: Routledge.

Vernon, B. (1982) *Ellen Wilkinson 1891–1947.* Beckenham, UK: Croom Helm.

Vernon, P.E. (ed.) (1957) *Secondary School Selection.* London: Methuen.

Walford, G. and Miller, H. (1991) *City Technology Colleges.* Buckingham, UK: Open University Press.

Wallace, R.G. (1981) 'The origins and authorship of the 1944 Education Act'. *History of Education*, Vol. 10, No. 4. pp. 283–90.

Webb, S. (1901) *The Educational Muddle and the Way Out.* London: Fabian Pamphlet.

Webster, D. and Parsons, K. (1999) 'British Labour Party policy on educational selection 1996–8: a sociological analysis'. *Journal of Education Policy*, Vol. 14, No. 5.

Wells, H.G. (1934) *Experiment in Autobiography: Discoveries and Conclusions of a Very Ordinary Brain.* London: Gollancz and the Cresset Press.

White, M. (2002) 'Blair: a closet Tory?'. *Guardian* 12.2.

Wilderspin, S. (1923) 'On the Importance of Educating the Infant Children of the Poor', quoted in Simon 1960, pp. 237–8, 262.

Williams, P.M. (1979) *Hugh Gaitskell: A Political Biography*. London: Jonathan Cape.

Woods, P., Jeffrey, B. and Troman, G. (2001) 'The impact of New Labour's educational policy on primary schools', in M. Fielding (ed.).

Young, M. (1958) *The Rise of the Meritocracy*. Harmondsworth, UK: Penguin.

Young, M.F.D. (1971) *Knowledge and Control*. Collier Macmillan.

Index